Managing People in a Conten Context

The worldwide financial crash and the ensuing recession have coincided with other significant long-term changes for the Western economies of Europe and the USA, especially the growing strength of newly developed economies, demographic and technological change, institutional crises, and political uncertainty. The interconnected nature of businesses and societies means the competitive landscape is being transformed, and new economic pressures and opportunities are producing new business models, a rebalancing of economies, and a new human resources management.

The application of new technology to the processes and systems of people management is spreading, in a world where competitive advantage is increasingly about how smart the management processes are, and how well people are managed. This text is the first book to analyse the way these contextual pressures are producing a game change in the human resource (HR) function of management.

For anyone who has an HR role, or who is a line manager or a student of management, and for those who teach, research, or consult in the field, this book encapsulates these critically important trends and what they mean for managing people in the twenty-first century.

Emma Parry is a Reader in Human Resource Management at Cranfield University School of Management. Her research focuses on the influence of context on managing people, specifically the influence of national context, demographic changes, and technological advancement. She has authored a number of publications in this area.

Shaun Tyson is Emeritus Professor of Human Resource Management at Cranfield University School of Management. Following senior management experience in industry and the public sector, he was Director of a research centre and Professor for 20 years. He has published widely in the field.

Managing People in a Contemporary Context

Emma Parry and Shaun Tyson

Routledge
Taylor & Francis Group

LONDON AND NEW YORK

First published 2014
by Routledge
2 Park Square, Milton Park, Abingdon, Oxon OX14 4RN

and by Routledge
711 Third Avenue, New York, NY 10017

Routledge is an imprint of the Taylor & Francis Group, an informa business

British Library Cataloguing in Publication Data
A catalogue record for this book is available from the British Library

Library of Congress Cataloguing in Publication Data
  Managing people in a contemporary context / Emma Parry and Shaun Tyson.
    pages cm
  Includes bibliographical references and index.
  1. Personnel management.   2. Personnel management – Technological
  innovations.   I. Tyson, S. (Shaun)   II. Title.
  HF5549.P2838 2013
  658.3–dc23
  2013013669

ISBN: 978-0-415-53311-9 (hbk)
ISBN: 978-0-415-53312-6 (pbk)
ISBN: 978-1-315-88587-2 (ebk)

Typeset in Times New Roman
by Out of House Publishing

Printed and bound in Great Britain by
TJ International Ltd, Padstow, Cornwall

Contents

vi *Contents*

Figures

Tables

Acknowledgements

We must first thank Jayne Ashley for her tireless enthusiasm and incredibly hard work in putting this manuscript together.

There are also a number of individuals who were interviewed or provided data or case study information for various chapters throughout this book. These individuals deserved to be thanked by name: Matt Alder, Michael Dickmann, Paul Flowers, Anna Holm, Randall Schuler, Hugh Scullion, and Angela Ralph; Tay McNamara and the team at Boston Center for Ageing and Work; and Catherine Schlieben and the recruitment team at ITV. A special thanks must also go to the members of the Cranet network for collecting the data that we have used in several places throughout this text.

We would also like to acknowledge with thanks the permission to reproduce in this book the material from the following works, granted by the publishers and authors listed below:

Figure 5.1 reproduced from Dyer and Shafer (1999), with kind permission from Emerald Publishing Group. Table 7.1 reproduced from Paik *et al.* (2011), with kind permission from John Wiley and Sons. Figure 7.1 reproduced from Dickmann and Müller-Camen (2006), with kind permission from Taylor & Francis. Table 8.1 reproduced from Mannix and Neale (2005), with kind permission from Sage Publications. Figure 9.1 reproduced from Wood (2010), with kind permission from Blackwell Publishing Limited and the British Academy of Management. Figure 13.1 reproduced from Cooper and Cartwright (1994), with kind permission from Sage Publications.

1 Introduction

Managing people in a contemporary context

Across the globe all nations are facing unprecedented economic challenges. In developed and developing economies, the recession which began in the West in 2008 has had an impact which is far reaching. The people who work in organizations and those who manage them have borne the brunt of the changes which have ensued. At the same time, new technologies and changes to society which were already occurring have been creating a new context in which organizations of all sizes and in all sectors have sought to operate successfully. This backdrop raises questions about how those responsible for managing human resources can overcome the new challenges, in order that their organizations can prosper into the future. That is the subject of this book.

The emerging context

The economic and social changes already facing organizations were sufficiently taxing without the sudden banking failures and the subsequent events in financial markets and economies of Western nations. Demographic shifts towards an ageing population together with generational differences presented difficulties for pension schemes, health and social welfare budgets, as well as problems in workforce planning, lifestyle changes, elder care, promotion policies, talent management, and rewards. New technology enabled whole new generations of products, and new ways of doing business through faster communications of all kinds, and vast amounts of data made available to all. Such developments were exciting and brought new business opportunities, but new technology is also a great leveller, and the costs of entry to a new business, or even a new geographical area, were suddenly diminished, encouraging greater competition. The emergence as major players of the BRIC countries (Brazil, Russia, India, and China) was part of a massive expansion of trade. Western economies were not able easily to compete on a basis of costs/prices, and nor eventually on quality. It is our contention that even if there had been no recession, the UK's economy was becoming uncompetitive, and that the economic policies prior to the recession were unsustainable. This is also true of many of the countries in the European Union (EU), where economic performance was sometimes based on false assumptions, about demand and property prices, for example.

However, these issues have become more critical as a result of the recession. Up until the financial crash, there was a widely held belief that recessions were cyclical over a short time period, a temporary halt on the march towards better living standards. Now, it is clear there are institutional changes required and that the return to long term competitiveness may take decades for many countries in Europe. The changes we see because of this confluence of circumstances lead us to believe that the effects will produce fundamental changes to people management, which are now becoming apparent. The scale of change required has been expressed by the leaders of all the major economies.

In the USA, still the largest economy in the world, President Obama, in his first inaugural address on 20 January 2009, set out the challenges when he said: 'Our economy is badly weakened, a consequence of greed and the irresponsibility of some, but also our collective failure to make hard choices and prepare the nation for a new age. Homes have been lost, jobs shed, businesses shuttered …' (extract from the President's speech released by the White House). The US economy has moved back into modest growth since that time, and unemployment in the USA has reduced. However, public spending has been massive. In the fiscal year to 2012, the US budget deficit reached $1.6 trillion, and the debt totalled $16 trillion, making tax reform efforts to reduce the deficit a priority. The absence of a bi-partisan agreement triggered 'sequestration', which resulted in budget cuts of $1.2 trillion being imposed over ten years. This was expected to lead to the loss of thousands of jobs (SHRM 2013). At his second inaugural address, on 21 January 2013, President Obama spoke of the need to change with the times: 'Our country cannot succeed when a shrinking few do well, and a growing many barely make it' (extract from the President's speech released by the White House).

The EU faces similar major problems, where in 2012 there was an unemployment rate of 12 per cent, as well as a rumbling political and currency crisis in the Eurozone countries. Angela Merkel, the German Chancellor, in her New Year television address to the nation on 31 December 2012, commented, on looking forward: 'In fact, the economic situation will not be easier, but more difficult' (CET Euronews 2012). The UK economy has been almost flatlining, stagnating with some employment growth, but little economic growth, and no real improvement to the indebtedness of the state. In early 2013, the UK lost its triple A credit rating, as the economic problems began to build. One of the major engines for growth in the Far East, China, downgraded its growth forecast for 2013, from 8 per cent to 7.5 per cent, and India, which originally forecast 7.6 per cent for 2013, reduced this forecast to 5 per cent. In addition, India has a large fiscal and current account deficit to tackle.

One aspect of the recession which may be affecting management thinking is to bring the interconnectivity of the world's economies into the foreground. These interconnections between nations and trading blocs, between international businesses and the major powers, influenced by geopolitical trends, all have an impact on opportunities and competitiveness. Institutional and political uncertainty feed through into trading conditions, exports, jobs, and the pressure on costs, especially labour costs and productivity. The global aspects of trading provide important foundations for strategically important commodities such as oil and gas, grain, and raw materials, with consequences for energy and food prices, and hence for inflation. There is institutional uncertainty; for example, the Euro crisis, the reforms of the EU, and the political fallout of the austerity measures in Greece, Italy, Portugal, and Spain. There are wider problems of uncertainty, such as the problems affecting religious institutions, the difficulties arising from the revolutions initiated in 'the Arab Spring', and uncertainty about local political situations, such as the UK's relations with the EU, the threats from North Korea, and the ongoing threats from terrorists in Africa, and in Afghanistan and Pakistan. The list of potential political flashpoints around the world at any one time seems to be growing. These issues can delay investments, or tip the balance in decisions on where to make an investment. They disrupt trade and aid, and result in tensions reflected in stock market performance, and share price volatility. The atmosphere of change and uncertainty brings opportunities as well as problems. In our account of the impact of the recent changes on people management, we are conscious of the underlying economic and social issues and perspectives, which inform management strategies, and therefore the management of people.

Our view is that the political, social, and economic context nationally, and increasingly internationally, establishes the choices and the opportunities companies and governments can make, and that business or organizational strategy is influenced by these choices. This position is consistent with contingency theory (Lawrence and Lorsch 1967), but does not take a deterministic stance. Our position is also in tune with the view that we are moving from what is seen as the modernist conception of the world into a postmodern world, at different rates of development, where the individual is simultaneously attached to the local community and to global trends, exposed to products, ideas, and opinions from around the world, as well as the institutions of the economic and state structures which seek to mediate them. Giddens (1991) argued that we are living more in a world of 'radicalized modernity' than of postmodernity. Radicalized modernity takes a more positive view of the trends and institutional forces shaping our lives than is found in postmodernism. There would seem to be elements of both in our analysis, but we do find it possible 'to identify the institutional developments which create a sense of fragmentation and dispersal' (p. 50) and we are able to see 'day to day life as an active complex of reactions to abstract systems, involving appropriation as well as loss' (p. 50) which Giddens saw as two of the eight features which identify radicalized modernism. However, we also 'theorize powerlessness which individuals feel in the face of globalising tendencies' (p. 50) which he defined as one of the characteristics of postmodernity.

The effects of contextual change on managing people

The initial context for the firm is the industry sector which affects how influential these wider trends are for managers in their analysis of factors when making strategies, policies, and decisions, as seen, for example, in how industries develop and change (MacGahan 2000). There is a long-established theoretical and empirical tradition of research on organizations, and on people management policies and practices in particular, which acknowledges the significance of the environmental context. Early studies of human resource (HR) policies and practices followed the contingency approach found in the work of Burns and Stalker (1961) and Emery and Trist (1965), which showed how ways of organizing work are contingent upon the degree of change, the complexity, and the type of technology in the organization, and that as a consequence different types of environment produce different organization structures and working systems. Similarly, early studies of HR policies by Ackermann (1986), Schuler and Jackson (1987), and Delery and Doty (1996) showed that organization size and industry sector were, among other causes, the reasons for differences in HR policies and practices. There is also empirical research which seeks to relate data in human resource management (HRM) research to the institutional context, for example by acknowledging the effects of trade union membership on HRM and performance (Arthur 1992).

The point of departure for this book is the impact of the various contextual factors on people management in organizations. We take the HR function of management to be the whole range of activities under the control of management which are intended to affect the management of people in an organization. This definition therefore covers first-level supervisors, line managers, and directors, as well as the specialists in the HR Department, all of whom have some part of the responsibility for managing people at work. The context of the changes experienced in organizations since the financial crash we see as the social, economic, and institutional forces and influences which have shaped the responses of organizations to the threats and opportunities they face. Some of these threats are part of a long term trend, such as the demographic shift to an ageing population, while some, such as the austerity packages adopted or wished upon governments, have suddenly been deemed necessary for survival, and were unexpected, with immediate effects such as redundancy on the employees concerned.

The economic context and the social context are experienced by employees through economic and social institutions. Of the institutions of the market place, those of the labour market have a major impact on the life chances of employees. If we take Dunlop's old (1970) notion of the industrial relations system, there are three main actors: employers' associations, trade unions, and the government. These institutions have been subject to long term changes. Employers' associations in the UK and elsewhere have seen bargaining and dispute resolution in the case of most associations move to the company level. In the East of Europe, employers' associations in those countries that were once dominated by the Soviet Union had to make rapid changes after the fall of the Berlin Wall, from being organs of the Communist Party to becoming more focused on trade and on the representation of employers' interests (Croucher *et al.* 2006). In the West also, employers' associations have shifted their emphasis to providing services more for their members and (as employer representatives) to acting as lobbyists and in a public relations role. Trade unions in the UK have retained their role in bargaining, but membership has been subject to steady decline, from a peak of 13.2 million members in 1979, to 7.2 million in 2012 (Certification Officer Report 2012). Public sector unions have become more prominent and there has been a decline of manufacturing employment where there were traditions of membership because of the nature of working conditions. Other reasons for the reduction in trade union membership include the effects of the rise of small businesses (there has been a rise in the number of self-employed to 367,000 people in the four years to 2012), increases in unemployment, and the legislation of the Conservative government in the 1980s. The state's direct influence on industrial relations is mostly through employment law, which covers a massive range of topics, such as redundancy procedures, bargaining rights, health and safety, and individual aspects of employment contracts, such as unfair dismissal, discrimination, and employees' rights. Indirectly, of course, the state influences the employment relationship through economic policies giving rise to unemployment or increases in demand, changes to inflation, and interest rates.

These changes to laws show how there has been an evolution of industrial relations. Nevertheless, the shift from the collective to individual relationships charts a movement which is found in society generally. The individualization of employment relations and the changes in social behaviour with more single parents, more single households, and demographic changes, goes alongside changing social norms, such as falling church attendance, more alcoholism, drug abuse, and increases in mental health problems, especially depression and anxiety. Perhaps coincidentally, there is now more individual entertainment (computer games and television, with more television and radio channels and internet entertainment, as well as more take-up of individual games such as tennis, golf, squash rather than team sports). All these factors paint a picture of a changing society.

Paradoxically, new developments in information systems have enabled mass electronic relationships to form via social media such as Facebook and Twitter, emails, and the possibilities of the Internet. There is more overseas travel, more intercultural understanding through immigration and 24/7 TV news, all trends which encourage a more global mindset. The Canadian pop star Justin Bieber, perhaps the first internet pop idol, has created an image and a massive following across the globe due to his appeal to teenagers everywhere, with millions of fans following his blogs and music around the world in 2013. His prodigious number of tweets and blogs have excited the interest of corporations which have, as they have with other pop stars, seen the possibilities of gaining access to millions of teenagers and their families through sponsorship deals, giving opportunities for sales and perhaps chances to use add-ons on websites as part of their marketing and merchandising strategies (IEG 2013). New technology has proved to be a game changing development. Offering instant communications and access to masses of data on every topic, due to the interactive nature of the Internet, its transparency, and wide availability, the Internet can now be seen as a new societal institution.

New technology has also revolutionized work. Robots now build our cars, computers help us to drive, and keep our railways and airports safe, and our traffic moving. There are no jobs however menial where computers are not at some point involved, whether it is in the scheduling of work or the operation of complex systems in laboratories, nuclear power stations, and in schools, concert halls, hotels, offices, shops, government buildings, tax systems, banks and money transfer, in air-conditioning systems, water supply, and in the logistics which deliver food to supermarkets and other outlets. A small failure, such as has occurred in bank cash machines (ATMs), can affect millions. So pervasive are the effects of new technology that we do not always realize that our lives now depend on these systems working.

The effects of the developments in new technology such as the dramatic impact of social media on recruitment we will examine in detail in Chapter 6, but here we should note that there are significant effects on employment relationships from the use, for example, of online surveys intended to inform frequent evaluations of HR policies and strategies, and the growing extensive use of e-learning. These kinds of changes show how new technology is making the HR function different – more driven by an employee's own needs and views, encouraging greater transparency and employee involvement.

The changes to HRM brought about by the financial crash and the following recession are aspects of the economic context which are central to this book's purpose. While acknowledging the long term trends which are impacting economies, such as in the UK, where there were pre-existing structural problems of an un-balanced economy, with an overconcentration on the service sector rather than the manufacturing industries, and the north-south divide of investment and industries, the impact of the recession has brought about a sea change, a shift in the tectonic plates of the economy. This requires a transformation in the way we think about our future, and the kind of life we will be able to live. There is a gradual realization that, as President Obama said, there is the coming of a new age especially for the Western economies in Europe and the USA, where we all have to come to accept that our standard of living may not continue to rise, that we cannot afford to live as we used to, and that survival depends upon us finding a new mission, a new vision for the future, in which there is a return to long term competitiveness.

The economic context has a multiplier effect on all the other trends, social, institutional, and technological, and interactive effects on the various aspects of the economy. The effects of the sudden downturn can be seen in pay, redundancies, workforce restructuring, and changes to business models.

These changes affect recruitment, retention, reward, and development at the policy and individual employee level. There are also issues about the climate of employment relations which the economic downturn has created. In the public sector this has been one of hostility to the cuts, and in the UK and in other European countries, such as Greece, Italy, Spain, and Portugal, large scale demonstrations, where public sector and other workers express their anger at the reduction in their life chances which austerity has brought. The recession has therefore acted as a catalyst, bringing together long-run failures which had not been addressed, with the immediate problems of unsustainable levels of debt.

Some of the failures are social and political, as much as commercial. There is a widespread belief in the UK that the educational and training systems have not delivered on their promise. This is one reason for major problems with the economy, and why many British employers fill vacancies with migrant workers, especially from Eastern Europe, because in addition to their skills, migrants often possess a strong work ethic, and flexibility. The LSE Growth Commission (2013) in its report, drawing on secondary data sources, pointed to the failures in UK schools to teach to a sufficiently high standard. The report argues that intermediate skills and the transition from school to workplace are said to be poor in the UK. However, employers in the UK have also too often failed to provide apprenticeships of sufficient length and quality, compared to our European rivals. The UK government has now made a number of interventions to increase the number of apprenticeships.

The recession may well have resulted in reductions in training spend by many employers, who are aggressively seeking value for money in their search for solutions to the problems of balancing needs against a shrinking training budget. The changes that have been occurring are also opportunities for organization development, and there are now many variations in approach that can be taken, using models of action learning such as collaborative enquiry. The management of change is made more difficult when the circumstances of impending closure of the business are apparent. It is too late at this stage. As with many HR interventions, the time for major development initiatives is usually when there is a consensus among the board that there needs to be a change in direction, in order to grow the business more, or to restructure in advance of change.

Themes in the contemporary context of people management and the book's structure

Our book focuses on the new and emerging trends and activities in HRM, and there is a strong emphasis on the way the external context shapes these trends. There are a number of themes from our analysis, which emerge throughout the book. We can summarize these themes briefly in the following list.

- Organizational effectiveness and competitive advantage, as a necessity for survival, and the development of organizational agility by dynamic capabilities and in response to rapid change.
- Talent management, the psychological contract, and the linkages through the marketing role of HRM into total rewards.
- The impact of new technology via e-HRM, in support of HR policies, and within the work itself, in manufacturing processes, as well as in the new methods of service delivery.
- The changing focus and role of HRM and that of line managers, as reductions in costs force a re-evaluation of the advantages of outsourcing, and as IT advances change modes of service delivery, structure, and the nature of specialist and HR generalist roles.
- Changing values and employment relationships at the individual level, with increasing diversity, attempts to align employee and employer values, found in engagement practices, total rewards, and the growing interest in corporate social responsibility, in the face of the social pressures on individuals to become more isolated.
- Uncertainty, the role of the state and supra-national bodies and the internationalization of work, both through the trading conditions, outsourcing, and the globalization of brands, and also through international workforces working locally, and the convergence of management practices, including those of the HR function.

These themes are not distinct individual lines of enquiry. They are woven together, with a variety of interdependencies and in an emerging picture of management re-evaluation of the commercial objectives the company is trying to achieve, despite unpredictable and rapid exogenous pressures for change.

We have resisted the temptation to structure the book around these themes because we do see them as a closely knit pattern of pressures and reactions to both new issues and long-standing problems within the management of people area. In order to trace how these issues are influencing people management, we have structured the book in three parts, the first of which sets out the social, economic, and organizational context against which changes to HRM have occurred; the second part discusses a number of broad changes impacting on the organization and HR function specifically; and the third part examines what is happening in a number of human resource management policy areas. The chapters include a brief summary of the argument at the end of each chapter, and these are drawn together in a concluding chapter at the end of the book.

Our approach is to combine literature and secondary data with our own research and experience, adding case material examples as appropriate. The purpose of the book is not to present new research, but to discuss existing evidence about HRM in the light of the changing context.

The reasons for writing the book and the intended audience

There are large numbers of texts available about the nuts and bolts of HRM, and quite a number of more academic texts which seek to examine some of the empirical evidence available to prove or disprove various theses advanced by academics on the subject. This book is not about the basics of people management practices, nor is it intended as a comprehensive discussion of HR activities. We aim to address the strategic issues. However, both authors have experienced a degree of dissatisfaction at the absence of texts which give full accounts of the changing contexts in which HRM takes place. Although the significance of context is readily acknowledged in HR textbooks, for example, it is much more difficult to tease out the differences and to explain these differences, between countries, legal jurisdictions, industry sectors, organization sizes, and geographical areas, to say nothing of the differences between the HR policies applied to different occupational groups. Both authors have a long-standing interest in the impact of context upon HRM, and the advent of the recession and ongoing changes to the social context has made apparent the significance of context, and brought into sharp relief the changes to the meaning of the concepts so often found in HR texts. We wanted to capture the confluence of the long term changing social and technological context with economic, financial, and institutional pressures, at this time, in order to point to the new directions in HRM which are emerging. We also think we should provide a counter-weight to those books on HRM which imply 'business as usual', so that researchers, managers, and students of HRM will have a basis for discussing the issues of the present and the future.

The recession itself has, of course, affected industries and countries differently. This made the task of writing the book even more problematic, as inevitably we will be driven towards some generalization. The main differences we believe are between those countries experiencing economic growth at levels which are not too much reduced from pre-financial crash days, and European, the USA, and similar economies which have all been badly affected. Our book, therefore, wherever possible draws examples and data from those most affected by the recession, but as we are based in the UK we are aware that we have a mostly Anglo Saxon version of events. The changes and trends are, however, impacting all major economies, and we have drawn on data from many countries in our descriptions and examples. The question of whether there is a convergence between countries in HR policies and practices is open to debate, but although there are differences in policies reflecting the different country contexts, commentators seem to agree there is a degree of commonality in the objectives of HR policies (Mayrhofer *et al.* 2011).

We believe the book will be a timely reminder that the HR field of study has altered. While writing the book we were cheered to find there were academic articles beginning to come out where there was a recognition of the economic changes, for example the special issue of the *International Journal of Human Resource Management* of July 2012. Although organizational agility had already been recognized as a growing aspect of HR strategy (Dyer and Schafer 2003; Boxall and Purcell 2011), the article by Nijessen and Paauwe (2012) is a sign that the need for organizations to be more responsive to their contexts if they are to survive is now normal currency. We intend our book to be a contribution to the debate about the effect of long term and immediate unpredictable change on HRM and to set out the consequences for the development of the function. We seek to explain the impact of changes by our analysis, using theories to help to explain the nature of the changes and the consequences for managing people at work.

The recession we see as marking the end of an era. There will be no return in the foreseeable future to the expansionist carelessness of the first few years of this century. This does mean there will be controlled growth, but as we set out to explain, the social and economic issues we are resolving require a more responsible capitalism, with important social objectives to achieve. We think the book will be of interest, therefore, to thinking practitioners and academics alike, to those who specialize in HRM, and to managers with responsibilities for strategy. We have also seen our natural readership as students who specialize in HRM, and those who are researching in the field.

Part I
The new context

2 The new social context of HRM

Human resource management (HRM) as an activity and as a field of study has derived from three dominant forces. These are: economic influences and trends, social and legal institutions, and influences within organizations. The view that HRM has always been influenced in this way is not a new thought. Since the 1950s and 1960s, there has been research into the role of HR specialists and what they do, and organizational factors as well as the traditions of industries were seen as important influences. The unique feature of HRM at the organizational level of analysis is its role in bringing together these influences on employees and reinterpreting and legitimating the meaning of HRM activities according to organizational needs (Tyson 1997). In this chapter, we will focus on the social and institutional environment. The economic environment will be considered in Chapter 3.

The development of HRM is affected by the social context in which an organization and its employees operate. As the social context changes, so will the needs of employees and the requirements for people management. The 'human' in HRM, is, after all, the most important element in any organization, without which nothing would be achieved or created. Institutional theory and neo-institutionalism imply that legal institutions and laws, the pressure of societal norms, demographic trends, religious institutions, class or caste, and cultural traditions have a powerful effect on behaviour, driving organizations towards convergence in HR policies and other management practices (DiMaggio and Powell 1983). Indeed, organizational practices, including HR practices, are seen as having been directly shaped by the rules and structures built into their larger environments (Powell 1998). These isomorphic tendencies are not totally deterministic, as there are countervailing pressures, so there is a constant process of adapting, compromising, and adjusting by organizations in order to ensure survival.

DiMaggio and Powell (1983) suggest three institutional mechanisms that influence the adoption of practices by organizations: first, coercive mechanisms which arise from political influence and legitimacy such as trade unions, employment legislation, and the government; second, mimetic mechanisms which arise from standard responses to uncertainty, such as imitating competitors or following management fashions; and finally, normative mechanisms, related to the professionalization of (in this case) human resource management, such as the influence of HR qualifications and professional bodies, for example the Chartered Institute of Personnel and Development (CIPD) and Society for Human Resource Management (SHRM) (Paauwe and Boselie 2003). Paauwe and Boselie (2003) suggested that it is these three mechanisms, rather than the need to create unique resources in order to achieve competitive advantage (as argued in the resource based view) that drives the development of particular HR practices and trends. Neo-institutionalism therefore provides a useful lens through which to examine the impact of the social environment on HRM.

The impact of the social environment can be illustrated by looking at the way in which multinational corporations often shape the HR practices of their subsidiaries to the national context in which that subsidiary is operating. For example, Brewster *et al.* (2008) have produced data to show that although multinational corporations (MNCs) try to use common policies across the globe, there are pressures wherever they are based locally to conform to host country norms. The compromises on policies that are used are evidence that, in spite of the desire of MNCs for convergence and standardization of policies, the host country pressures, for example from laws, labour markets, and local institutions, lead to a mixture of host country and home country policies being adopted. In truth, the adoption of HRM practices is a combination of the deterministic influences of the institutional environment and the strategic choices of the organization, depending on how much agency or leeway the organization has (Boon *et al.* 2009). In this way, the choice of HR practices will not only be affected by coercive mechanisms but also by less deterministic mimetic and normative factors.

Long term trends in HRM are shaped in a similar way to HRM practices in MNCs, as the coercive, mimetic, and normative influences offered by the social context change over time. The social environment therefore has a key role in shaping the nature of HRM. This idea is central to the thesis of this book as a whole: throughout this text we will discuss how recent trends in HRM can be connected to changes in the external context. The question addressed by this chapter is therefore: what are the major social changes which are impacting on employment and the work of HRM?

The social context in which people live and work has changed considerably since the end of the last century. This means that the nature of HRM also needs to develop in order to accommodate the evolving environment in which organizations and their employees operate. In this chapter we will divide these changes to the social context into a number of themes and discuss these in turn: first, we will look at developments in the labour market, both as a result of the economic downturn and changes to international borders, as well as examining the impact of workforce and family demographics; second, we will look at how the expectations of employees have changed, in particular changes to career structures and the psychological contract; and finally we will discuss the evolving role of employment law, which not only follows important change in values and mirrors societal trends, but also shapes HRM. It is the combination of these factors that reflects the needs of the workforce and therefore impacts on the development of HRM.

Labour markets and demographics

Since the banking crisis, and the subsequent recession, employment opportunities have become reduced and new labour force entrants in the 16–24 year old bracket have been particularly badly affected. The USA has experienced an unusually high unemployment rate over the past two years – 8.3 per cent in 2012 compared to 5.7 per cent in 2009. In the UK the unemployment rate has also risen steadily, reaching 8.4 per cent in January 2012, although this had dropped to 7.8 per cent in December 2012. Unemployment is a particular problem for young people: between November 2011 and January 2012 1.04 million (22.5 per cent) 16–24 year olds were unemployed, a rise of 7 per cent on the same quarter in 2011 (Office for National Statistics (ONS) 2012a). The situation is even worse in other areas of Europe, with over 50 per cent of young people unemployed in Spain and Greece, and in the USA youth unemployment rates rose from around 10 per cent in July 2007 to over 18 per cent in July 2011.

The state of the labour market can be related, at least in part, to educational structures and standards within a country. For example, youth unemployment in the UK has been blamed to some extent on the failure of the UK educational system to prepare young people to enter the workforce. Indeed, general numeracy and literacy in the UK is poor, with a 2011 Government study suggesting that 24 per cent of UK adults would struggle to count up to 1,000, meaning that they had the number skills of a child aged nine or younger. The study also found that 15 per cent of UK adults had the reading and writing age of a child aged 11 or younger (Shepherd 2011). There has also been some suggestion in the popular media that young people lack the communication, interpersonal, and self-presentation and self-management skills that employers require. These difficulties present obvious challenges to HRM practitioners in recruiting and developing their employees.

The nature of the workforce and labour market itself is also changing. In Europe, many employers have taken advantage of the effects of wider European Community membership, and are now able to choose from a larger labour market. In addition, employers have also benefited from the mass migrations from developing countries in the early years of this century. For example, in the UK, net migration in the year up to June 2011 was 250,000, with these immigrants most commonly coming from India (11.9 per cent), Pakistan (5.8 per cent), Poland (5.4 per cent), Australia (5.2 per cent), and China (5.2 per cent). In addition, the increased mobility offered by EU membership has meant that immigration from Eastern European countries into the UK has risen considerably, from 5,000 in 2009 to 40,000 in 2010 (ONS 2012b). This will increase further following the removal of restrictions on the movement of Bulgarian and Romanian nationals within the EU in 2014. It has been estimated that around 50,000 people will immigrate to the UK from Bulgaria and Romania per year (BBC Online 2013). As a consequence of increasing immigration, many UK organizations have an international workforce, working domestically. This is also true of other European states, and of the USA, where there is a continuous stream of migrants from South and Central America. In the 2009 USA Census Bureau's American Community Survey, immigrants made up 12.5 per cent of the US population. In addition, the proportion of non-white ethnic groups within both the UK and USA is increasing, as earlier immigrants to these countries have first and second generation British or American children. For example, in the UK, the proportion of non-white British grew by 40 per cent within eight years, to 9.1 million (approximately 1 in 6) (Bentham 2011). This group is predicted to grow to 20 per cent of the UK population by 2051 (BBC Online 2010). The existence of a multicultural workforce not only means that employers must develop policies and practices that account for cultural, ethnic, and religious differences, but also that they can no longer count on shared values in the organization, unless they can create them for themselves.

Ethnic and cultural origin is not the only basis on which the workforce is becoming more diverse. The proportion of women in the labour market has been increasing steadily over the past few years. According to the EU Labour Force Survey, 64.4 per cent of women of working age within the EU were active in the labour force in 2010. Despite the fact that workforce participation of men has declined slightly (International Labour Office (ILO) 2010) the proportion of working age women active in the workforce is still considerably lower than the proportion of working age men (77.6 per cent) (Eurostat 2010), although the percentage point gap between the proportion of men and women working is narrowing (ILO 2010). Data suggest that women represent around 40 per cent of people working worldwide (ILO 2010). In addition to the increase in women at work generally, there has also been a move away from the tendency for women to work in vulnerable occupations such as self-employed and family work into waged and salaried employment (ILO 2010). However, it should be noted that in some countries, such as those in which women lack even the right to make basic choices such as how to contribute economically to the household, there is still much that needs to be done to encourage and advocate for women's rights in the labour force (ILO 2010). Women also appear to have been hit slightly harder internationally by the global economic crisis with the global female unemployment rate rising from 6 per cent to 7 per cent compared to male unemployment rising from 5.5 per cent to 6.3 per cent, with past research suggesting that women are generally slower to return to work during economic recovery compared to men (ILO 2010).

It should also not be news to anyone that the population is ageing, as this has been much talked about by the media and governments over the past decade. Taking the UK as an example, it is projected that by 2050 there will be around 19 million people over 65 – around a quarter of the population. The numbers of individuals over age 80 grows even faster, with the number of over 80 year olds projected to be 8 million by 2050. This change is due to increases in life expectancy – this has risen by around 3 years in the last decade with the life expectancy now at an average of 80.17 in the UK, 81.90 in Australia, 81.48 in Canada, and 78.49 in the USA (CIA Factbook 2013). This, coupled with lower birth rates (the number of births per 1,000 population worldwide has fallen from 37.2 in 1950–55 to 21.2 in 2000–5 (United Nations 2008)), means that there has been an overall increase in the age of the world's population. This in turn leads to an increasing strain on social security and pension funds. In fact, the ratio of people of working age to every pensioner in the UK is projected to fall to 2.8 by 2033 (ONS 2008). For employers, the ageing popu-lation means that there are fewer younger workers entering the workforce so that competition to recruit younger people has increased. In addition, increas-ing life expectancy, pressure on pension funds, and the removal of mandatory retirement in countries such as the UK and Canada has meant that people are staying in the workforce for longer if they can. Indeed in the UK, data from the Office for National Statistics (2012a) shows that the average age at which people leave the workforce rose from 63.8 to 64.6 for men and from 61.2 to 62.3 for women between 2004 and 2010. All of these developments in the make-up of the workforce have implications for HRM, in the potential differ-ences in the preferences and needs of these groups. These will be discussed in more detail in Chapter 8 on equality and diversity, later in this text.

Technology and means of communication

In addition to changes to the workforce itself and to the expectations of employees, technological advancement has brought significant changes to the way that people work, play, and communicate. Information technology (IT) has had a dramatic impact on the workplace, with manufacturing being transformed by the use of technology such as computer controlled and auto-mated machine tools, computerized diagnostic and testing equipment, and computer assisted design (Handel 2003). IT has also transformed the office environment through the introduction of computers, email, word processing, and data entry and analysis software. Over the past 20 years, the Internet has revolutionized both the workplace and home environment by providing easy access to information and connections between people regardless of where they are in the world and at what time. Internet usage has grown from only 0.4 per cent of the world population in December 1995 to 28.7 per cent in June 2010 (www.allaboutmarketresearch.com). Recent research in the UK found that 77 per cent of households had internet access (ONS 2008). The Internet itself has recently evolved from a platform that provides information to users (web 1.0) to one that promotes two-way communication, collaboration, and interaction (web 2.0) through the use of social media tools such as blogs, wikis, social networking sites, and RSS feeds. Indeed, recent UK research found that 91 per cent of 16–24 year olds took part in social networking sites such as Facebook or Twitter (ONS 2008). Web 2.0 has not been limited to personal interactions, with many organizations adopting social media technology to promote collaboration and knowledge sharing among employees and with many individuals choosing to use professional networking sites such as LinkedIn to develop contacts and seek work (see Chapter 6). The way that people access the Internet has also changed with the development of wireless and more recently mobile and Cloud technology. Data show that 45 per cent of UK internet users used a mobile phone to connect to the Internet and 6 million people had accessed the Internet using a mobile phone for the first time in the 12 months up until January 2011. Around 6.8 per cent of internet use in the UK was from non-PC sources in 2011 (Arthur 2011), but this is bound to rise over the next few years. At the time of writing, over 20 per cent of internet use within the USA was via smartphones and tablet computers (Rougeau 2012), with 14.6 per cent of all internet surfing undertaken on smartphones and 5.6 per cent on tablets. We will discuss the impact of technology on HRM in more detail later in this text (see Chapter 6), but it is important here to note that technological advances have completely changed the way that people communicate and interact and that this, in turn, must surely have an impact on their expectations for work. We mention below the hypothesized impact of technology on work values through our discussion of generations. Indeed, the change in the technological environment has had an enormous and permanent impact on the values and expectations of employees and also on the way in which HRM is undertaken.

Values and expectations of the workforce

The changes in the nature of the workforce and external environment have an impact on the values of individuals and society as a whole. Values can be defined as 'an enduring belief that a specific mode of conduct or end-state of existence is personally or socially preferable to an opposite or converse mode of conduct or end-state of existence' (Rokeach 1973: 5), so values are seen as defining what people believe to be fundamentally right or wrong in both life and at work. Values are generally developed as an individual grows up and are affected by social interactions such as those with parents, teachers, friends, and other role models. Individual values are generally presumed to remain roughly the same over the course of an individual's life. However, the values of society as a whole are driven to a large extent by the external environment. For example, a large body of literature has discussed the impact of national culture on work values (for example, Schwartz 1992, 1994; Hofstede 1996) in that individuals who grow up in different national contexts have different values and preferences. Similarly, more recently much attention has been given to the impact of age, or more specifically year of birth, on values, through the study of generational diversity (Strauss and Howe 1991; Smola and Sutton 2002; Lyons *et al.* 2007; Twenge and Campbell 2008).

Table 2.1 Definitions of generational groups currently in the workforce

Generation	Years of birth	Also known as
Veterans	1925–42	Silent Generation, Matures, Traditionalists
Baby Boomers	1943–60	
Generation X	1961–81	Thirteenth, Baby Busters, Lost Generation
Generation Y	1982–	Millennials, Nexters, Echo Boomers

Source: Parry and Urwin (2011).

As the idea of generational diversity in values is based firmly on the idea that the external context affects the values of a cohort of individuals, it is worth pausing to consider this in more detail. A 'generation' is often very broadly defined as, for example, 'an identifiable group that shares birth years, age, location and significant life events at critical developmental stages' (Kupperschmidt 2000: 66). Within Western economies, most of the attention has focused on the four generations of Veterans, Baby Boomers, Generation X, and Generation Y. These four generations are defined in Table 2.1 above (taken from Parry and Urwin 2011).

Veterans are now moving out of the workforce but, more recently, discussion has also moved to a fifth generation – called Generation Z, M (multitasking), C (Connected), or N (Net) – born after 1990. Little is known about this group so far. Theoretically, members of the same generation share the same year of birth so have a common location in the historical dimension of the social process. This limits them to a specific range of potential experience, predisposing them to a certain characteristic mode of thought and experience (Mannheim 1952). According to Mannheim (1952), there are two important elements to the term 'generation'. First, a common location in historical time and second a 'distinct consciousness of that historical position ... shaped by the events and experiences of that time' (Gilleard 2004: 108). Therefore the grouping of individuals within the four or five generations discussed above is based on the belief that they each share a different set of values and attitudes, as a result of shared events and experiences as they grew up. For example, some consider that Generation X saw their parents being made redundant in the 1980s and this shaped their perceptions of work in a time of economic uncertainty. It is suggested that this led to a tendency for them to see each job as temporary and each company as a 'stepping stone' to something else (Filipczak 1994). Similarly, the characteristics of Generations Y and Z are seen as having been shaped by the existence of internet technology meaning that they expect constant and immediate feedback. We will discuss generational differences and their relationship to equality and diversity within organizations in more detail in Chapter 8.

It can be seen how the values, needs, and preferences of different age cohorts, and ethnic and cultural groups in the workforce might have an impact on the nature of HRM within an organization. Other factors also affect the needs and values of employees. Social life within the UK and USA at least has changed through the collapse of the traditional family. For example, a high proportion of families are now dependent on a single parent. In the UK, 26 per cent of households with dependent children are single parent families (92 per cent are women) with over 2 million single parents in Britain in total. This has increased considerably since the 1970s (only 8 per cent in 1971) but has remained relatively consistent since the mid 1990s. There are over 3 million children in the UK in single parent families (Gingerbread 2012). Within the USA, there are 13.7 million single parents of 21.8 million children (About.com 2012). On top of this change to the structure of a family, teenage pregnancy is now relatively common, particularly in the UK which has higher teenage pregnancy rates than most of the rest of Europe. However, the rate of pregnancy in under 18s fell slightly recently to 34,633 in 2010 compared to 38,259 in 2009 (a fall of 9.5 per cent). The rate of pregnancies in under 16 year olds has also fallen to 6,674 in 2010, from 7,158 in 2009 (a 6.8 per cent drop) (ONS 2012a). On top of these figures, and cause for greater concern, is the fact that the rate of child poverty is high – 18 per cent of UK children in 2010–11 lived in households earning less than 60 per cent of the median UK income. Figures suggest, however, that child poverty is considerably higher in particular areas of the UK, for example 47 per cent in Central Manchester and 42 per cent in the Bethnal Green and Bow areas of London (BBC Online 2013).

These changes in the make-up of the population all have an impact on individuals' values and therefore have resulted in changes in the overall needs and expectations of the employee population.

Working patterns

For instance, the steady growth in female participation in the labour market in the Western world means that there is an increased requirement for flexible working and other policies that address the needs of those with caring responsibilities. Indeed, many EU countries, including the UK, have introduced legislation that ensures that individuals with young dependent children have the right to request flexible working arrangements from their organization. The fact that people are working for longer, up to and past retirement, has also led to an increased demand for work–life balance. In many countries organizations have introduced 'bridge employment' practices that include a range of part time and other flexible working practices that people engage in as they approach retirement (Schultz 2003). Since the early 1990s a number of new patterns of working have appeared, such as widespread home-working, part time working, and flexibility of time, task, location, and contract. For example, data from a recent survey of HRM policies and practices in

33 countries worldwide (Cranet 2009) showed that just under 80 per cent of organizations used part time work and around 65 per cent used flexitime. The recession has actually given these practices a new impetus, with many organizations choosing to move a number of individual employees onto part time contracts rather than undertake more permanent downsizing. In addition, data on younger workers, known as Generations X and Y, suggest an increased emphasis on work–life balance as being important in their requirements for employment. We will discuss flexible working in light of the changes to organizational structures in Chapter 4.

Career structures and the psychological contract

Fifty years ago, careers were viewed as being simple, linear structures (Super 1957). Typically, an individual would work for only one or two employers and would move up in an organization hierarchically until they were no longer able to do so due to a lack of capability or because they had reached retirement. This meant that the psychological contract – the implicit mutual obligations perceived between an employee and employer, which specify what each party expects to give and receive (Kotter 1973) – could be conceived mainly as the employer's provision of a stable 'job for life' in return for the employee's loyalty and hard work. It can be seen that this career structure and formation of the psychological contract was based upon a period when change was slow, job security was high, and labour turnover was low. Over the past 20 years in particular, this situation has changed to one where frequent organizational restructuring has meant that organizational change is more common and job security is no longer the norm. This has led to a decline in the traditional long term career spent in one or two organizations (Hall and Mirvis 1996; Sullivan 1999), in that workers have been forced to move in and out of several organizations during their careers and that their willingness to be loyal to an employer is reduced. This has led to changes in both the nature of careers and the psychological contract.

In order to account for some of these changes, a number of new theories and structures for careers have been proposed. For instance, Arthur and Rousseau's (1996) theory of 'boundaryless' careers and Hall and Moss's (1998) 'protean' career theory suggested first that the responsibility for career development had shifted from the organization to the individual, and second, that an individual creates their own career identity using mobility between employers as a means of career development and maintaining allegiance to themselves rather than a single employing body. Boundaryless careers involve both objective (e.g. physical mobility) and subjective (attitudinal) features, but a common factor in all of these is the independence from (rather than dependence on) traditional career arrangements (Arthur and Rousseau 1996).

Alongside these changes in career structures, there has also been a change in the psychological contract and the expectations of employees. Rousseau

(1995) describes this as a transition from a long term 'relational' psychological contract that involved a long term investment from both parties, to a short term 'transactional' contract that focuses on economic rewards and low employee commitment. Indeed, much of the media attention on the younger generations in the workforce – Generations X and Y – has described them having a low level of loyalty to their employers, and seeking the development of their marketable skills rather than a long term employment relationship. As the emphasis for career management moves more onto the individual to manage and to support through education and learning, employee expectations now include the individualization of the contract and of the reward package, and a more explicit statement of requirements from employers regarding behaviour at work, and what is permissible (see Chapter 12).

Employment law

It would be remiss of us not to mention employment legislation here, although the purpose of this book is not to discuss the impact of employment law changes in any detail. The amount of protection offered to employees by the state differs by country, with those coordinated market economies which have high trade union influence such as Germany and the Netherlands offering more protection than liberal market economies such as the UK and the USA. As a general trend, regardless of the national context, employment law (supported for instance by European Union legislation) has grown annually to become a massive and complex web of rights and obligations. This means that employers now need to deal with a myriad of laws pertaining to wage regulation, working time, child care, health and safety, occupational pensions, equality, and discrimination.

The increasingly legislative environment for employment adds greatly to the complexity of the work undertaken by HR practitioners. The HR function within an organization is responsible for ensuring that the organization complies with employment law, and also for training other managers and employees to comply with these laws. The HR function is therefore responsible for ensuring that all HR activity – recruitment, selection, promotion, training and development, career development, compensation and benefits, employment relations, redundancy and retirement – is undertaken within the limits set out by a country's employment legislation. The systems of regulation which apply in most developed economies may well encourage litigiousness, and result in rigidities in the labour market. Although this does not result in more formal employment contracts, important freedoms are protected.

Conclusions

We have provided an overview of the main changes to the social context in which organizations are operating today. There are undoubtedly others – few would agree that the social environment of work today is in any way similar to that of 40 years ago. We now live in a more atomistic society, there are fewer traditional families, more people living alone, less sense of community, fewer shared values, new working practices, more travel, and more communication.

HR practitioners in contemporary organizations are faced with a labour market and population that are changing dramatically – resulting in increased diversity of gender, ethnicity, and age among other dimensions within the workforce. This leads to the increased need for employers to address discrimination and promote equality within their organization in order to operate within anti-discrimination legislation set up as a response to increased diversity in the population and to promote fairness for their workforce. Employers also, however, need to find ways in which to leverage and take advantage of this diversity in order to improve their competitive advantage. We will discuss this further in Chapter 8 of this text.

The development of new technologies is an ongoing trend, from the industrial revolution to the changing faces of the Internet that permeate every aspect of virtually every individual's life, both inside and outside work. Over the past 20 years, internet technology has developed incredibly quickly – it is up to the HR function to keep pace with this, in order to both benefit from the value of these technologies in managing people efficiently and effectively, and also to meet the expectations of today's workers. We will examine the impact of technology on HRM in some detail in Chapter 6.

Finally, we see that the expectations of workers of their employers, careers, and life in general are also shifting with time, and as the external context changes. This shift has led to the need for corresponding changes in the nature of careers, working patterns, and psychological contracts and has also led to significant interest in the idea of generational differences – a concept that has face validity for HR practitioners attempting to deal with work values and preferences that differ by the age group of employees. Once again, it is within the remit of the HR function, as well as of line managers, to address these changing values in their design of terms and conditions, working environments, career structures, and rewards, in order to promote the retention and satisfaction of employees.

The above changes in the external social context mean that both the HR function and line managers have had to change the ways in which they manage people, the systems and policies that are in place, and their approach to attracting and retaining the individuals that they need within the organization. This is not a single step change, but an ongoing process of change as trends in demographics, technological advancement, and attitudinal change are ongoing. We will examine these changes and the resulting trends in contemporary HRM throughout this text.

3 The new economic context of HRM

The economic state of nations has come to determine the political agenda of most of the developed countries in the world. The significance of the economic context is such that economic performance has come to dominate the thinking of entrepreneurs, working people, managers, and of the wider society. We therefore see this area as a super-ordinate contextual factor which dictates the options available to governments, and the policy choices made in such diverse fields as health provision, education, defence, government support for business, and welfare support. In this chapter we examine the impact of the economic context upon human resource management (HRM). We therefore will discuss the consequences of economic uncertainty and volatility, the issues of unemployment and changes to the labour market, skills and organizational capabilities, competitive advantage, different forms of capitalism, and the prospects for HRM.

Recession

At the time of writing, most economies are in the midst of an economic downturn, following the financial crash of 2008. We have not yet quite reached the same position as after the Wall Street crash of 1929. In the decade of the late 1920s to late 1930s there were never less than 10 per cent of people unemployed in the UK, and similar figures in other European countries and in the USA. Although unemployment rates are lower currently, there is considerable youth unemployment, there are major problems of debt and there has been a financial crash. Recessions create the conditions for fundamental change, by shifting irrevocably political agendas and social reality, so that there is a sharper focus, not just on political and economic issues, but also in working life where social and cultural experiences are embedded. In 1939, on the eve of the Second World War, W.H. Auden wrote:

> I sit in one of the dives
> On Fifty-second Street
> Uncertain and afraid

As the clever hopes expire
Of a low dishonest decade.
Waves of anger and fear
Circulate over the bright
And darkened lands of the earth,
Obsessing our private lives ...

September 1, 1939

Our past decade has included the major financial crash of the banks in the UK and the USA, producing a general feeling of distrust directed at bankers and politicians. The decade covers in addition: the Presidency of George Bush, the attacks on 9/11, the Iraq and Afghan Wars, Prime Minister Blair's premiership and the 'dodgy dossier', the scandals of the UK parliament over expenses, and of bankers over bonuses, the collapse of Lehman Bros. Bank, the sub-prime mortgage fiasco, and the time when the Royal Bank of Scotland posted the biggest loss in British corporate history, ending up with a part nationalization in order to protect its customers.

The excessive debts, first of individuals, then of companies, and now of sovereign states have produced a secondary crisis of the Euro currency in the European Union, where even some of the larger economies are seen to be at risk due to unsustainable borrowing by some EU countries, and the exposure of banks in other countries to risks should there be a default on loans already made. The USA, as with its European counterparts, also has debts comprising a large percentage of its annual GDP, and along with the UK, has lost the coveted 'triple A' rating. The markets suspect that the long cycle of growth in the older economies is coming to an end, and are turning more and more to China, India, and to countries such as Brazil to be the engines of future growth, suggesting that the fault lines are appearing in the doctrine of progress for the West. This is the back story to economic development and business strategy from now onwards.

The economic events of the last decade have created a sense of uncertainty and have dashed the hopes of millions of people. The recession and the fear of a slump have an intensely private as well as a public presence in the lives of people. High unemployment, uncertainty over the future, and a reduced role for the state in protecting individuals from the effects of major economic change, have produced a realization of the fragility of our prosperity. 'In 2007 the sub-prime market, so favoured up to this point, collapsed. This would be the catalyst that would herald the beginning of the end of the post-war capitalist financial model as we know it' (Moyo 2011: 69). The significance of this crisis is that the full employment society, with booming house prices and share prices, and ever improving state support for health, education and welfare, expensive defence projects, and the expanding administration of government support, has gone from the West for the foreseeable future.

The effects of the slowdown and long term competitiveness

The economic crisis has brought an exogenous shock to the system, and hence to employers and employees. The first important effect has been the creation of uncertainty, for employers, for employees, and for investors alike. Speculative investors can no longer anticipate high returns: the desired home for investments is a safe, if less remunerative opportunity. The UK and the USA have enjoyed low interest rates and low long term inflation during the last five years. This may lead to caution and risk aversion, and also to a desire to sweat the firm's assets before commitment of any future investment in expansion. Many companies have become cash rich, and less inclined to borrow. Banks are also cautious about loans, since they have to maintain larger fiduciary deposits, and may themselves be exposed to unexpected defaults. Banks in Europe and in the USA have been put under more scrutiny through new regulatory regimes, with improvements to corporate governance, more transparency about their balance sheets, their transactions, and reward systems. In particular, the 'bonus' culture was widely regarded as having caused the risky decision making which led to disasters – for example the risks associated with the Royal Bank of Scotland's acquisition of ABM Amro.

Second, the workforce is now in two separate tiers. In the UK, the Government has adopted a policy which seeks to rebalance the economy, away from the public, towards the private sector, and towards manufacturing, and away from the service sector. There are those with a secure full time job, for example in manufacturing, and those who find it impossible to climb back onto the employment ladder, or who may never have had a job. For these people, there may be part time work, casual work, internships, and similar roles. They are the true victims of the recession, including both older workers made redundant, women who left the workforce to have a baby and are now without a recent employment record or skills, whose skills are perceived to be obsolete, and many young university graduates whose hopes of a great career are being destroyed. In future, such people will have to be more opportunistic, and prepared to move to find work, and to change their ambitions more rapidly.

There are longer term issues. To what extent are businesses in the West able to compete against the emerging economies of Brazil, Russia, India, and China (the BRIC countries) and other giants growing in the background, such as Indonesia, Turkey, Canada, Australia, and South Africa? It could be argued that even without the banking crisis, the basis for development in the UK and USA was on shaky foundations, since increasingly we had become reliant on the Far East to be the engine of growth for the world economy, and some developed economies were becoming less competitive on costs and even on quality with some products and services. In Europe, countries such as Germany and France have largely maintained their competitive advantage in view of their skill base and engineering traditions and well founded education systems, but also because of the structure of their economies (for example state owned and family owned businesses in France, and close linkages between the banks and manufacturing businesses in Germany). The governments in both of these countries seem to have espoused industrial policies, which are long term and which therefore provide support and direction over decades to companies. For many European Union companies, high tax rates with considerable and expensive social benefits, including holidays, pensions, and social security are driving them out of business. It seems probable that the banking crisis may have masked these weaknesses when demand faltered, and the reality of uncompetitive working practices, products, and labour costs became apparent.

The lack of competitiveness remains an issue for European companies. As German Chancellor, Angela Merkel said in an interview with the *Financial Times*:

> Europe will have to work very hard to maintain the most generous welfare system in the world, and remain globally competitive. If Europe today accounts for just over 7 per cent of the world's population, produces around 25 per cent of global GDP, and has to finance 50 per cent of global social spending, then it is obvious that it will have to work very hard to maintain its prosperity and way of life.
>
> (Peel 2012)

A study for the European Union (EORY's ENTR06/054 2011), examining the cost competitiveness of European manufacturing industries of 16 EU countries comparing unit labour costs at sectoral level with those in Brazil, China, and India, showed that EU country unit labour cost competitiveness deteriorated over the period 2000–7, due to the lower costs in China at that time. Unit labour costs in Greece, Portugal, Spain, and Italy increased compared to the average for ten of the EU's most competitive economies over that period. The study 'also shows that there is no simple, consistent relationship between trends in the trade balance and trends in REERs' (p. 11; REERs refers to real effective exchange rates). Other issues as, if not more, important as labour costs were cited as research and development expenditure in industries such as pharmaceuticals, chemicals, engineering, electrical machinery, and restructuring in industries such as textiles, and a number of other local factors.

However, although there are now many European countries where wage costs are falling, in manufacturing (by 2012, Spain, Greece, Ireland, and Portugal had reduced by around 15 per cent since 2009), improved competition does not necessarily produce growth, because falling domestic demand, structural unemployment, and a lack of investment stifle any revival. Problems with growth in Europe as a whole have begun to affect growth in other countries such as France and Germany, which were initially unaffected (Janson 2012). In the USA, there are improvements in competitiveness. Kell (2012), using data from the Boston Consulting Group and William Mercer consultancy, described how the USA had become uncompetitive, with an average manufacturing wage rate 23 times higher than China, which had improved to 11 times higher by 2012, and was projected to be only 6 times higher by 2015. If the productivity of US workers is taken into account, this will be adjusted to 2.3 times higher than in China by then. In addition, Chinese wage rates are projected to rise as the country becomes wealthier, and its middle class continues to grow. The main constraint, in the USA as well as China, is the shortage of talent. This is reflected in pay rates.

By contrast, UK productivity is still a cause for concern. Aston (2013) points to the Office of National Statistics (ONS) Survey, which showed UK output per hour as 15 per cent below the average for the G7 countries, in 2011, and the output per worker at 20 per cent lower than the average for the G7. The US Bureau of Labor Statistics Report (2012) showed that unit labour costs fell in the USA in the period 2000–7, while they rose in the UK, but fell in Germany. In the period 2007–10, unit labour costs rose at a higher rate in the UK than in the USA and Germany. The UK has a long term productivity problem, which would need to be addressed to ensure growth.

Competitiveness and the resource based view

The situation created by the economic crisis provides a test for the resource based view (RBV) of competitive business strategy, a theoretical construct which has become accepted as an underlying theory which can be utilized in the study of HRM (Wernerfelt 1984; Barney 1991; Wright *et al.* 2001). The reason for the prominence of the RBV is no doubt due to its concentration on the contribution of internal firm resources to competitive advantage. The central tenet of the theory is that firms create and sustain competitive advantage over their rivals in any given industry by developing resources which are rare, valuable, inimitable, and non-substitutable. The RBV makes two simplifying assumptions about firms: that a firm's performance is a consequence of various allocation and resource decisions made over time which produce what might be described as its unique combination of resources (a path dependency assumption), and that it is able to be competitive with other firms because of firm heterogeneity; and that firms are different from each other because they possess attributes and a history which others cannot easily imitate (Lockett *et al.* 2009). The idea that firms are idiosyncratic with their own particular history, and hence have a 'footprint' of resources, has high face validity. This becomes more easily seen if, in the 'resources' category, we include organizational routines and methods for learning from mistakes and responding to market changes, which develops capability in functions such as marketing, production, and human resources over time.

The question then arises of what happens to these resources when the economy changes dramatically and the path of development no longer offers a guide to the future? The strategic inflection point we discussed earlier was a game changing series of events, and this leads on to what are the dynamic capabilities, and the missing link in the RBV is the enabling capability which we will describe in Chapter 4 on organizations as 'organizational agility'. An enabling capability brings to the fore the capacity to adapt competence or firm attributes, so that the firm can adapt. We call this 'agility'. There are, of course, other critiques of the RBV, which comment inter alia on the functionality of the resources, and the apparent tautology of the thesis because differences in firm performance are attributed to differences in firms (Lockett *et al.* 2009).

Gaining competitive advantage through innovation

In spite of its weaknesses, the RBV reminds us that sudden economic change is disruptive to firm performance. HRM policies and practices must therefore be geared to helping organizations respond rapidly to the changes. The RBV does help to explain how some companies have managed to survive recessions and major market changes. The RBV can be used as a basis for discussion of other sources of change which are equally important. Some changes can have a very rapid effect, for example changes to retailing as a consequence of the revolution of shopping online. The changes to shopping patterns were not unexpected. Retailers such as Waitrose/John Lewis Partnership have been selling online for around ten years, but no one could easily predict when customers would become more inclined to buy online, nor what the effects would be on the stores, as there is some evidence that online customers may also be more likely to go into the shops as well as make purchases online.

However, there is no doubt that many shops are closing in the main streets/ high streets in the USA and Europe, with consequential job losses. Some of these closures may be due to the retailers who are not doing well, lacking the competencies to develop online business, and so relatively quickly, their human resources have moved from being a source of competitive advantage, to just being a cost. The issue is therefore as much about developing employee competencies, so that employees become more perceptive, and highly adaptable, whatever the rarity of the competencies. Strategic change means that firms need to understand quickly what competencies they need to survive.

New technology developments, as we shall see from Chapter 6 on the impact of technology on HRM, arrive quickly, and the key issue is the take-up rate, in this case by customers. The firm has to know what their customers are typically likely to do when new methods of purchasing products and services become available. The problem is that firms may know how their customers used to react before the recession, but the crisis has changed behaviour, and therefore predicting how customers will react to a new situation is difficult. Path dependency does not help in this situation.

It is not just in the services sector that firms have to revolutionize their way of doing business. In manufacturing there are developments beyond the creation of intelligent robots in factories and warehouses. Additive manufacturing, for example, is a technology which utilizes the breakthroughs in printing from computers to three-dimensional printers. This means that customization can be achieved more extensively by customers designing their own product adjustments or adaptations and sending these online to be produced by a machine which layers the dimensions into a three-dimensional product, for example the mould of a product, which is then manufactured in modern materials. We are moving from the consumer communicating needs electronically to service providers and producers, to the consumer as designer sending the design to a remotely located manufacturer. Greater specificity and customization is achieved therefore. Specialist designers become advisors and consultants, geared to a wide range of requirements. In a world where consumer choice is expressed through an 'app', creating attributes which are rare, un-substitutable, valuable, and inimitable will be a new challenge for HR specialists and other managers alike.

The RBV approach to strategy suggests that companies should be investing in and developing their human assets as a way to overtake the competition. However, the future is not so much about the rather mechanistic competencies pre-recession: the emphasis has now largely shifted to highly flexible systems and imaginative ways of doing business, built on insights gained from a wide experience of the industry. In the current economic context, competition seems to be most likely on cost/price for any given level of quality, quantity, or product or service. However, as the BRIC countries and the new entrants to the EU become equally competitive on cost and quality, the RBV has less to offer as a guide to survival for companies. Innovation and an imaginative approach seem likely to help organizations to be competitive in the new environment. The process of helping the organization to change offers opportunities for employees to learn new capabilities. Innovations in the process of management would be within the RBV of the firm, which might be structural, for example, problem solving groups, research teams, and similar methods (see Chapter 4).

Varieties of capitalism

Our commitment to free trade means that, at present, competition cannot be managed by trade rules. The full force of competition as well as the free movement of labour within the EU therefore produces high levels of unemployment, which national governments can do little to alleviate. There is a potential danger here of a race to the bottom, a reduction in wages and living standards to become more competitive against countries where there are substantially lower wages and less protection for the employee, lower levels of health care, and fewer costs associated with our Western way of life. Within strong democracies, where the voters are reluctant to lose pension, welfare, health, and other benefits, the most likely reaction would be to vote out the politicians who failed them in this way, and to insist on some form of limited protectionism, probably at the supra-national level, for example the European Union or North American level. Although this would bring a temporary respite, the long term result would endanger export markets, and produce a downturn in international trade. These are the dynamics at the heart of the European crisis, for countries such as Greece, Italy, and Portugal, where the challenge to make the country competitive with the low cost emerging economies will be extremely challenging, especially where countries do not have the opportunity to devalue their currencies, as the USA and the UK can do.

The debate has shifted to a series of questions within the field of political economy. In essence, the choices faced by the West are as much political as economic. The inarticulate, but emotionally charged attacks on 'capitalism' found in the movements and sit-ins in New York's Wall Street, and on the steps of Saint Paul's Cathedral in London, blamed capitalism, red in tooth and claw. Capitalism is also blamed in the media, and by some politicians, for creating an atmosphere where excessive risks have been taken with savings and investments by the banks. Increasingly, companies are international in their operations, and outlook. The interconnections between companies are intensified by new technology, by 'just-in-time working', by the vertical integration of companies, and by the tendencies for companies to seek cost reductions through outsourcing aspects of the business to lower cost countries, as well as the need to service clients/customers throughout the world, to beat the competition.

The clash of ideologies which underlies this debate is described in the theoretical discussions about the different forms of capitalism. One robust response to the protestors would have been that at this time what is needed is not less capitalism, but more capitalism. Only by capital formation and investment with more successful businesses will a secure future be built in an uncertain world, it might be said. However, this begs the question of whether there are some forms of capitalism which are more successful or more acceptable than others. Street protesters, including those from the 'Occupy' movement, were trying to draw attention to the question of who should benefit from capitalism? Should this just be the investors, and the rich few who run the businesses, or should there be a public value outcome? The protests in the streets of Spain, Greece, Italy, and Portugal about the austerity packages that have been wished upon the populace, may be because the EU had never been conceived as a 'rich person's club', but through the Social Chapter and the EU mechanisms for assisting social development, was intended to bring social value to the whole society. And yet, as the German Chancellor has pointed out, many of these benefits are no longer affordable. This helps to explain the sense of betrayal felt by those for whom the European dream has become a nightmare.

The long-standing debate on different varieties of capitalism posits two different forms: liberal market economies, and coordinated market economies (Hall and Soskice 2001). Liberal market economies (LMEs) create competitive markets through formal institutions and legal relations with formal contracting, and firms adjust the supply of goods and services in response to demand and price signals. These firms access finance through stock markets and formal hierarchical means. Coordinated market economies (CMEs) through their culture, traditions, and institutions enable firms to coordinate their activities with a strategic relationship with other firms, there being a greater emphasis on networks, on mechanisms for 'deliberation', that is, consultation, for example with trade unions as in the German system of two-tier boards, and its tradition of co-determination (Lawrence 1993).

These two different varieties of capitalism address the common problems of coordination, LMEs through market mechanisms, and CMEs by networks, cultural, social, institutional, and non-market mechanisms. CME approaches to coordination could be through industry level bodies, or group based coordination, i.e. through groups of companies operating in different industries as in Japan's keiretsu type of coordination, or employers' associations, as in Western Europe.

The countries in the OECD that could be classified within the 'varieties of capitalism' literature as typical LMEs are the USA, the UK, Australia, Canada, New Zealand, and Ireland. By contrast, Germany, Japan, Switzerland, the Netherlands, Belgium, Sweden, Norway, Denmark, Finland, and Austria could be classified as CMEs. France, Italy, Spain, Portugal, Greece, and Turkey are a mixture of both types (Hancke 2009). One of the problems of the varieties of capitalism approach is apparent here, since the LMEs seem to be Anglo Saxon countries – all having been British colonies at some time – whereas the CMEs are Northern European and Scandinavian countries. The detailed reasons for these differences need not detain us here, but it is noticeable that the recession has only really hit the USA, UK, and Ireland, of the LMEs, and that the largely Mediterranean countries of those with a mixed approach were most affected by sovereign debt problems. One of the criticisms of the 'varieties of capitalism' theory is that only two varieties were found (Howell 2003), whereas there are perhaps a number of countries where there are mixed forms of the two main types.

The issue for us is the effect of the recession on different countries, and the extent to which different types of capitalist economy are influencing the HRM response to the crisis. One conclusion we might draw is that LMEs can be affected quickly by economic downturns, but also might recover more quickly (as in the USA), since the market is ultimately rational in its outcomes, and responds to good levels of profitability, and to good dividends, but is not so susceptible, for example, to changes of ownership, or to unemployment unless the levels reach a position where demand is badly depressed as a result. LMEs have been less affected by the recession, but where this has occurred, as in Japan, recovery has taken much longer. The mixed approach countries, with the exception of France and Turkey, have had the greatest difficulty in recovery (perhaps because there are no dominant varieties of capitalism in these countries, due to an insufficient number of companies in each type of capitalism), so they are unable to take advantage of the opportunities of each type, but still have the disadvantages. When considering the impact of the economic crisis on HRM we should be mindful of the differential effects on the HR policies and practices of the labour market institutions, and the ways of doing businesses in LMEs and CMEs.

This is illustrated by the German case. Hall and Soskice (2009) describe the complementarities across the subsystems in the German CME companies. These systems work in conjunction, so that there are corporate governance systems which permit long range finance, enabling education and training systems which put skilled employees in powerful positions, in an industrial relations system which provides wage moderation and employee cooperation, and a system of intercompany relations which allows standard setting and technology transfer, which provides reputational monitoring and lower external labour market competition (an aspect of corporate governance).

Conclusions

How will companies compete in the future? In this chapter, we have sought to explore the economic effects of the most significant change to Western economies since the end of the Second World War. The recession can be seen as a wake-up call to Western economies, which were already becoming uncompetitive due to the rise of successful economies from the BRIC countries. This implies that in addition to overcoming the problems of the shock of the crisis, companies should work with their governments to create an industrial policy which helps them to develop strategically over a longer time period.

The further outcome from the analysis stresses the need for companies to develop the competencies which help the firm to adjust to the process of rapid change, as a part of normal business. These agility competencies are more about the way the work is done, and require senior staff to develop insightful capabilities, the challenge for HR being to find techniques for developing high quality, resourceful leaders, who are industry insiders, but who have a wide experience of innovation and the marketing abilities alongside technical knowledge to translate good ideas into products and services. The inimitable competencies reside in the capacity to develop these people as well as the company systems built on successful survival of crises such as the present one. There are clear benefits for companies to develop their business processes by taking advantage of the type of capitalism well developed in the country where they are operating. HR needs to find ways to embed the business in the appropriate market and institutional mechanisms. This might include, for example, linking in to industry bodies, or into local company networks, if appropriate, whereas in LMEs, solutions such as all employee share schemes, formal work on corporate governance arrangements on green issues, and building the employer brand, may well be worthwhile and valued in that society.

Success for companies will only be achieved if there are serious attempts to help to solve the problems of unemployment. These will have to be sustainable jobs. The need for solutions to unemployment problems are central to economic recovery, and were increasingly accepted towards the end of the 1930s recession, when there was a debate about the ideas found in the works of the economist John Maynard Keynes, who saw recovery as contingent upon wages driving demand, and consumption. It is clear on both sides of the Atlantic, and most especially in Europe, that the model most governments are adopting is of organic growth, but with various stimuli, such as 'quantitative easing' and fewer of the massive infrastructure projects, which policy makers in the UK have tended to introduce in a piecemeal way, too late and too little.

Instead, there is more than a touch of allowing the forces of creative destruction, as Joseph Schumpeter described them, to hold sway, in a kind of general belief that the market would right itself (Say's Law), and that letting companies go bust was a way to clean out the inefficient businesses anyway. For example, when Woolworths in the UK failed, commentators were quick to refer to its long term decline, as was said about many other businesses, such as Wedgewood pottery. Schumpeter emphasized sociological factors, especially the cultural institutions and the extent to which societies encouraged entrepreneurial activity. He saw growth as emerging from the development of new products and investment in new technology. Most commentators take a mixture of these ideas from the political economists and economic thinkers from the past, which have entered into the ways of thinking about slumps and recessions. Ultimately, there seems to be an acceptance that whatever model of capitalism is adopted, economic prosperity only comes when companies are successful in the markets where they trade.

There are a number of specific impacts on HRM of the strategic point we have reached. The economic changes have increased the importance of finding the key to growth. These opportunities are likely to come from international development such as collaboration with international businesses, exporting, and by recruiting a more international workforce. The signs of increased pressure on competitiveness are readily seen. Recruitment and employee development are under pressure, in spite of high levels of unemployment, because of the high standards and exacting competencies needed, and the lack of preparedness of companies to compromise in their hunt for talent. Total reward approaches are becoming more popular, as an aspect of the drive to find ways to engage and motivate people, which, along with employee training and development, are often seen as the best way to achieve the possession of those unique and rare resources – often found and expressed in organization cultures and employer brands. The uncertainty which characterizes the current period has turned the attention of HR practitioners towards developing organizational capability. Organization development and change management are organizational capabilities which are the composite terms used to describe the processes and techniques which enable organizations to adjust, to change, to survive, and to succeed. These will occupy our discussions in the remaining chapters in this volume.

4   Changes to organizations

Human resource management (HRM) is an organization-specific activity. Societal and economic contexts heavily influence policies in people management because these contextual factors affect how organizations do business, the demand for their products and services, and their strategic intent.

In this chapter, we discuss how organizations are responding to contextual changes, in the way they are structured, and what this means for the management of people. From the late twentieth century onwards, we have seen many new developments. Organization structure was often shown as a part of the technical system, this being the arrangements and routines of activities and relationships within the organization which were perceived to be the most efficient formation to deliver products and services to customers and other stakeholders. The pace of change, and the need for more openness and involvement, with greater choice for customers and a freer flow of information for employees and suppliers to improve decision making, has prompted attempts to move away from rigid bureaucratic structures towards more 'organic' forms. This trend has been reinforced by the need to adapt to new opportunities, to avoid the threats from a recessionary economic crisis, in a world where trade is increasingly globalized and technological change forces new ways of operating. In order to survive, companies now put a greater priority on adapting to new challenges, which may come in the form of new products and services, and mean using new technologies to improve efficiency, and to add more value for customers.

The increasingly flexible use of labour could be both a cause and an effect of the business strategy changes. A more flexible human resource is more in tune with the flexible use of capital and other resources. There are more joint agreements and alliances between organizations, including marketing and joint production activities, often of an international nature (as for example with Airbus Industries) and companies move into different ownership patterns through, for example, private equity holdings and sovereign wealth funds. The notion that there is a degree of flexibility in the cost base of a company, where people costs are a significant part of total costs, could be seen as positive for rapid changes of direction, and be a part of the value of the business. However, taking the resource based view, where the employees are seen as a source of competitive advantage, there is the question of how embedded in the company are the strategically significant groups of people? The value in most businesses resides in at least some of the specialists and experienced personnel employed, in the work processes and the experience of those who created them. For HR managers and senior line managers, there are new challenges. As Roehling *et al.* (2005) pointed out, managing people is now more about developing and sustaining organizational effectiveness.

What is, or is not, an effective organization structure is a function of many different factors. These include: the relationship between structure and strategy, the balance between risk and control that is adopted, the types of occupational groups employed and the way their work is to be organized, the management of increasing flexibility and complexity in organizations, and the extent to which competitive advantages can be gained by organizing around new technological processes.

We will examine each of these factors, and discuss the inherent people management issues which are likely to emerge. We are assuming throughout that the context is changing rapidly, as is reflected in stock market volatility in all the main Exchanges. The HRM responses to volatility and to economic uncertainty in what is becoming the worst recession faced globally for almost a century are also worth noting and form a significant part of the organizational reaction to context.

The relationship between business strategy and organization structure

There are many definitions of 'business strategy' which cover the different ways the term is used, for example in private or in public sector organizations. We will take a good general definition drawn from the well respected textbook on strategy by Johnson *et al.* (2008: 3): 'Strategy is the direction and scope of an organization over the long term, which achieves advantage in a changing environment through its configuration of resources and competences with the aim of fulfilling stakeholder expectations'. This definition stresses both the sense of senior managers seeking to move the organization to achieve a competitive advantage in the face of continuous change, and the responsibility to stakeholders, these being shareholders, customers, employees, and suppliers, as well as the wider social responsibility to communities.

There are well documented critiques on the subject of whether strategy is mostly espoused but not enacted, and the view in this period of rapid change must be that it is usually emergent. Strategic decisions are taken in response to changes and to new ideas, and strategic plans are not rigid, immovable blueprints. Rather, the strategy is the starting point which shows the direction of travel for the business; it is a statement of strategic intent which may contain a number of strategic objectives, but management must keep the strategy under review. Although in capital intensive businesses there may be long term plans for many years ahead, in most businesses, a more dynamic approach is favoured in the face of continuing uncertainty, with some appropriate contingency thinking.

Some of the disjunctions between espoused and realized strategies are because of sectoral differences. Sectoral differences reflect different planning time horizons, the changes of customer requirements, fashions, emerging trends, innovations and technical developments, and not least new economic and social circumstances. For example, one could compare companies in the retail sector with those constructing power generation stations. Retail activities are highly susceptible to the invention of new products, to fashion and social trends, and to spending patterns. Marks and Spencer, a highly sophisticated and experienced retail business, was, for example, caught out in its clothing sales by the unpredictable weather in the UK during May to July 2012, when record rainfall occurred. Tesco, an equally well known and professional business, experienced falling sales in some of its products due to fierce price discounting by rivals during the Christmas period 2011–12 in the UK. There were impacts on the profits of these companies in each case. Such sudden changes of fortune are unpredictable, and what matters is that there are contingency plans for a rapid response, not that one should find fault with the original strategy. Constructing power stations is a long term activity, with ten year plus planning horizons, so one would expect long term strategies for that period. However, there will always be surprises, for example after the tsunami and nuclear accident at Japan's power stations, Germany decided to abandon its plans for more nuclear power stations, and the UK found that the consortium to build its new nuclear power stations in which a German company was due to participate was no longer viable. Even with a legitimate long term plan, responsiveness to the changing context is essential.

Many of the early theories about 'corporate' and business strategies suggested that there are differences between these two forms. Corporate strategy was concerned with the survival and adaptive capacity of the corporation, rather than any particular business stream. This tended to see strategy as the preserve of the larger corporations. One of the famous axioms of Alfred Chandler (1962) was that structure should follow strategy, in order to improve efficiencies and allow for different businesses to follow different strategies within conglomerates. So Chandler cited the way that diversification may require a divisional structure to be formed, with the centre following a corporate strategy and performing central functions, such as raising finance, and managing the portfolio of businesses. These central operations in multinational businesses, for example, might well have some central HR functions, such as management development, succession planning, and talent management, for high performers and rewards for the senior management teams, including performance management.

However, following Chandler, if there were to be changes in strategy, there would need to be changes in structure. In a counter argument, Mintzberg (1990) argued that changing structures is costly, and produces inefficiencies. Rather than have rigid structures, one of the conditions for agreeing to a particular structure perhaps should be that any structure should be capable of accommodating changes to new contexts and needs.

Creating value

Business organization structures exist to create and to sustain the business model. A business model is defined as 'a way of doing business' (Hamel 2000). To discover the business model in use, one has only to ask a senior manager how their company conducts its business to make money; the networks of business processes, which are usually a mixture of information flows, procedures and systems, and relationships between sections or departments and with suppliers and customers, will be described in the response.

From these interchanges, we discover that the business processes and supporting systems follow the process from order taking to production or service and on to delivery, in a model which shows how value is added. Value creation is seen by one stream of research as arising from the customer–firm interaction, occurring at those times when the customers perceive use value, exchange value, and relationship value. Other researchers examine the creation of value by the firm at the point of offering the product or service (the point of proposition). Building on Bowman and Ambrosini's (2000) flow chart description of use value from the firm becoming a new use value for the customer, these models adopt a systems theory approach where value as a concept is broken down into outputs for one firm being the inputs to another, in a business to business relationship. Research by O'Cass and Ngo (2011) showed that a firm's offering has four components: a performance value for the customer, pricing value, relationship building value, and co-creation value (for example, helping to customize the offering), and that these correlated elements produce a multidimensional construct which drives customer acquisition, customer satisfaction, customer retention, and the possibilities for add-on selling.

These aspects of value creation were also captured in the well known case study by Rucci *et al.* (1998) on the turnaround at the Sears retail store in the USA. What they described as 'The Employee-Customer Profit Chain' was shown as a model in which employee attitudes about their jobs and about the company were described as indicators of employee behaviour and as influences on employee retention. The effects of employee behaviour were seen to have an impact on customer impressions, which drove customer retention and customer recommendations. These effects on the customer were said to produce a return on assets, operating margins, and revenue growth. The central contention was that a 5 unit increase in employee attitude score drove a 1.3 unit improvement in customer impression and this produced a 0.5 per cent increase in company revenue. The Organization Development (OD) type interventions with considerable employee involvement, which were reported to have created these positive results, were a mixture of line management, consultancy, and HR activity. The case has been hailed as an example of how people management practices can have a direct effect on the bottom line. The success of the Sears change depended on people acting outside their formal roles, in task groups and teams, and communications through large 'town hall' type meetings. We can see that flexibility in structure is necessary for organizations to be able to change quickly, in this case by creating parallel structures. Adding value does require the managers in the organization to take some risks.

The balance between risk and control

Organization structures are created to support whatever initiative or business model the company decides in order to create more value: that is the imperative for the organization. This view of the organization concentrates on the performance function of organizations. There is also a control function of organizations. They are structured to provide control with defined levels of authority and lines of reporting. These structures are also used to maintain the rules of work for employees. Control is felt to be necessary for management boards in order to implement strategy, and to deliver the added value created. The classic bureaucracy is one in which a pyramid-type structure is formed, with a number of levels according to the number of people needed to perform the work and the span of control at each level.

Such structures also produce organization cultures, and develop systems, procedures, and the processes for creating value through the human resources in the organization whose employment sustains the knowledge base and the skills to perform the work. However, bureaucracies are also seen as impersonal, embodying the values of professionalism, impartiality, a concentration on efficiency, and the avoidance of nepotism and corruption (Weber 1947). There is, of course, a downside in the formal, evidence based, rule based decision making processes which are slow, and where staff may also find difficulty in dealing with new, unprogrammed events and challenges for which there is no precedent and no rules to apply.

These two approaches to organization structures are not mutually exclusive, but they do represent different managerial emphases. Organization structure concepts are being reframed due to the changes which we outlined in the previous two chapters. New forms of organization have important consequences for HR strategy.

Examples of the two different emphases can be found in the way, following deregulation of the banks in the 1980s (the 'big bang'), financial institutions of all kinds were encouraged to put value creation for their shareholders and for themselves at the heart of their business models. This resulted in a massive expansion of the financial sectors on both sides of the Atlantic, and considerable increase in wealth generation with benefits for the public and private sector investors, for pension funds, and for the general standard of living in Europe and in the population around the world. From this unfettered approach to money making, there were also the unforeseen consequences of unsustainable levels of debt at the individual level, a boom in unsecured loans, and ultimately a crisis in the banking sector, due to excessive leveraging and the failure in controls.

Since the 2008–9 crash the governments in the USA, UK, and other European countries have sought to rein in this emphasis in favour of more controls and supervision by central banks, regulators, and governments. In the UK, and possibly elsewhere in Europe, this seems set to result in a separation to be imposed between the 'casino' style operations of the banks, where they are lending to other financial institutions, and the retail operations which serve retail customers in the more mundane task of looking after millions of current and deposit accounts and mortgages for house purchases, as well as loans to business. The separation will mean a shift back to a machine bureaucracy for the retail side. It is thought that this would improve control and decision making for both sides of the business, would isolate the risky side of banking, and protect retail customers from the consequences of failure. Above all, it would mean the public would not have to bail out the banks if there is a future failure, and it would restore the sense of moral hazard to the risk taking operations. This follows the ideas of separation based on different markets as proposed by Alfred Chandler.

One effect of the recession on organizations therefore is for managers to ensure there is a more balanced approach to control and risk. The appropriateness of the response to risk depends very much on the nature of the business. All capitalist economies depend on entrepreneurs taking risks with their capital, and in a recession we need more of such risk takers not fewer if unemployment is to be reduced, and businesses are to grow. There are, as we discussed in Chapter 3, varieties of capitalism – but the element of risk cannot be removed. The recession and downturn in demand have put a strain on those companies and countries where many years of continuous growth and improving living standards have led employees and governments to believe in the doctrine of progress, and that there are no limits to growth. However, there will always be the requirement for both risk taking and controls to coexist.

Paradoxes of this kind are likely to continue because of the degree of change companies face. Smith and Lewis (2011) argued that cyclical management responses to paradoxical tensions can produce an integrative process. According to Poole and Van de Ven (1989), tension should be seen as normal in organizations, due to the plurality of stakeholders with competing strategies and goals. Smith and Lewis (2011) proposed an integrative model, which they see as a dynamic equilibrium model of organizing. The purpose of their model is to show paradoxical tensions as both inherent within the system, and socially constructed. Making latent tensions explicit encourages organizational leaders to adopt strategies to address them, and to deal with opposing paradoxes simultaneously, enabling a virtuous circle through acceptance and resolution. Acceptance implies working with and through the problems surfaced, and resolution might involve using various OD techniques, looking for common ground and integrating different perspectives, as well as splitting off the differences and seeking creative solutions to them. As they explain, 'a dynamic equilibrium enables sustainability through three mechanisms: (1) enabling, learning and creativity (2) fostering flexibility and resilience, and (3) unleashing human potential' (Smith and Lewis 2011: 393). There are a number of people policy areas and types of expertise required to support and develop these processes, especially the capacity for consultancy-style interventions, a 'learning organization' approach (Senge 1990), talent management policies, and high level OD capacities, which would need to be available at board level.

Occupational groups and the organization of work

The tensions in organizations are often resolved through changes to new structural forms. For example, various types of matrix structure are commonly created to avoid conflicts over resource allocation, so that specialists can be deployed across a variety of projects efficiently. Similarly, matrix structures allow project managers to take responsibility for decisions and control on projects with varying levels of involvement, thus providing a coordination function. Staff who have both a local interest in the project or unit, but also wider responsibilities to maintain standards and control over an area of expertise in the organization as a whole, can also find matrix structures useful, for example accountants or HR staff with reporting lines to the centre as well as to whoever is in charge of the business unit.

Matrix structures are also a source of frustration for managers and project teams. The problem of priorities being different when seen from different perspectives can result in miscommunication and conflict. Matrix structures are often found in multinational companies. Here, the reporting lines can be two, three, or four dimensional, for example local management or country management, regional management (with regions such as EMEA, EU countries, Asia-Pacific), functional or product group management, and accountability to head office. These relationships become increasingly complex due to the global reach of businesses, cross border mergers, and acquisitions. Such multiple relationships are facilitated by improved technical facilities, so that virtual teams can be created, and video links and teleconferences, webinars, etc. can be used. Whatever the format of the matrix, whether it be national or international in scope, performance should be improved if there is clarity from the outset about the accountabilities of the different groups, team members or projects, and others involved. Good communication is the most important attribute in matrix structures, and research has shown teams will function far better if the members have already met beforehand, and have shared perceptions of the process to be adopted (Harrison *et al.* 2003; Kijkuit and Van den Ende 2007). The matrix structure form is favoured in project teams and research teams, in sectors such as pharmaceuticals, engineering, and health care, government departments, and anywhere that specialists and professional employees are found.

Professional groups do not always fit naturally into traditional bureaucratic structures, favouring, as professionals typically do, autonomy and a high degree of freedom from control, as well as owing an allegiance to their professions and their own codes of conduct. There has been an expansion in the numbers of occupations called 'professions', and this is a broad church, including security specialists, engineers, chefs, actuaries, designers, and anyone who is called 'professional' just because they specialize in one kind of work – as in 'professional drivers'. Even if we stick with the old notion of professions there has been a substantial increase in the numbers as one of the features of our modern society: accountants, lawyers, teachers … the list could go on. If we take lawyers as one of the more conservative groups, even here The Law Society, which regulates solicitors (lawyers) in England and Wales, showed that from 1981 to 2011 the total number of solicitors holding a practising certificate had increased by 206.4 per cent, at an annual rate of increase of 3.8 per cent. Solicitors are now employed in companies, as corporate lawyers, in large practices, and in government departments, as well as in their own large and small partnerships. However, solicitors also illustrate another significant social trend which affects organizations. Following the UK's Legal Services Act of 2007, the range of people who can provide some of the basic legal services was expanded to introduce more competition, to give more consumer choice. This is another trend – with the expansion of professional roles and of the service sector has come a multiplicity of different kinds of providers. The people management implications are found, for example, in widening choice of employee benefit providers and consultants, more outsourcing choice, with more sub-contracting to niche providers, as well as the organizational requirement for high quality general management and project management.

Increased complexity and flexibility – new structures emerging

The lessons of consensual management and the need to move away from a simple machine bureaucracy were generally accepted in the larger business organizations in the developed economies by the end of the twentieth century. However, there are newer trends in structures which have been emerging as a result of the more deregulated and flexible era of the early part of the twenty-first century. The growth of emerging markets, new global trading patterns, increased internationalization of business, new technologies, a more individualized psychological contract, and the intensification of work as a result of the constant pressure on companies to improve short term profitability could all be cited as causes of the pressure for change on organizations, even before the financial crash.

Among the trends which first became apparent, the broad concept of the 'boundaryless organization' sums up the ethos of a new approach to organizing. In their book, *The Boundaryless Organization*, Ashkenas *et al.* (1995) argued that managers should reframe the main questions in organizations. 'To reframe the question, management first view the organization not as a set of functional boxes but as a set of shared resources and competencies that collectively define the organization's range of activities' (p. 126). They went on to suggest organizations should make all their resources support the creation of added value for customers.

At first sight, the idea of boundaryless organizations seems to be a contradiction in terms. However, Ashkenas *et al.* (1995) used the term to describe a different approach to organizational hierarchies in place of the traditional bureaucracy. Instead, they urge strengthening the value chain, and see the organization as one part of the process for delivering services and products to customers, while other parts are outside the formal organization. The internal structural issues should in this view be designed purely to deliver, not to sustain horizontal and vertical boundaries. They describe the future success factors as speed, flexibility, integration, and innovation. These attributes, they argue, are best created through a learning culture, a strong focus on teams working without regard to hierarchy or narrow functional specialism, and with a collaborative attitude towards customers and suppliers who should be seen as partners. This means permeability between horizontal and vertical boundaries, more use of self-managed teams, and an open approach to learning with feedback and a rapid response to needs. This revolution was already occurring in the 1980s and 1990s, with HR and line managers working together to improve efficiency and competitiveness. For example, early in that period there was a long tradition in what is sometimes called socio-technical systems which suggested that the technical system and the social system in the organization should be seen as interdependent, therefore work design and job design as well as organization design were seen as important. The de-layering of organizations and managing the interface between the organization and its customers were also well known. The move to horizontal reporting structures, more autonomy for sub-units, and more federal structures (Handy 1989), clearer channels to market (Whitaker 1992), greater interest in Japanese management practices (Thurley 1983; Abegglen and Stalk 1985), and similar studies were already well publicized. O'Toole (1985) described US vanguard companies where there were examples of more employee participation in decision making, freedom of expression, and lifelong learning.

The HR narrative in this chapter is consistent, and relatively easy to explain. Changes to business strategy which produce a different business model or affect the value chain need to be supported by new HR practices. Hence, HR has adopted a supporting and at times a leading role in producing organization cultures, which have in the 1980s through to the first part of the twenty-first century sought to change organizations to make them more effective. These policies have included de-layering, knowledge management, learning interventions, and OD practices, as well as policies on rewards, talent management, well-being, and corporate social responsibility. In the chapters that follow, we will look in detail at these policy areas. Nevertheless, we now see that these interventions were in support of expansion and were based on the presumption of growth. The challenges now are to cope with austerity and the recession, and at the same time become competitive with emerging economies and the new areas for growth.

There is increased complexity and variety in the way organizations operate. In commenting on what has been a silent transformation, O'Toole and Lawler (2006) commented: 'The shifts to services, high speed product development, global operations and high value added activities by large American corporations have led them to create ever-more complex organizations' (p. 35).

Complexity in organizational forms is not just a US phenomenon. All international businesses have to resolve multiple accountabilities across many different jurisdictions and time zones. The 'M' form organization, with subsidiaries in divisional structures, following Chandler's axiom, provides operational management and a business strategy for the company or product group. Finding the best route for communicating in such structures is a challenge in itself. So many people have to be involved in decisions, or kept informed or have to be consulted, that fast action is not often possible and some confusion is unsurprising. Head offices can take different roles according to the degree of control they exercise over, for example, budgets, and issues such as planning and new product development (Goold and Campbell 1987). The head office role can change, with new senior managers and their brief; for example, a marketing director might have more interest in one product group than another, or a company in the group could be under greater scrutiny than another because of some previous failing. Similarly, ownership by a controlling family could put the head office in a different position on areas of the business of interest to family members.

Complexity in structures has an effect on the sense of identity felt by employees and those in leadership roles. L'Oreal, the French cosmetics international giant, is an interesting example of how to deal with this. The company has four divisions, representing the product groups, the regions of the world, and national country management, as well as a head office in Paris. This means employees would typically be in a reporting relationship with a wide group of people. However, so effective has the company been in creating a strong, distinctive, and pervasive culture that communications are excellent, and information flows around the company and around the world rapidly. HR policies which stress high quality talent management, openness, and continuous feedback, with an emphasis on learning, and the rotation of staff through different countries and different functions, help to sustain the culture and a strong identification with the brands. This type of leadership is one which can build intergroup relational identity (Hogg *et al.* 2012). The culture in L'Oreal enables managers to be accepted as leaders who can shape the employees' understanding of a common identity, achieved through role modelling, rhetoric, and boundary spanning leadership – based on shared goals and collaboration.

To meet the long-standing challenge of improving the cost structure of their businesses, companies often turn to offshoring and/or outsourcing approaches. Outsourcing meets the logic of company strategies where cost competition is the critical issue. Offshoring implies there would be cost or logistic benefits in moving parts of the company operation to a location which is cheaper due to lower labour costs, and lower operating costs, sometimes as an outcome of a work simplification, or industrial re-engineering programme.

Outsourcing is not a new phenomenon. Most organizations have for many years depended on other businesses for products and services they use, but do not produce or supply themselves, such as legal services, training services, logistic and transport, IT services, building services, etc., as well as sub-contracting aspects of production. Rilla and Squicciarini (2011) helpfully set out a taxonomy of outsourcing activities. Offshoring is defined as activities or processes which are moved to a country other than the home country. The OECD (2007) referred to offshoring as 'outsourcing abroad'. Under this definition, therefore, companies which purchase goods and services domestically are 'onshoring'. More practically, outsourcing is defined as moving activities which were normally performed within the company, to be outside the boundary of the organization. As discussed earlier, deciding what is outside organizations is more difficult than it might at first seem.

This has led to further refinements, so that activities conducted by vertically integrated affiliates are defined as 'captive offshoring' (Rilla and Squicciarini 2011: 395). Rilla and Squicciarini suggested a broader definition of offshoring as the relocation of in-house activities to other often 'low cost' countries, whatever the contractual agreement and whether or not affiliated companies are involved. In the recession, there are potential employment effects of moving jobs abroad to low paid economies which produce an adverse effect on pay levels in the country losing the jobs. Such concerns are also sometimes linked to the fear that child labour may be used in those countries, and that workers in those countries may have fewer rights and be exploited. However, on the case of research and development (R&D) outsourcing and offshoring, Rilla and Squicciarini (2011) reported that the reasons most often given were as an alternative to purchasing services from outside providers, and the inability to attract talent in home labour markets. R&D activities were outsourced to environments where innovation was well supported, for example where there was IT enabled integration in a company's operations, and where top management were committed to innovation.

There are a number of consequences of outsourcing. Assuming the supplier is efficient and there is satisfaction with the delivery of the service, one result is a reduction in headcount and employment costs, while the core capability of the business is not affected, although there is a loss of control. There are questions to be dealt with, for example: is the competitive advantage of the company due in part to the integrated nature of the various functions? Without this integration, does the company lose the advantages? For example, the benefits that problems are dealt with quickly and effectively because there is a shared company membership, new products and services are more easily launched, there is better feedback from customers, and faster response times to new business, product developments.

Table 4.1 Trends in flexible working in Germany, France, UK, and USA (organizations where there are >50% of employees who are covered by these flexible working practices)

>50%	France		Germany		UK		USA	
	2004	*2009*	*2004*	*2009*	*2004*	*2009*	*2004*	*2009*
Home based work	0	0	0.3	0	0	2.9	0.4	0
Compressed working week	0	0	0	2.0	1.4	4.0	5.5	4.5
Flexitime	2.6	6.1	53.2	67.6	11.4	16.8	16.3	16.2
Temporary/casual work	0	0	0	0.5	0.9	1.1	0.8	0.5
Fixed term contracts	0.8	0	1.2	4.6	0.8	4.6	2.4	1.2
Annual hours contract	49.6	30.1	9.5	9.0	4.4	11.5	3.7	6.0
Part time working	0.8	1.4	2.0	3.2	5.8	4.0	4.7	1.9
Job share	0	0.8	0	0.3	0.2	0	0	0.2
Weekend work	11.7	11.4	10.9	8.8	9.8	10.8	9.1	6.9
Shift work	32.3	22.9	19.1	13.5	21.0	16.9	10.3	9.3
Overtime	7.9	14.7	7.3	7.3	14.8	16.9	7.5	9.8

Source: Cranet survey data gathered in 2004 and 2009.

Potential downsides to outsourcing could include damage to the brand image, and a subsequent loss of competitiveness. Although suppliers could agree not to offer the same service to the company's competitors, such a loss of business opportunities could come at a premium. Without that clause, competitors can easily replicate the service provided, so that any competitive improvement would be short-lived. If other good providers of the service are easily found, there can be no long term competitive advantage from the outsourcing.

Clearly, precision on what is expected by the company and what can realistically be delivered by the supplier are important. In an HR due diligence exercise, an audit of the supplier's HR policies and practices and of the quality of their staff, covering stability in employment and quality of management, recruitment, and training policies should be undertaken, before letting the contract. All these steps to mitigate the risks outlined above will help, if there are regular reviews of the suppliers to ensure that all is well, before any problems emerge.

A quiet revolution in the flexible use of labour has been taking place in developed economies, in which outsourcing and offshoring are included. By far the most important and widespread changes in practices are found in the three main areas of contract, time, and task flexibility in employment. Contract flexibility includes part time, zero hours contracts, short term and temporary contracts, and various forms of sub-contracting. Contractual and time flexibility is often devised to meet the needs for a cost efficient, flexible work-force on the part of the employer, and flexibility for employee lifestyles. Task flexibility helps employers to create flexible teams, and to use labour flexibly. Employees gain a widening of their skills, and potential for job enlargement and job enrichment.

The figures in Table 4.1 indicate for the majority of organizations that weekend working has not changed except in the USA where there has been a small decline; there is a declining amount of shift working; and overtime has increased, especially in France. Annual hours contracts have declined in France and increased in the USA; job sharing has reduced in all four countries; and flexitime has increased except in the USA. There has been an increase in fixed term contracts in the UK and Germany, but a reduction elsewhere. The main conclusion from the data is that there are wide variations in the usage of these HR practices, which has its origin in factors which would be best explained through institutional theory – the different legislative and industrial context, with variations between different occupational groups. These figures were gathered before the full effect of the recession would have been felt, the US data probably being the closest to reactions to the emerging crisis.

Part time working has reduced in the USA where there was less labour hoarding, whereas in Germany this increase in part time working may reflect the desire to hang on to skills, awaiting the upturn. This would also explain the reduction in fixed term contracts – where these are the easiest group of employees to cut quickly. Similarly, annual hours contracts bring a benefit to the employer, who can gain the benefit of flexibility by the employee, to increase their hours to suit market conditions, without extra cost, unlike flexi-time where the employee makes the decision about when they come to work within the total hours contracted.

We see from this quick analysis of these figures that there is evidence of the widespread use of these flexible conditions, and that we might expect changes in the recession to reduce labour costs, and that the choices about whether to retain people on part time or reduced hours is a labour market strategy which European employers might be adopting.

The increased sense of complexity in organizations is partly a consequence of increased pressure of time – the need to complete tasks more and more quickly, and the rapidity of change. The extension of project management is found in the development of more temporary organizations. Although temporary organizations have always existed, for example in the construction industry, according to Bakker (2010) there are more and more businesses using this time bound mode to achieve specific outcomes. Examples are found in the entertainment industry, in film making, theatre productions, and sports events, such as the Olympics. But increasingly temporary structures are found in software development, advertising, television, fashion, biotechnology, and consulting. The temporary organization is defined as a 'set of organizational actors working together on a complex task over a limited period of time' (Bakker 2010: 468).

The characteristic feature of temporary organizations is time limitation, where systems are seen as linear, instead of cyclical, over a year. Teams therefore anticipate a limited period working together, so swift trust is required among team members and leadership on the soft issues of relationships and role related behaviours is important. There is a strong sense of task orientation, and a capacity for improvisation. Temporary structures thrive where innovation is desired. Temporary organizations need to be able to create their own cultures within a broader institutional environment. Rather like matrix structures, temporary organizations can create friction in bureaucracies, where the speed of their temporary organization's work, their desire to focus purely on the task through their own internal culture is a challenge for some organizational managers, who find communicating with temporary teams difficult. Temporary organizations can show signs of goal displacement when their period of operation comes to an end – the desire to invent a new purpose so they can continue in what are desirable work activities and cultures. NATO, originally established to counter potential threats from the Soviet Union, searched for another sense of purpose when the cold war came to an end, and became a broad military alliance of Europe and North America, for any military or humanitarian purpose. Temporary structures add to the fragmented nature of modern organizations, raising issues of identity for temporary team members. For HR managers of temporary organizations to create a sense of identity, and of status, one can see various strategies – for example in the Olympic Games in 2012 in the UK, volunteers who were used to give visitors and sportsmen and women a sense of belonging in a temporary home, were called 'Gamesmakers', and were trained and developed to be high quality hosts.

The impact of new technology on organizations

As discussed in Chapter 2, the most significant and pervasive change in the century is the onward march of developments in new information technology. Affecting every aspect of business and public sector organizations, the creation of the Internet and its widespread use across the world is as important as the invention of printing, the internal combustion engine, powered flight, or television. It has become another sense, like vision or touch, allowing us to communicate and to transfer information around the globe in fractions of a second.

According to Thomas Friedman's interpretation of history, this is the third great era of globalization, a process he suggested began with Christopher Columbus in 1492, followed by the expansion of world trading in the nineteenth century. This, the third era, is characterized by a flatter, more interconnected world, where information is freely available, ideas and causes are quickly spread, and we work, shop, and play globally.

As the world starts to move from a primarily vertical, command and control system for creating value to a more horizontal-connect and collaborative value creation model, and we blow away more walls, ceilings and floors at the same time, societies are going to find themselves facing a lot of profound changes all at once.

(Friedman 2005: 213)

New developments have had effects of course, on manufacturing and on service industries. New product development now happens at a frightening speed. South Korea, for example, has built its whole economic future on creating new ideas for applying technology to every aspect of the human condition, with thousands of employees working for companies such as Samsung, a company which has usurped Nokia, a one time market leader in the mobile phone market. Nokia was slow to enter the smartphone market, and paid the penalty. One characteristic of the new technologies is that they are a fertile ground for new applications, and the speed with which these are brought to market can make the difference between corporate success or failure.

The revolution brought by new technology has made a big impact on manufacturing processes. The use of robotic methods of manufacturing in production lines is well established. One consequence is that the modern factory is not a place for large scale employment. Furthermore, the invention of three-dimensional printing technologies and of new materials which can be moulded means a process known as additive manufacturing has been invented. This means anyone can, through computer aided design, send their design for a new product, for example tableware, vehicle bodywork, furniture, etc. directly to the manufacturer, who can reproduce the design in three dimensions from the printer and make the mould for the new materials, producing the article quickly and accurately. This means even fewer people need to be employed, with potential effects on retailers, designers, and production planners. Additive manufacturing can get rid of the middle person in the value chain.

We live in a world of micro multinationals, which can operate all over the world from one PC, wherever it is located. With reliable systems for passing money around the world, invoicing in another country is no longer a problem, although there are potential problems of duties and taxes which can often be dealt with online by the knowledgeable. This method of doing business is well suited to a number of services, for example graphic design, or some forms of consultancy. The main difficulties are in the need to establish a relationship online, and the legal systems, which often do not really recognize the new world of the Internet.

Conclusions

In this chapter we have reviewed some of the developments in those factors which have impacted on organizations, and the consequences for how organizations are changing, as employers. Features of the new era are the speed of change, the need therefore for organizations to adapt, and to be resilient, agile, and flexible. One of the conclusions we can draw is that new organizational forms are now seeking to match the new ways of working, the new business models. One of the consequences of the new world of work in new types of structure is the problem of how employees can find and sustain a sense of identity. This is the old problem of rapid change, what Durkheim called 'anomie'. This is a sense of normlessness, of being in a society where no one 'fits in'. The challenge for HRM is to move away from rules and towards organization cultures as a way to cope with this issue, to encourage innovation, and to enable agility. We will explore organizational agility and its relationship to dynamic capabilities in Chapter 5, on changes to HRM, when we discuss strategic capability.

The forces for risk taking are inherent in the capitalist system. There is currently a struggle between these natural energies to be competitive and to acquire wealth for shareholders and the forces of society seeking to moderate and reduce risk for fear of the consequences for society as a whole. This clash of interests is fought in financial organizations but with a spillover into the rest of the business world. This is also a global issue, as the financing of business is a global issue.

Much of the literature and the HR practices of organizations see the value chain as of more importance than the formal organization or company. The consequences for where work is done and who controls work are enormous; these include consequences for organizational identity and personal identity, a further dilemma which also becomes apparent in the effects of new technology applications. Most of the trends we discussed are global in scope, showing the mimetic processes at work as institutional theory suggests. New technologies are also spreading similar ways of operating, and the globalization of product sales brings similarities in working practices, for example spreadsheets, protocols for using the Internet, and security systems.

We will develop a number of the themes in the chapters that follow on HRM delivery and the trends of HRM, including talent management, the use of marketing in HRM, total rewards, equality and diversity, and employee well-being.

Part II

Changing HR roles and technology

5 The changing role of HRM

The changing role of HRM is a central concern of this book, as we examine the effects of the changing context on the management of people. In this chapter, we set out the new 'HR configurations' within the overall architecture of HRM (Lepak and Snell 1999), the broader approach to managing people in organizations by line managers, as well as the specialist HR department. This we describe as the HR function of management, which we see covering recruitment, selection, development, rewards, well-being and safety at work, and the wider field of employment relationships, which includes engagement, employee voice, trade union relationships, and collective bargaining.

We begin by looking at how these changes are part of long term developments in HRM, and at how new models of HRM, with the accent on the link to organizational performance, were already important. We then go on to consider the developments to the strategic role of HRM, and the theoretical bases which underpin these trends, which are advancing with the changing economic and organizational context.

The old order of HRM

There is an extensive literature on the history and development of the specialist occupation of 'personnel management', which has shown how the roles antecedent to HRM were equally confounded by ambiguity and by the questions about the efficacy of the work in this field (Niven 1967; Ritzer and Trice 1969; Watson 1977). The creation of a specialist role, and its 'professionalization' over time, resulted in questions concerning how such roles interact with line management, and what real decision making power such specialists possessed? Underlying much of this debate were questions about legitimacy, and the potential for anti-trade union activity by companies.

The use of the term 'human resource management' (HRM) arose in the 1980s and spread from the USA to the UK, and then via multinationals, into Western Europe. For many working in the field, with a variety of job titles, such as personnel officer, employment relations manager, labour officer, as well as personnel manager, and for the academic establishment, the term HRM represented a new concept. This produced different perspectives on managing people and shifted the terms of the debate (Guest and Peccei 1994), with an increasingly polarized argument about whether HRM was a new phenomenon, concentrating on the acquisition, maintenance, and development of human capital for a business, or merely the renaming of personnel management (Guest 1987). For some academic commentators, this was seen as the latest attempt to solve the old problems of legitimating the occupation, and to enable erstwhile personnel managers the opportunity to obtain a seat at the table of the senior management or main board of the company, with all the attendant improvements to their rewards and status (Legge 1995).

If we apply a contextual interpretation to the morphology of this shift in job titles, we can see that the changes coincided with new management contexts in the private sector. 'Industrial relations', with its emphasis on trade union relationships, was giving way to 'employee relationships', which were much more about employee engagement and direct communication with employees, at a time when trade union membership was falling, living standards were rising, and employment legislation was removing many individual grievances from workplace bargaining as well as redefining the legal position of trade unions. At the same time, trends such as internationalization and the rise of multinational enterprises were having a positive impact on growth, financial services were being deregulated in the 'big bang', along with new trading partnerships, such as the European Union. In this context, the notion of developing people to obtain a competitive advantage was readily accepted, and management could see how management development and organization restructuring, new reward practices, and more professional recruitment could help to change businesses to be more competitive, for example by removing barriers to change, improving competence and skills, and by innovative reward practices for individuals and teams. Japanese management practices, such as quality circles, were becoming popular, and these fed into the desire to put more effort into developing first line supervisors, and into changing the culture of a business.

These were the seeds of the early HR configurations. Not all companies developed their HRM at the same pace, and the varying contexts and institutions between countries and even within countries such as the variations in size, ownership patterns, and industries make generalization difficult. These factors produced different models of HRM (Tyson and Fell 1986), but because they affected all employing organizations, they produced a need to review what was being done by management to improve the competitiveness of the business, through their employees, in a more global competitive environment.

The old order changes

By the time of the crash in 2008–9 and the following recession, the concepts of HRM were well established in the public and private sectors around the world (Brewster and Mayrhofer 2012). These concepts did not represent a common model of people management, but it is the case that there were commonalities in the objectives for the function, and ways of organizing delivery of HR services to line management which had similar characteristics.

The main feature of HRM in the first decade of the millennium was, above all, a more strategic approach to managing people, based on using HR practices systematically to drive performance, especially performance management, employee and management development, reward, and talent management at the individual level. Tight labour markets made talent management a priority for many businesses, which feared losing high quality people to the competition, for example in the City of London, and on Wall Street, New York. This was the era when capital was easily obtained for projects and new ventures, but high quality people, with the right kind of experience for the role, were difficult to find and keep, in most industries. In many organizations, there were also attempts to produce coherence in pay and benefits and the various aspects of the employers' side of the psychological contract (the 'offer'), by creating a total reward philosophy.

Change in organizations was a constant, due to the fast pace of global trading, and the expansion of new markets in Eastern Europe, the Far East, and continuing expansion in the USA and in the Eurozone economies. There was a very active mergers and acquisitions agenda, so on the people side, projects such as creating new organization cultures, ensuring employee engagement, reorganizing and planning the use of resources, drew HR staff in as part of the top team and called for organization development (OD) type skills, and experience in organization design. The delivery of HR services and the HR departments themselves were also being reorganized. Following prescriptions advanced from consultancies, there were moves to establish shared services and call centres for HR policy administration. Many companies and public sector organizations introduced the role of HR 'business partner', following the popularity of the books of David Ulrich (1997). These were HR generalists who worked closely with line management colleagues to provide an HR service as close to the business as possible, running a department which used specialists in the internal centres of excellence to advise on the main policy areas on topics such as rewards, development, and employee relations, and, in larger businesses, supported by a call centre. As a part of the structure outlined above, new technology has played a major part in reducing the size of HR departments, and enabling new policies, making them user friendly and more extensive.

Human capital theory and the resource based view (RBV)

Early attempts to measure HRM in the 1980s were made first in the USA by introducing the concept of human asset accounting. Flamholtz and Lacey (1981) defined this as: 'the measurement and reporting of the cost and value of people as organizational resources' (p. 57). Human asset accounting required accounting for any investments in employees, such as training, their replacement cost, and the economic value of employees to the company. This latter idea of 'value' was measured by the difference between pay and marginal revenue product. Human asset and human capital accounting failed to attract much support, because they encapsulated too many unmeasurable variables, for example when measuring investments, whether the replacement cost or the historical or acquisition cost should be taken, and how to deal with the costs of education which are covered by society. Unlike physical or capital assets, human assets cannot be controlled; for example, employees can leave, or become ineffective for personal reasons, or due to low motivation.

Human capital theory generally provided a fertile ground for those interested in finding a basis for creating a theory with practical measurement applications which could give HR staff a framework for establishing the contribution of HR to organizational performance. There is an intellectual connection to the RBV, as human asset accounting treats people as part of the firm's resources, and encourages the view that these resources can be acquired and developed to the economic benefit of the business. The RBV takes this a stage further and argues that these assets are a significant source of competitive advantage. We should note that the shift in the theoretical stance occurred at a time when high quality labour was becoming more expensive, and the key issue for employers was not labour cost but the contribution to the business, as competition became global.

In their article outlining the idea of human resource architecture, Lepak and Snell (1999) argued that four different employment modes can be derived from the RBV, human capital theory, and transaction cost economics, in order to determine the key research questions centred around 'make or buy' questions implicit in decisions about what kind of employment contracts and policies to pursue. In their 2002 article, Lepak and Snell developed these ideas more fully. They tested a number of hypotheses to see whether the four employment modes, which include contractual work arrangements, alliances, knowledge based, and job based employment modes, correspond to the HR configurations they predict. They argue that the study supports the view that different employment modes are associated with variations in human capital, reflecting the choices regarding internal versus external employment modes. These findings are not surprising, showing that externalizing the workforce or moving to temporary labour has an impact on HR policies.

The study is also useful in demonstrating how the value of human capital and the practices within HRM vary between firms, and the bundles of HR practices vary often within firms, so we can see that 'human assets' can be managed in a variety of ways, even in the same firm. The fact that human capital theory could be adopted to support either a 'best practice' or a more contingent view of the firm's HR practices helps to explain why the RBV came to be seen as a theory suitable to underpin all forms of HRM.

Wright *et al.* (2001) summarized how the RBV came to be so essential to the study of HRM, describing the trail of research which sought to show how the 'human capital pool' (p. 703) and HR practices both form a part of competitive advantage. In this literature, authors were careful to place the 'human process advantage' alongside the behaviours and competences of individual employees (Snell *et al.* 1996; Boxall 1998).

What are the effects of the recession on HRM?

If the RBV can be applied in any context, then we should explore the question of how the financial crash and the subsequent recession have affected HRM, in terms of the 'human capital pool' and the 'human process advantage'. The central feature of the downturn is the new context, characterized by economic, political, and social uncertainty, since the recession has revealed institutional fault lines and produced a strong desire to review existing institutions. These changes are felt in the UK and in other parts of Europe, across the Middle East in the 'Arab Spring', and in the Far East, where there is also a downturn in the Chinese economy, as well as a once in a decade change to the leadership. The increasing lack of competitiveness of the West means we can no longer rely on the 'doctrine of progress'. There is nothing inevitable about any improvements to the lives of working people in the world of the future. This is not the context in which businesses can readily invest in the future, or feel secure about the business environment.

Although employment figures are holding up in parts of Europe and in the USA, there have been significant closures (for example, in October 2012 Ford of Europe closed a manufacturing plant in Belgium, with the loss of 4,000 jobs, and closures in the UK of two facilities with around 1,200 people affected). All such changes have knock-on effects on suppliers and on the local economies concerned. The difficulty with multinational corporations is that they are quite content to shift production to cheaper areas or closer to their markets. In the case of Ford, some of the production was moved to Turkey, and in another instance involving General Motors it became clear that when expanding into the Chinese market, the company preferred to set up a factory in China, rather than to export from its existing plants. This means we can no longer rely on developing economies for growth in manufacturing, unless the skills are so special that they are only found in the West. The realization is slowly dawning that in the West generally, we have lost our competitive advantage in most industries.

The economic conditions of the slowdown bring a fear of redundancy and dismissal on the part of the employee, and a reluctance to invest on the part of the employer because of the reduction in consumer demand. This is the vicious circle of the recession. The result is a fear of unemployment which dampens down demand, and, with little prospect of finding new work if they lose their jobs, people become more conservative about buying big ticket items and moving house.

Some organizations, especially the public sector in Europe, are reducing in size and reforming their service delivery models at the same time. In the private sector too, there is a need to reconfigure the business models, to find new ways to attract customers, and to revisit price structures. Some of these changes are, of course, brought about by different societal changes, such as the changing demographic profile of consumers, and it is difficult to pinpoint what is a consequence of the recession and what is a part of the 'background noise' of social change.

One issue for organizations facing a reduction in demand, or budget cuts in the public sector, is how to retain those groups of employees who will remain a source of competitive advantage, once the immediate crisis is over. This has produced new policy responses. If the assumption is that there will be sufficient a recovery to justify retaining staff over a period of months while the workload is reduced, organizations have proved imaginative in finding solutions. By their nature such deals are often private, but there are indicators of this happening. In the UK and in the USA, the total number of people in employment has been rising, in spite of the recession and high levels of unemployment. This is to some extent due to a rise in the number of part time workers. There are also some well publicized examples using zero and annualized hours contracts, and in Germany, 'mini' and 'midi' jobs have been created with employees able to work part time while the state pays benefits, as long as the hours at work are short (mini), or they are on reduced benefits where the time spent working for the employer is longer (midi). Employers have also instituted pay freezes as a way to reduce costs, instead of making employees redundant, and have agreed with trade unions deals whereby time off with pay is given, because of excess capacity or excess stock levels. This was the case for Vauxhall (General Motors) Vans in Luton, UK, on the basis that the employees would work longer hours later in the year on reduced pay levels. Of course, short time working is not unusual, but the difference here is that employers and trade unions have been looking for solutions which provide a degree of security for the employees, and some mitigation of lost earnings, and in return the employer retains skilled and experienced employees.

To return to the earlier question, the RBV is clearly relevant even in these new contextual circumstances. However, not all employers are willing or can afford to retain staff in the face of falling demand. What is rare, unsubstitutable, and valuable does change with the economy. The state of labour markets is a critical factor, since it impinges on the level of demand for the company's product or service, the cost of labour, and the rarity of skills and capability. In terms of human asset accounting, we can say that the asset value of employees can go down as well as up.

Labour turnover is dependent upon the particular labour market, and the type of work. There are negative as well as positive results for the employer from a reduction in turnover. The positive consequences are lower costs, in recruitment and training, and there is more continuity and less disruption; the downside is that there are fewer opportunities to restructure jobs, there is a lack of refreshment to the talent pool, and there are frustrated employees who would like to move on with their lives who are not able to obtain promotion or to leave because there are few alternatives. In this situation, demotivated employees are likely to underperform, not to go the extra mile for customers or to be creative in their work. The legislation on age discrimination in EU countries which means there is no normal retirement age could be seen as being to the disadvantage of an employer who is trying to provide more promotion opportunities.

With fewer promotion prospects and lower turnover, there would be lower training costs. In any case, training and development budgets have been cut, although with limited resources this has focused attention more on the strategically important groups of employees in talent management policies, which we discuss further in Chapter 10. Uncertainty about the long term future for business leads to doubt about what kinds of jobs will be needed. Changes to businesses, and public sector organizations, closures, restructuring, and new systems will take time for organizations to assimilate, and create difficulties for planning. We do not know what competencies will be needed in the future, how the various debt problems (with banks, businesses, and private debt) and the issues with economies and currencies, with political changes and their impact upon demand, prices, innovation, and the labour market will play out. These are all unpredictable variables which may affect HR policies in the future.

HRM and performance

In 1997, Paauwe and Richardson produced a summarized framework derived from the already extensive literature, which sets out to express the complex relationships between the many variables that affect the relationship between HR activity and organizational performance. The important insight from this framework was that rather than seek direct organizational outcomes from HR activities (recruitment, training, rewards, etc.), such as profit or financial turnover, they show there are intervening outcomes from HR policies and practices, for example labour turnover, motivation, and commitment, which in turn could be shown to relate to financial and marketing outcomes at the organizational level. Paauwe and Richardson acknowledged that there are possibilities of reverse causality, for example, that organizations which are more profitable could afford more advanced recruitment, and have bigger recruitment budgets. Similarly they acknowledged that there are contextual variables which could influence the relationships, such as organizational size, unionization, technology, etc., and that some of these variables may also be at the individual level, for example employee education level, experience, and knowledge.

In their review of this model, alongside the empirical studies on HR and performance between 1994 and 2003, Boselie *et al.* (2005) concluded that there were still serious problems in the empirical research to establish unequivocally how HR activities affect organizational performance (what is described as the 'black box' problem). As they put it: 'These concerns lead us to reiterate our earlier scepticism about the methodological validity of isolating the impact of an organization's HRM from all the other variables that might part determine financial success' (p. 79). Boselie *et al.* suggested more attention be paid to employee perceptions of HR policies and practices, which are a part of the psychological contract between the organization and the individual, and which are susceptible to influence by signals from management's attitude. This is the sentient level in Tyson's (1997) article, where employees look at what happens in the organization from their position in society, with their own sense of fairness and reciprocity.

Paauwe (2009) in a later article called for a more contextually based theory of HRM, which 'redirects attention away from a preoccupation with performance' (p. 137). The greater use of institutional theory and of path dependency might help both to ground theories in the organizational context, and show causation on a more longitudinal basis. The issues of context are becoming more salient, as the scale of the changes to economies becomes more widely understood, this being part of the rationale for writing this book.

In an attempt to analyse the 'black box', Boxall *et al.* (2011) tested a number of hypotheses. These included the relationship between the employee experience of espoused HR practices and customer oriented behaviour and performance. The study was of the operating staff of an Australian cinema chain of ten cinemas (around 750 people) in one state. The majority of employees were 'casual', employed at weekends, evening, holiday periods, and the company needed the staff to provide a standardized, high quality customer experience and to create customer loyalty. The findings from this research showed that what was effective was compliance behaviour, rather than empowerment, with adherence to particular scripts for customer facing staff, what is described as 'routinized efficiency', rather than personalized service. This has been described as the 'low involvement' route to high performance. This may well be a common type of HR goal, for the many similar types of businesses in the service sector, which indicates that HR policies can demonstrate a direct impact in the service environment, as in the Sears case (see Chapter 4). The difficulty is in unpacking the black box in the more complex organizations with more actors involved, with different kinds of customers, and less obvious products or services.

The recession has created new opportunities for reviews of institutions and for renewal, and the forces for change in HRM go beyond economic disruption. The new strategic realities mean HR functions must play a significant role in the management of change. This leads us to look in detail at the effects of contextual change on HR strategy.

Human resource strategy

Human resource strategy has been defined as: 'a set of ideas, policies and practices which management adopt in order to achieve a people management objective' (Tyson 1995: 3). It is argued that strategy is emergent and that often there are variations between intended and realized strategies. The concept of strategy in the business context has at least three meanings. It can be seen as a policy or a stream of policies and practices, as a means of manoeuvring or outwitting the opposition, and is sometimes (in a rather confusing way) stated as the objective. As we discussed earlier in Chapter 4, there are also business strategies within business units, and broader corporate strategies which are concerned with the portfolio of businesses. We will be using the concept here as meaning a stream or bundle of HR policies designed to meet the business unit's objectives and the corporate objectives of the organization as a whole.

Most organizations will have some formal intentions, the period of planning being dependent on the volatility of the context, whether or not the industry is capital intensive, and the industry sector. Most businesses will not wish to plan too far ahead in view of the economic environment, and plans of three or even two years would be likely currently. Arising from these plans, in some circumstances HR strategies will be imposed, in that they arise from the logic of the overall company plan, while in more volatile industries and times, HR strategies are more likely to be emergent. Similarly, strategy may be created by a form of logical incrementalism, where it is produced one step at a time, after analysing the options available. HR strategies should always be seen as integrated with the business plan or strategy, as they are one means to give effect to the plan (Schuler 1992).

HR strategy is a practical way to describe the various HR policies which are designed to deliver the business objectives, but it also represents, through the choices made, the particular policies adopted and, from the way the strategy is implemented, the desired philosophy of management within the organization (Tyson 1997). The integration of the HR strategy with the business strategy and the desired business model give the HR strategy its legitimacy and value. HR strategies could therefore affect the whole organization's effectiveness, and also impact the psychological contract at the individual level. There are three main ways that HR strategy gives effect to the business strategy: through the 'fit' of HR strategy to business strategy, through developing resources to sustain competitive advantage, and through creating an agile approach to the pressures and opportunities in the organizational context. These are not mutually exclusive, but for the sake of clarity, we will consider each of these in turn.

The notion of fit has a number of dimensions. There is the 'fit' between the HR strategy and the business strategy (Dyer 1984), the fit between the different components of the HR strategy, to produce coherence in the HR policies and practices (Delery 1998), and the fit of the HR strategy to the organizational context (Toh *et al.* 2008). As an overall approach, the way that companies manage the types of 'fit' could be seen as indicators of the different varieties of capitalism in which they are engaged.

Witcher and Chau (2012) argued that following the crash of 2008, international firms are becoming more conscious of the need to integrate their internal cohesion with their responses to the changes in the market place. Taking Nissan as an example, they argued that multinational companies are moving towards a more holistic approach to strategic management. The integrated management within Nissan, they suggested, is exemplified by the Japanese concept of *hoshin kanri*, which is a system for incorporating strategic priorities throughout the business. The article used the strategic concepts developed by Baden-Fuller (1995) of 'outside-in' and 'inside-out'. Outside-in strategic approaches look to the external environment, in terms of an industry's continuing attractiveness, to decide how the firm should be positioned to compete in the future, whereas inside-out looks at the internal resources and the firm's capability to be competitive (in a similar fashion to the RBV). The integration of these two perspectives, Witcher and Chau argued, comes from the *hoshin kanri* methodology, where: 'Functional objectives are reviewed inside-out for their continuing impact on the mission of the firm, and cross functional objectives are reviewed outside-in for their impact on moving the firm to a new substantial strategic change based on the vision' (p. 67). They go on to suggest that 'outside-in' would be attractive in liberal market economies and that 'inside-out' is in tune with coordinated market economies. The inside-out, and outside-in perspectives equate to the different kinds of strategic fit described above. This is interesting because the post-recessionary business world clearly requires a more integrated and coherent approach, so that working across functional boundaries has implications for the way the HR strategy fits the business strategy.

As we intimated earlier in the chapter, the RBV is central to HRM, because it concentrates on the development of internal resources through recruiting high quality people, talent management, organizational learning, and ensuring responsiveness of the internal fit to the needs of the business. The belief that competitive advantage, all things being equal, depends upon superior advantage gained through all the various resources, including the people, research and development, the systems for quality and for creating firm specific knowledge, all play well to the HR management agenda. However, the RBV, although central to HR strategy, may be less attractive as an underpinning concept when labour markets are not so tight, and when there is a shortage of investment capital rather than of human capital.

In the new era of HRM, HR strategies which focus on the development of those organizational capabilities which enable rapid, market sensitive change are likely to be of pressing importance. We see organizational agility as the keystone for strategic approaches in the future. The idea of organizational agility applied to HRM is not new. Dyer and Shafer (1989) defined this as 'the capacity to be infinitely adaptable without having to change' (p. 6). The need is for organizations to be so close to their respective markets, clients, and customers that they are constantly making the relatively minor adjustments to accommodate new conditions, new technologies, and economic and social change at a faster pace than ever, so that adjustments have to be immediate, not part of some long overdue change programme. The competition does not wait for its rivals to catch up. In agile organizations, change is the norm. The idea of the agile organization is portrayed in Figure 5.1.

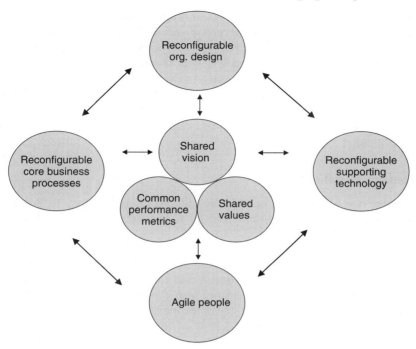

Figure 5.1 Agile organizational capability
Source: Dyer and Shafer (1999).

As shown, the central feature is a strong organization culture based on shared values and common performance metrics. One might consider the notion of juxtaposing a strong culture with agility to be paradoxical. However, without a central core around which people and their structures and technologies can flex, agility would descend into chaos. It is the adherence to these shared vision/values which forms the glue, and allows invention, resourcefulness, and market sensitivity. The figure shows flexible organization design interacting with frequent reviews of business processes, and with supporting technologies, which in turn feed back into the agile people management processes of the HR function.

We can return to the example of L'Oreal cited in Chapter 4 to illustrate agility. Its strong culture is encapsulated in its cherished brands, common performance metrics in its global operations, its reliance on the budget process, and shared vision. This enables the company to absorb new brands quickly, and to manage operations around the world in the knowledge that the same business processes are being adopted but that local variations in the offering to customers may be made, according to local requirements. Employees are moved between functions and between countries, usually within the same division, and there are well instituted processes for enabling new ideas and innovations to be brought up to board level rapidly. There is a heavy investment in employee development, and close attention to the quality of recruitment.

In a fast moving business world where opportunities have to be grasped quickly, the agile organization concept is very appropriate. We should note that what is being described here is not a perspective limited to the HR function, but one which is integrated throughout the organization, hence the importance of organizational culture. As the problems of falling demand have mounted, organizations are becoming more interested in other sources of competitive advantage. In addition to capabilities for agility, there are other questions about how organizations can cope with a dynamic uncertain environment.

Dynamic capabilities

In their review of the dynamic capability literature, Ambrosini and Bowman (2009) examined the various definitions of the construct, and summarize the most common features.

> These definitions reflect that dynamic capabilities are organizational processes in the most general sense, and that their role is to change the firm's resource base. The literature also explains that dynamic capabilities are built rather than bought in the market … are path dependent … and are embedded in the firm.
>
> (p. 38)

Dynamic capabilities must be systematic, routine, be persistent in the organization, and it is through these organizational processes that it is possible to reconstruct core capabilities in response to rapid changes in the economic environment. It is the environment which is dynamic – the capabilities in the organization are marshalled to deal with unpredictable change. Capabilities which can develop new responses ahead of competitors and which can produce new responses to modify the resource base are likely to be able to create a competitive advantage. Such capabilities could be within a number of functions – marketing, operations management, and finance, for example, as well as in human resources, and any mixture of these.

The strategy literature has shown much interest in dynamic capabilities since the 1990s (Teece *et al.* 1997), and there is an ongoing debate in which the HR function of management (not necessarily the HR Department) provides an important bundle of policies and practices in gaining competitive advantage. Some commentators believe that these capabilities are difficult to sustain in high velocity markets. Easterby-Smith and Prieto (2008) see a linkage between dynamic capabilities and the ability to manage knowledge and learning. The organizational learning literature is associated with the 'absorptive capacity' of the organization, which is regarded as an important capacity whereby new knowledge is recognized and assimilated by the organization (Sun and Anderson 2010). Absorptive capacity is very much a part of all management concerns, but the systematic nature which is needed to embed this would be within the remit of a strategic HR specialist. Absorptive capacity is seen as a dynamic capability, in view of the connection between learning and change (Zahra and George 2002).

In addition to the learning capability, agile organizations also have change capabilities and innovative capabilities. Employee knowledge can be characterized as the human capital which, combined with learning, produces the innovative capability of the firm, according to the processes of management by the HR function (Borney-Barrachina *et al.* 2012). The change capability is a consequence of the way employee relationships and the dynamic capabilities are closely attuned to the market place as well as the emphasis on feedback as a part of learning.

The model of HRM which is emerging

In their article in 2005, Boselie *et al.* (2005) described the top four HR practices cited in studies reflecting what was thought to be 'Strategic HRM'. These were: recruitment and selection, training and development, reward, and performance management. These may seem rather prosaic activities. This reminds us not to be too carried away with strategic rhetoric, and that, at its heart, HRM is practical as well as conceptual work, concerned with administering people management in the organization, working in support of the business strategy, and helping to deliver performance according to the business model in place.

In their article, Boselie *et al.* referred to the 'signalling effects' that HRM has on employees. Even routine HR matters portray organizational values and a prevailing management style. Under the broad headings of recruitment, development, and reward, come activities associated with building and sustaining dynamic capabilities, maintaining the systems of talent management, for example, and the incentives within the psychological contract which drive performance. It is the very routineness of excellence and the systematic approach of HRM which produces the competitive advantage. Superior performance, according to the RBV, comes from ensuring the organization can routinely possess high quality methods of working, as well as high quality people, and that this accomplishment is not an accident.

What models of HRM will emerge from the recession? Many of the existing trends will continue. Developments in new technology, in flexible working, and new forms of contracting have a momentum which, if anything, will be given a boost by the recession. Many organizations are pursuing the twin tracks of retrenchment and cost cutting, as well as repositioning, changing the service or the project, which creates contextual ambiguity for HRM (Boyne and Meier 2009). The intention is to emerge from the recession with a flexible, scaleable workforce, having achieved long term savings. This suggests organizations should plan for the upturn in demand when it comes, without committing resources beyond what is needed at the present time. Efficiency savings will continue to be sought and organizations are more likely to plan for a size and shape which does not assume an expansion in employee numbers proportionate to an increase in demand.

HR outsourcing (HRO) can provide a buffer to future uncertainty. Organizations providing HR outsourcing (HROs) could therefore be expected to take the risk in future. Interest in HRO has continued to grow during the recession. The opportunities are changing, for example, towards e-learning and webinars, as cost effective learning solutions. Recruitment process outsourcing (RPO) can bring specialist knowledge with particular occupational groups, and avoid the costs of the retention of specialist recruiters inside organizations.

At the HR Outsourcing European Summit in 2011 for HROs, the five 'game changers' for the future of the industry were identified. These were: the technologies that make possible employee involvement in the creation of strategy through surveys, for example using social computing and conferencing; the better use of social media in employee search; greater use of e-learning; using 'big data' capability through the use of predictive analytics; and employee branding with global talent management. They also saw HROs becoming more involved directly with line management, with direct support to senior line managers, including areas previously covered by centres of expertise in HRM.

So how do we describe the role of HRM specialists in this new order? There have been many attempts to devise descriptions of 'ideal types' of HRM, starting with Tyson and Fell in 1986. The model which became most popular in the early part of the twenty-first century was Ulrich's (1997) concept of the four key roles for HR-administrative efficiency, keeping employees committed to corporate goals, change agency, and strategy execution. The roles identified with these activities were: administrative experts, employee champions, change agents, and strategic partners. Although in time, the dominant role came to be that of strategic partner, which caught the imagination of practitioners, all the other roles were said to be of equal importance. So popular had these classifications become among practitioners, that companies began reorganizing their HR departments under these headings, often adopting the term 'business partners', an interesting case of life imitating art. Business partners were often given an area of the business for which to take the HR responsibility, so that HR development and policy formation could go hand in hand with the development of the business.

In spite of the potential for HRM to take advantage of the opportunities to play a more strategic role, the evidence so far is disappointing. In a regular survey of 200 US companies, funded by SHRM, Lawler and Boudreau (2012) found from the 2010 results that 'HR executives often are not strategic partners, they are administrators, and on occasion business partners' (p. 58). They point out that the results show that the HR function is too often concerned with cost control, and running the systems, rather than addressing the key challenges of improving productivity and quality, talent management, developing business strategies, managing knowledge, and facilitating mergers and acquisitions. They attribute this failure to achieve a strategic role to the lack of data driven policy, and the lack of metrics. There is too great an accent placed on efficiency and not a sufficient emphasis on effectiveness, or on the impact of the function on the business.

Conclusions

We have outlined above the strategic role for HRM. The operational role is being pulled in two different directions. On the one hand, we see the generalist HRM role only surviving in a general management capacity, or as an internal change consultant, managing the department and the outsourced contracts, with a remit to produce the HR strategy and to ensure coherence in the way the various bundles of policies support the business model, and the long term mission of the organization. On the other hand, there is now what was predicted to be the balkanization of HRM (Tyson 1987), where sub-specialisms develop to the point of becoming separate experts with their own knowledge base and external recognition. The growth of employment law, for example, has reached the stage where there are specialists in various types of employment law (for example discrimination law), and in rewards for particular levels of employees (for example sales commissions, executive-level pay, expatriate reward) in all Western countries. The organizational manifestation of these sub-specialisms is in centres of excellence within these fields, where a lifetime career could be spent. The reorganization of management, succession planning, and the recruitment of staff under the category of talent management is a good example of a sub-specialism being turned into a separate field of knowledge.

The general management of HRM requires competence in the business, and a close relationship with the line, and in project management, and knowledge of areas such as finance and marketing. The other growing role within general HR management is concerned with organization development and change management. This group of activities now links into employee relations, via communications, employee voice and organizational citizenship, and into employee and management development through techniques such as collaborative and appreciative enquiry, and action centred learning generally.

The linkage between the theoretical approaches in this chapter shows how theories about people management have built a picture of HRM and how it is changing. As we have shown, the RBV is central to the study of strategic HRM, since the theory explains the rationale for the HRM mission to deliver competitive advantage through the processes of creating organizational capability in the people and in the systems and routines unique to each business.

Human resource strategy has to 'fit' the business strategy, and it is argued here that the different kinds of 'fit' and the different ways of relating the organization to the context are each based on one of the main varieties of capitalism. The method by which company strategy links into changing contexts is explained by the way organizations seek to remain agile in the face of unpredictable change. The mechanism for making organizations capable of adjusting and reacting to contextual change is through dynamic capabilities, these being mostly organizational learning and knowledge management routines, and systematic adjustments to the external environment. These dynamic capabilities could be seen as aspects of the RBV's competitive capabilities in the organization.

As the context has become more unpredictable, competitive HR strategies which major on those dynamic capabilities have enabled organizations to adjust and to survive and prosper. Globalization and new technology increase the speed of change, and the spread of new ideas and techniques, so that competitiveness is dependent on how quickly and accurately organizations respond to the new challenges such as new products and processes (for example, additive manufacturing, and new methods of marketing, such as via Cloud and mobile technology).

The focus of HRM in the recession has been on cost reduction and switching into products and services which deliver the best value to the business. The overall capability of organizational agility gives HRM a central role in managing the core culture, and requires a technology enabled function, run by business minded general managers, with access to specialists in the HR subjects, either in house or from an external provider. The long term survival of HRM as a strategically important function depends on delivering the high quality needed for competitive advantage, on the ability to sustain employment relationships on a good footing and to ensure the employer brand remains attractive in the face of unpredictable challenges.

6 Technology and e-HRM

> The e-enablement of human resources (e-HR) is one of the most important recent developments in human resource management (HRM) ... e-HR has the potential to result in a radically changed or even virtualized function.
>
> Martin and Reddington (2010: 1553)

Undoubtedly, one of the most significant contextual influences on human resource management (HRM) over the past 20 years has been the development of information and communication technologies (ICT), including the Internet. As discussed in Chapter 2, technology has not only revolutionized the way that people live and work but has also changed the way in which HRM itself is delivered. The development of ICT, coupled with increasing globalization, has meant that people are no longer restricted by geographical borders or by the need to be co-located in order to work together. This has led to an increase in globally dispersed teams that interact virtually, the ability to connect with a mobile workforce and virtual organizations generally (see Chapter 4). Indirectly, technology has also had a profound effect on the expectations of employees, especially the younger generations, who now expect to communicate electronically. This chapter will examine the impact of technology in HRM in more detail: first, we will look at the significant impact that technology has had on the delivery of HRM activities, through a detailed examination of the growth of e-HRM; second, we will look at the impact of e-HRM on the HR function; and third, we will examine recent advances in technology itself, such as web 2.0 and social media technologies, and the ways in which these have been used within HRM.

The growth of e-HRM

The use of technology in HRM has not only grown generally, but has evolved over time. Initially, the use of technology in HRM was centred on the use of human resource information systems (HRIS), defined as systems 'used to acquire, store, manipulate, analyse, retrieve and distribute pertinent information regarding an organization's human resources ... it includes people, forms, policies and procedures and data' (Kavanagh *et al.* 1990: 29). As the nature of technology generally has developed, these typically one way systems have developed into that which is known as e-HRM. E-HRM is the '(planning, implementation and) application of information technology for both net-working and supporting at least two individual or collective actors in their shared performing of HR activities' (Strohmeier 2007: 20). Strohmeier use-fully splits this definition into two parts: first, that technology is needed to connect usually segregated individuals regardless of their physical location; and second, that technology supports actors by partially or completely sub-stituting for them in undertaking HR activities.

An alternative definition of e-HRM is provided by Ruel *et al.* (2004: 281): 'a way of implementing HR strategies, policies and practices in organizations through a conscious and directed support of and/or with the full use of web-technology-based channels'. Ruel *et al.* (2004) and other authors have taken care to distinguish between e-HRM and HRIS in that HRIS are used basi-cally by the HR department itself whereas e-HRM is used by a wider range of organizational stakeholders such as managers and employees, and is con-cerned with changing the interactions between the HR function and these stakeholders 'from a pure face to face relationship to a technology mediated one' (Martin and Reddington 2010: 1554). This has allowed the use of self-service technology whereby line managers and employees conduct HR activi-ties themselves. Indeed, Florowski and Olivas-Lujan (2006) reflected on the transition to a technology centred approach to HR delivery where a large proportion of administrative or transactional HR activities are now deliv-ered electronically. Thite and Kavanagh (2009), however, noted that the use of e-HRM was not limited only to transactional HR but could also be used for 'traditional' HR activities such as recruitment, selection, training, compensa-tion, and managing performance, for value adding transformational activities or for managing HR across the whole employee life cycle. In this way, the use of e-HRM has mirrored the use of the Internet more generally, from its beginnings as an information provider, to a platform for communication and interaction, and activities such as shopping.

More recently, technology in HRM has evolved into the use of more inter-active web 2.0 technologies, mobile technology (Martin and Reddington 2010), and even gaming applications, in which employees, potential job appli-cants, and learners interact, at least partly, with a technological platform rather than an individual. These developments have occurred in tandem with the move towards open access to learning tools: at the time of writing, many educational and training institutions were focusing on the development of 'Massive Open Online Courses' (MOOCS). The use of web 2.0 and social media will be dis-cussed in more detail later in this chapter. First, we will focus on the more gen-eral growth in the use of e-HRM as a delivery mode for HRM activities, and the impact of the use of these technologies on the HR function.

Table 6.1 below draws on the results of survey data in eight selected coun-tries (Cranet 2009) to show that e-HRM is now used by the majority of

Table 6.1 Proportion of organizations using
e-HRM in eight countries

Country	N	% organizations
United Kingdom	204	91
Germany	418	92
Italy	155	84
Norway	95	98
Switzerland	96	90
USA	484	85
Australia	96	84
South Africa	187	84

Source: Data taken from Cranet survey 2009

Table 6.2 Activities e-HRM is used for (%) (N=1735)

HR activity	% organizations
Personnel records	83
Payroll	93
Attendance	79
Recruitment and selection	42
Training and development	52
Performance management	40
Career development	20
Work scheduling	40
Health and safety	26
Measurement of HR performance	25
Providing HR information	42

Source: Data taken from Cranet survey 2009

organizations. Data from the same survey also showed that 48 per cent of surveyed organizations (in 33 countries) used manager self-service and 39 per cent used employee self-service.

When we look at Table 6.2, we can see that e-HRM is not used equally across all HR activities. Despite the evolution from HRIS to e-HRM, technology is still most commonly used for transactional activities such as record keeping, payroll, and attendance and is less commonly used for traditional or transformational HR activities such as recruitment and selection, training and development, performance management, or career development. This supports the assertion of Burbach and Dundon (2005) that technology in HRM is used for administrative rather than strategic purposes. Marler (2009) drew on Strang and Macy (2001) to explain that the adoption of e-HRM might also be limited by inertia and scepticism in some organizations. She went on to explain that this was evident in the originally slow adoption of HR technology followed by rapid growth in the 2000s.

The growth of e-HRM can be explained using neo-institutionalism (DiMaggio and Powell 1983) in the same way as other trends in HRM. As discussed in Chapter 2, there are three institutional mechanisms that influence the adoption of practices by organizations: coercive, normative, and mimetic forces. While e-HRM has not yet been subject to the coercive forces of government and legislation, there is evidence that its growth has been driven, at least in part, by normative and mimetic forces. The use of technology in HRM has been adopted as part of 'best practice' guidelines by professional bodies such as the Chartered Institute of Personnel and Development (CIPD) in the UK and the Society for Human Resource Management (SHRM) in the USA, therefore encouraging its adoption by members of those institutions. The use of e-HRM has also been driven by mimetic forces as successful businesses are seen to adopt e-HRM. Indeed, Marler (2009) described how the adoption of e-HRM might be fuelled by obsession with management fashions, as in uncertain environments organizations turn to success stories from other organizations for a source of information and future practice. Our own work (Parry and Wilson 2009) supported this suggestion through the finding that the adoption of one area of e-HRM, e-recruitment, was driven by subjective norms, that is perceptions that other organizations in the same industry were adopting these methods. In addition to being influenced by the adoption of e-HRM by competitors, the use of technology in managing people is also driven by the expectations of employees. Indeed, work by the Ministry of Manpower (2003) suggested that, in parallel with emergence of e-HRM and new technologies outside of the workplace, employees have begun to request the same 24/7 access to information from their employers as they do from other providers. This means that employers are encouraged to adopt ICT in order to satisfy employee expectations.

The development of e-HRM can also been seen as part of wider pressures on the HR function to change its role, from one that is mainly administrative to one that has more strategic value and acts as a 'business partner' (Ulrich 1997; Ministry of Manpower 2003). In this text we have discussed the changing role of HRM in more detail in Chapter 5; however, it is important to realize that the evolution of e-HRM has happened hand in hand with the development of the HR role. Indeed, Voermans and van Veldhoven (2006) suggested that changes in the HR role and the implementation of e-HRM should not be considered separately as they are closely related. Voermans and van Veldhoven see the implementation of e-HRM as a deliberate move on the part of the HR function to offload administrative work, therefore allowing them to focus more on strategic activity. The proposal that the use of e-HRM can enable a more strategic role for the HR function has been much debated in the literature and will be discussed in more detail below. However, the pressure on the HR function to become more strategic and the idea that e-HRM might facilitate such a transition might be an important factor in the rapid uptake of e-HRM by organizations. In this way, it can be seen as another aspect of the institutional context that drives the use of e-HRM in that the pressure to become strategic is driven both by mimetic and normative forces, and this, in turn, encourages the use of e-HRM in order to facilitate this change.

The impact of e-HRM

Having considered the factors driving the adoption of e-HRM, we will now move on to look at the impacts that e-HRM has both on HR outcomes and the role of the HR function itself. These are typically split into consequences in three areas: HR efficiency, HR effectiveness, and the HR role.

Lepak and Snell (1998b) were one of the first sets of authors to divide the impact of IT into these three areas. They proposed that IT can influence: first, operational aspects of HR by reducing administration and streamlining HR processes; second, relational aspects of HR by improving the service that the HR function provides to managers and employees through the provision of remote access to HR information and the ability to connect with other parts of the organization; and third, IT can play a transformational role by enabling people to communicate across geographic boundaries, therefore eliminating barriers of time and space. These three aspects of IT's influence on HR were discussed further by Ruel *et al.* (2004) who suggested three goals for e-HRM: improving the strategic orientation of HRM, cost reduction/efficiency gains, and client service improvements/facilitating management of employees. Based upon their empirical work Ruel *et al.* (2004) confirmed these goals and added a fourth – improving the global orientation of HRM. Similarly, Hendrickson (2003) divided e-HRM into those technologies designed to promote increased efficiency, increased effectiveness, and IT enabled processes such as e-learning. In order to give further examples of the impact of technology on the HR function, we will briefly look at each of these potential outcomes of e-HRM in turn. We will draw on our own research (previously published as Parry 2011; Parry and Tyson 2011) as well as that of others as part of this process.

Efficiency

Efficiency gains are probably the most commonly discussed goal for the implementation of e-HRM (Ruel *et al.* 2004). E-HRM has been related to a reduction in the costs of performing HRM activities. By providing a means by which transactional or administrative HR tasks can be performed automatically and devolving many basic HR tasks onto employees and line managers, e-HRM reduces the need for HR practitioners to perform these activities, therefore potentially reducing HR headcount. This suggestion was contradicted by our quantitative survey results (Parry 2011) that failed to find a significant relationship between e-HRM and the ratio of HR practitioners to employees within an organization (HR headcount). However, an analysis of qualitative case study data from another study (Parry and Tyson 2011) showed that nine of the ten case studies analysed reported that they had experienced cost or efficiency savings as a result of introducing e-HRM, including those from the reduction of HR headcount. Specifically, interviewees suggested that the automation of processes and direct entry of HR information by managers (rather than by an HR administrator) had not only increased the speed of HR transactions but had also reduced the need for so many HR staff to be available.

While this case study data directly contradicts our quantitative survey results, it does also explain that the successful use of e-HRM and resulting efficiency gains are dependent on a number of conditions. First, an e-HRM system must be developed in such a way that promotes usability and lends itself to the easy achievement of efficiency gains. Second, efficiency gains may not be realized where potential users are either not familiar with the technology or where they are not engaged with the introduction of the new system. Indeed, the value of employee engagement with a new technological system is supported by more general research into technology implementation and acceptance (Davis 1989). Third, e-HRM will only result in reduced HR headcount if those individuals who would otherwise be employed in undertaking the transactional or administrative HR tasks performed by the e-HRM technology are removed from the organization. In some cases these individuals are actually redeployed into other roles rather than being made redundant.

Effectiveness

Past research has provided some evidence for a positive impact of e-HRM on HR service delivery through the simplification of processes or more accurate data entry (Gardner *et al.* 2003). Our case study research (Parry and Tyson 2011) found that some improvements to HR service delivery were being realized, in that seven of the ten case study organizations suggested that such improvements had occurred as a result of the introduction of e-HRM. These improvements were: first, increased accuracy of the data entered into HR systems due to the removal of the need for duplicate information keying; second, access to training or HR materials contained in HR systems; and third, more readily available information for management decision making.

Lepak and Snell (1998b) discussed the 'relational' effects of e-HRM on service delivery such as the ability to provide managers and employees with remote access to HR information and therefore increase their ability to connect to other parts of the organization and to other organizations, enabling them to perform many HR activities themselves. Indeed, Bondarouk *et al.* (2009) suggested that, in organizations where HR practitioners have used e-HRM to delegate their administrative HR tasks to line managers and employees, we might expect that the main goal of the introduction of e-HRM would be to improve the perceived effectiveness of HR to a range of stakeholders. This idea is related to the more general discussion of strategic HRM that includes the devolution of HR activities to managers as an important characteristic (Larsen and Brewster 2003; Whittaker and Marchington 2003). Our survey results (Parry 2011) actually demonstrated a negative relationship between e-HRM sophistication and the devolution of HR tasks to the line, an association that was therefore in the opposite direction to that expected. This suggests that organizations are using e-HRM as an alternative to devolving HR activities to the line rather than as a means to facilitate devolution. The qualitative case studies also failed to provide strong evidence for the empowerment of managers to perform HR duties. Six of our ten case study organizations (Parry and Tyson 2011) stated that the development of management capability to perform HR tasks was an objective for their introduction of e-HRM, but only three of the organizations provided any evidence that this goal was being realized. The evidence for the impact of e-HRM on service delivery or HR effectiveness is therefore mixed.

Again, this might be to some extent dependent on the usability of the technological tools themselves (particularly in the case of manager and employee self-service tools) and on the level to which managers and employees had bought into the use of such technology. The empowerment of managers to conduct a higher level of HR tasks is dependent on their willingness to take on this responsibility. An improvement in service delivery might also require the HR team to develop new skills such as consultancy. Authors such as Zhang and Wang (2006) have commented that a lack of competent HR staff might impede the realization of the benefits of e-HRM.

The role of the HR function

The 'transformational' impact of e-HRM has been much discussed in the literature (Lepak and Snell 1998b) with considerable disagreement existing between authors about whether the use of e-HRM can really facilitate the transition to an HR function playing the strategic role of 'business partner'. A number of authors, including Ruel *et al.* (2004), have suggested that e-HRM has the potential to transform the HR function into one that is more strategic, whereby 'strategic' refers to an involvement in the strategic management of the business (Wright and McMahan 1992). The HR function would therefore become one which spends less time focusing on transactional or administrative activities and more time focusing on activities that are central to the organization's strategy (Hendrickson 2003; Lawler and Mohrman 2003; Shrivastiva and Shaw 2004; Ruel *et al.* 2006). On one side of this debate, a number of authors have concluded that e-HRM can indeed help the HR function to play a more strategic role. For example, Ruel *et al.* (2004) and Olivas-Lujan *et al.* (2007) found a link between the use of e-HRM and the integration of the HR function with the firm strategy.

On the other hand, Tansley *et al.* (2001) concluded that e-HRM had not yet realized its potential to facilitate a more strategic role for HR. Burbach and Dundon (2005) suggested that the focus of e-HRM was most commonly on administrative activities rather than on strategic decision making, and Gardner *et al.* (2003) suggested that the use of e-HRM simply meant that administrative tasks were replaced with technological rather than strategic activities. Marler (2009) suggested that the impact of e-HRM on the role of the HR function was actually dependent on the nature of that function, with administratively oriented HR departments being more likely to have efficiency related goals for e-HRM. Alternatively, HR departments that already function strategically were more likely to have strategic goals for the use of e-HRM.

Our quantitative study did find a positive relationship between the use of e-HRM and the strategic nature of the HR function, and interviewees from seven of our ten case study organizations described effects of the introduction of e-HRM that could be related to an increase in strategic HR activity. In line with the literature, these changes were related to the increased availability of accurate and detailed HR information or to additional time available to the HR team as a result of e-HRM use. The data from both studies therefore provide some tentative evidence that the introduction of e-HRM might allow the HR function to have a greater involvement in the strategic activity of the firm rather than focusing purely on transactional and administrative tasks. However, it should be noted that this evidence is mainly anecdotal and may not actually reflect an increased involvement in the development or implementation of business strategy. The move of HR practitioners into more strategic roles is again dependent on the skills and experience of those individuals. In order to adopt a strategic role, HR practitioners need a very different set of skills to those needed to fulfil a transactional or administrative function. The HR function needs to develop skills such as data analysis, strategy formulation, and project management in order to be able to truly play a business partner role.

The answer to the above debate and mixed findings with regard to the impact of e-HRM might lie within the organizational context. Marler (2009) noted that, while the HR function might perform several roles, there is usually a primary role – typically as an administrative expert, strategic partner, or capability builder (Ulrich 1997; Ulrich and Brockbank 2005). She proposed that the primary role of HR will have an impact on the goals for e-HRM introduction, in that organizations whose HR role is primarily administrative will have e-HRM goals focusing on cost savings; those in which the HR role is primarily as a strategic partner will have e-HRM goals focusing on achieving alignment with business strategy and those with an HR role as capability builder will have e-HRM goals that focus on building human capital resources. It might be, therefore, that the outcomes of e-HRM depend at least partially on the wider context of the HR function and organizational objectives. Marler's theorizing is interesting to us, not only because it provides a possible explanation of the mixed findings with regard to the outcomes of e-HRM, but also because it suggests a contextual influence on these outcomes. In this way, Marler's suggestion is similar to the earlier contingency theories of the HR and performance link (see, for example, Jackson and Schuler 1987) suggesting that the outcomes of HRM are dependent on its alignment with the HR strategy.

The impact of new trends in technology

Over the past ten years, the world has seen the growth of a powerful group of new technologies – known generally as web 2.0, enterprise 2.0, or social media technologies. These technologies include online blogs, social networking sites, wikis, media sharing, RSS feeds, social bookmarking, and versions of gaming technologies such as virtual worlds; delivered through a variety of media such as desktop and laptop computers, tablets such as the iPad, and mobile 'smart' phones. The main difference with these technologies, in contrast to earlier ICT and internet technology, is that the emphasis has changed from accessing information (web 1.0) to 'the use of technology as a platform for social interaction, communication and collaboration (web 2.0)' (Denyer *et al.* 2011: 375). Alongside these advances have been developments in mobile and Cloud technology enabling both individuals and organizations to access information, communicate, and collaborate from a multitude of locations and devices.

The evolution of social media has undoubtedly changed the way in which individuals live and work (see Chapter 2). Organizations are increasingly adopting these technologies for a range of uses, not least within HRM. For HR practitioners, the potential of these technologies has been espoused as the ability to develop organizational social capital by: promoting collaboration among employees, customers, suppliers, and partners; second, sharing these stakeholders' knowledge and experiences to create organizational learning; third, facilitating communication with and learning from a new (virtual) generation of employees which have grown up with such media; fourth, helping organizations, employees, and potential employees learn more about each other; and fifth, giving customers, business partners, and employees more opportunity and control over authentic forms of 'voice' on issues that matter to them which are also relevant to organizations (Lai and Turban 2008; Martin *et al.* 2009). Some examples of the use of web 2.0 technologies within organizations are given in Table 6.3 below (taken from Denyer *et al.* 2011).

What is interesting about the evolution of social media technology is that it is developing at a faster speed than HR can keep up with. Therefore, typically organizations are not making use of the most recent technology for managing people. At the time of writing, personal use of technology is again being revolutionized by the rapid increase in the use of tablet and mobile access to the Internet. As discussed in Chapter 2, more and more people are now accessing the Internet via smartphones and tablet computers. Individuals are increasingly using 'the Cloud' to store information so that they can access it easily and on demand. Despite advances in individuals' use of technology, even those organizations that can be described as pioneers in the use of social media are only just beginning to adopt tools and approaches to HRM that make use of social media, Cloud, and mobile technology. It is also important for employers to realize that not all approaches to managing people are appropriate for translation onto new technologies. For example, it is not

Table 6.3 Selected examples of social media use

Organization	Web 2.0 use
Sun Microsystems	Blogging policy to encourage employees, partners, customers, analysts, and other interested parties to comment on Sun and its products (Gordon 2006)
Dresdner Kleinwort bank	Wikis to complement standard collaboration tools within its global teams. The wikis provide a comprehensive audit trail (Lai and Turban 2008)
Eli Lilly	'Innocentive' was created to provide an eBay-style interface to connect Research and Development departments of large firms to a global network of innovators (Tapscott and Williams 2007: 97)
Linklaters	Linkpedia, an internal version of Wikipedia, has been developed to allow employees to organize and share knowledge (The Lawyer Contributors 2007)
AMD	A virtual Second Life pavilion has been created where current and previous employees can meet, network, attend lectures and training courses, or visit the exhibition hall (Libert and Spector 2008: 31)
British National Physical Laboratory	Creation of an avatar based 'Nanotechnology Island' to facilitate scientific discussions and meetings (Humphrys 2008: 41)
General Motors	Formation of an executive blog, 'FastLane' (Economist Intelligence Unit 2007: 3)
Royal Bank of Scotland, KPMG, and Wells Fargo	Recruitment fairs in Second Life (Hoover 2007: 25)

Source: Denyer *et al.* (2011).

appropriate to ask job seekers to undertake long essay questions on a mobile or tablet device.

Most attention with regard to social media has related to two areas: communication or collaboration and recruitment. We will consider each of these briefly in turn in order to obtain some insight into the use and impact of social media technologies on HRM.

Collaboration and communication

As we can see from the discussion above, the main distinction between web 2.0 and web 1.0 is the facility for two way interaction, hence the term 'social media'. It is therefore not surprising that one of the main uses of web 2.0 within organizations is to promote communication and collaboration between employees. We will illustrate the use of web 2.0 for communication and collaboration through the use of an anonymous case study (originally published in Denyer *et al.* 2011) with an organization described as a pioneer in the use of social media technologies. This case study allows us not only to examine the potential of web 2.0 within organizations, but also to identify the issues or barriers that might be faced with regard to the technology keeping its promise of improving communication and collaboration within the organization.

Telco's use of web 2.0 for communication and collaboration

The case study organization (that we shall call Telco) is a large UK telecommunications company, widely regarded as one of the pioneers of using web 2.0. Telco has increasingly used web 2.0 technology since 2004, following the appointment of a new CEO for the business unit responsible for IT and network development, and a second appointment of an 'outspoken advocate' of web 2.0 technology in 2006. The company has fundamentally changed the way that it operates to include web 2.0 use, including the adoption of blogs and podcasts by senior leaders, development of corporate blogging policies, guidelines, and standardized tools for using web 2.0 and RSS feeds. This has been accompanied by a number of campaigns to encourage usage. In addition, Telco has founded an internal version of Wikipedia, an internal version of MySpace, and the extension of the online news service to include spaces for discussion. A number of internal professional communities of interest also extensively use social media to share information and an initiative to encourage people to create video podcasts as part of the learning and development agenda has been piloted. Second Life avatars (a representative of a real person in a virtual world) have been developed as part of a web 2.0 talent academy.

Despite the extensive development of web 2.0 tools, the success of these tools within Telco has been mixed. In some departments, web 2.0 has proved to be a cost and time efficient means of promoting communication and collaboration. However, despite the suggestion in the literature that social media can result in business benefits such as improved productivity, knowledge retention, business agility, increased transparency, and competitive advantage (Hinchcliffe 2009), little evidence of this was found in our case study. While managers did have increased access to social and organizational resources, some users struggled to make sense of the new technologies, were unclear whether these were meant to replace other communication methods and suffered from information overload. A number of issues relating to the power and politics within the organization were also apparent: in many cases communication was seen as only one way; being used to inform rather than engage with employees. Some employees feared repercussions if they spoke up honestly using the technology and others described the use of the tools as 'propaganda'. In summary, the technology did not uniformly live up to its promise in increasing communication and collaboration between managers and employees as it was subject to the same constraints as other forms of communication; namely the existing management relationships and culture of the organization.

This case study is interesting for us as it shows that, while these new technologies do have the potential to change the ways in which people communicate and collaborate; rather than being revolutionary as some commentators have suggested, they are actually subject to the same contextual forces as previous communication channels, namely the characteristics of the organizational environment and the attitudes of individual managers and employees.

Recruitment

It is perhaps in recruitment that social media technology has been most readily adopted by organizations. In fact, in this area, social media have the capacity to have perhaps the most significant impact in changing the nature of the recruitment process, and allowing access for recruiters to a wider pool of passive job seekers. Girard and Fallery (2009) summarize this potential change as the move from 'e-recruitment 1.0' that focuses on the use of career websites, jobs boards, and online recruitment systems to 'e-recruitment 2.0' that draws on social capital to tap into both active and passive job seekers' online social networks through the use of social media such as Facebook or LinkedIn, as well as other web 2.0 tools such as blogs, RSS feeds, and virtual worlds. Girard and Fallery (2010) suggest that web 2.0 'gives companies the possibility to increase their social capital' (p. 6) and directly contact individuals who are not actively seeking work. Of course, the use of networks for recruitment is not new: executive search agents have always relied on such systems to identify potential candidates for senior positions. The real difference that the evolution of social media brings is that organizations now have easy access to a wide variety of social networks, without the need to employ an executive search agent. Websites such as Facebook, LinkedIn, and Twitter contain a significant amount of information about potential employees that can be accessed relatively easily.

Again, the best way for us to illustrate the use of social media for recruitment is through a case study.

ITV's use of social media for recruitment

ITV is the largest commercial television network in the UK. It operates a family of channels including ITV1 and delivers content across multiple platforms. ITV Studios produces and sells programmes and formats across the UK and worldwide. ITV has around 4,000 employees on permanent or fixed term contracts and another 200–300 contractors. ITV is governed by a management team which is overseen by a Board of Directors. Human Resource Management is headed up by their Group HR Director, who sits on the Management Board. Each business area has an HR representative at HR Director, Head of HR, and HR Manager level. Centres of Expertise exist within the HR Business Partner structure in Pensions, Reward, Operations and Systems, Learning and Development, Internal Communications, and Recruitment.

Up until 18 months before this case study, ITV did not have a recruitment function. Recruitment of fixed term and permanent paid employees was undertaken by line managers with support from HR and relied heavily on the use of agencies. A new Head of Recruitment was employed in 2010 in order to review recruitment practices within the organization. She created an in-house recruitment team (of nine people at the time of data collection) and facilitated the move from agency recruitment to direct sourcing in order to reduce costs; to ensure ownership of recruitment; and to create a robust recruitment process. In addition, the move represented a desire to take a longer term view of recruitment and to recruit employees for future as well as current company requirements. At the time of writing, 97 per cent of recruitment was undertaken directly rather than via the use of agencies.

The recruitment process now relies heavily on social media tools, specifically LinkedIn and Twitter. The choice of social media tools was based upon the need to communicate the company's brand and to access passive, as well as active, job seekers. It was felt that ITV had a well known brand generally, but not as an employer. In addition, it was felt that the target employee audience for ITV was typically online.

ITV subscribe to LinkedIn so that it has access to the profiles of all LinkedIn members. In addition to this access, ITV has developed a number of careers pages on LinkedIn. The pages contain information about ITV's employer brand, the jobs that are available, and testimonials from employees. These pages are bespoke to particular job roles or areas. The functionality on LinkedIn means that members entering the ITV careers pages will automatically be directed to the page that is relevant to their work experience (based on an analysis of the information on their profile). ITV can also search profiles for particular skills and contact LinkedIn members directly. They allow applicants to apply for jobs via their careers website using their LinkedIn profile, rather than having to create a separate CV.

The company's use of LinkedIn has been very successful. ITV careers now has over 16,000 'followers' and is the second most popular company with students on LinkedIn. It was felt that LinkedIn provided applicants of the required quality for ITV.

ITV also has an ITV careers page and account on Twitter. It regularly 'tweets' content and news via this account and links readers to its ITV careers website. It uses a Twitter scheduling tool to send previously created tweets at particular times. It also encourages candidates to tweet about their experiences. The tweets are then retweeted (recirculated) by the main ITV Twitter account that has millions of followers. ITV careers also makes sure that it uses popular hashtags (subject areas) so that they are found by people searching Twitter. For example, ITV launched a graduate recruitment scheme on Twitter by sending two tweets a day about the scheme for two weeks prior to the launch and then encouraged both recruiters and candidates to tweet during the assessment process. It also provided a number of 30 minute Twitter 'chats' for potential applicants.

Twitter has also proved to be a successful tool for recruitment. In particular, it is very cheap. Twitter itself costs nothing to use and the scheduling tool costs very little. It is particularly easy for ITV to use Twitter as it has an existing, popular brand. However, it was also felt that smaller organizations could use Twitter effectively by sending interesting tweets and encouraging contacts to retweet these, therefore building their networks. It was noted that Twitter has produced a high quantity of applicants but these are not necessarily of the required quality so the use of some form of online sifting technology on the website is essential. ITV uses a number of online tests that are sent out automatically via the applicant tracking system.

The use of social media is supported by an applicant tracking system and company careers website. ITV also uses Google Analytics in order to track where applications have originated and therefore assess the success of their social media promotions, and has done a lot of work on search engine optimization in order to ensure that they are located by search engines. It is the combination of social media tools and online support mechanisms such as these that allows ITV to use social media effectively.

The most significant challenge in introducing social media for recruitment was obtaining the buy-in of line managers within the organization. More broadly, as the recruitment team and the move to in-house recruiting was new, there was a need to encourage managers to use and trust the team. They achieved this by demonstrating successful results and through internal communications. For example, there has been a perception that social media is not an appropriate tool for recruiting senior managers. They are challenging this by providing examples of successful senior manager recruitment using social media.

Resourcing the use of social media is also a challenge. It takes a lot of time, effort, and creativity to engage with potential employees via social media such as Twitter. ITV overcame some of this challenge by using external experts to set up its social media pages and to train its team. However, it is still time consuming, for example, to set up the necessary tweets. ITV has overcome this by setting up a rota for the responsibility for Twitter communications. It has also set some rules and guidelines around the use of Twitter, both for employees generally but also for the recruitment team.

The above case studies provide some illustration of both the potential impact of web 2.0 technologies on HR and also of the barriers and challenges that exist for organizations hoping to realize the potential of these technologies. Their use is also increasing in other areas such as e-learning. Indeed, Falch (2004) suggested that the use of new multimedia technology and the Internet improved the quality of learning by facilitating access to resources and services as well as remote exchanges and collaboration. The use of technologies for learning and development will be considered in more detail in our chapter on talent management, but it is important to realize here that training has also been affected to a great degree by the introduction of new technologies, perhaps most importantly by mobile technology with a recent significant rise in the use of mobile devices for e-learning (Norman 2011; Johnson *et al.* 2011).

Conclusions

Our brief consideration of the impact of these technologies on both the ways in which people work and upon HR delivery is sufficient to show that they are an aspect of the contextual environment that has had a profound effect on the way that we manage people.

In this chapter we have focused on one aspect of the contextual environment – that of technological development. Over the past 20 years, we have seen dramatic evolution in the nature and use of technology from the development of ICT, to the Internet, through web 1.0 platforms, and now to the more interactive web 2.0 or social media tools, 'the Cloud', and mobile technology. This technological development has had a major effect on human resource management in the ways in which people work, communicate and collaborate, and are managed.

We have shown that the nature of the impact of technology on HRM does not occur in isolation. This technological revolution has occurred hand in hand with changes in the expectations of individuals and organizations, both for the use of technology but also for the role that the HR function plays within a firm. Indeed, the use of e-HRM has been long associated with a change in the HR function to one that is more efficient, effective, and plays a more strategic role in the organization. In fact, e-HRM has been seen as an enabler for this change in the HR function, facilitating the move to a business partner role by allowing more efficiency and permitting an improved level of service delivery by empowering managers and employees to engage in HRM activities themselves.

Our own research has shown, however, that the relationship between e-HRM and the role of the HR function is not as simplistic as others have suggested, and in fact might be dependent on other aspects of the organizational context. The impact of e-HRM depends on the existing role or approach of the HR function and the skills and engagement of both HR and non-HR employees within the organization.

Our examination of new technologies such as web 2.0 and social media and their impact on HRM has painted a similar picture. While the potential impact of web 2.0 on communication and collaboration has often been discussed in the media, our case study in a telecommunications organization demonstrates that this potential is not easily realized, even in organizations that are seen as pioneers of this technology. In fact, these technologies are subject to the same forces (e.g. the culture and attitudes within the organization) as other means of communication. Social media also has the capacity to revolutionize other aspects of HRM such as recruitment, as evidenced by our case study with ITV.

An examination of the impact of technological development on HRM is therefore particularly interesting in reference to our focus on the influence of context in shaping HRM, as not only can technological development be seen as an aspect of the context that shapes HRM, its impact on HRM is also affected by other aspects of the contextual background. This provides us with a useful illustration of the complex interactions between contextual factors in shaping HRM and its outcomes within organizations.

7   HRM across national boundaries

The globalization of business is increasing at an unprecedented rate and its impact on the management of human resources has become critical to the success of global business.

Paik *et al.* (2011: 648)

Over the past 40 years or so, we have seen rapid increases in globalization. Factors such as world trade agreements, membership of the expanding European Union (EU), the need to find new markets and reduce costs, global communication, the development of new technology, and increased travel and migration have led to the increasing interaction, interconnectedness, and integration of people, companies, cultures, and countries (Briscoe *et al.* 2012). As internationalization continues to increase, firms operate more across national borders and, as such, foreign direct investment and the number of multinational corporations (MNCs) is also growing. In many of the economies suffering from recession and long run decline in manufacturing, the hopes for economic recovery are based on the expansion of exports, and are very dependent upon countries such as China and India, the USA, and on the EU's economy. This raises questions about how the context at the country or regional level impacts on the management of people? How countries can improve their people management practices is a vital aspect of HR strategy development. Since there are few technological advantages over the competition which can be maintained for long, one of the critical sources of competitive advantage comes from the way people are managed.

This chapter explores the impact of context and the significant national differentiators, in terms of culture, the institutional context, and the effectiveness of the practices that are adopted. The need to operate across a number of different national contexts means that employers also need to develop ways of attracting, selecting, rewarding, developing, deploying, and retaining people at an international level. At the very least, globalization considerably increases the level of complexity that is encountered in managing people effectively.

Two areas of scholarship deal with the impact of national context on HRM: first, international HRM concerns 'the strategies, structures, policies and processes used to manage people in organizations that operate in more than one country' (Dickmann forthcoming: 332); second, comparative HRM examines the differences between approaches to HRM in different countries. Lazarova *et al.* (2012) divided this dichotomy into three fields: first, 'international HRM' as concerned with HRM in an MNC; second, 'comparative HRM' looking at national patterns of HRM as an outcome of institutions and the historical development of countries; and third, 'cross cultural' HRM that examines the impact of national culture on HRM practice. For the purpose of this chapter, however, we will treat comparative and cross cultural HRM as a single field (hereafter described as comparative HRM), that focuses on the impact of national context on the nature of HRM. This is in line with Boxall (1995) who highlighted the distinction between comparative HRM and international HRM.

Brewster *et al.* (2007) have noted that, although comparative and international HRM were originally different fields of study,

> the increasing reliance on strategic partnerships and joint ventures coupled with a trend towards localization, has made the need to understand how HRM is delivered in different country contexts more important. Consequently there has been a degree of convergence in thinking between the comparative and international HRM fields.
>
> (p. 950)

Indeed, in order for organizations to operate across national boundaries, it is important for them to develop an understanding of both the international and comparative HRM areas. This chapter will therefore also discuss both comparative and international HRM in our discussion of how the need to operate across national borders has affected HRM. It is not within the remit (or space) of this text to analyse all aspects of international and comparative HRM in detail. Besides, there are a number of good texts available that are devoted to this topic (see, for instance, Dickmann and Baruch 2011 for an analysis of global careers). It is our job here to provide an overview of the main discussions within this area and to examine how the external context, in this case the national and transnational context, might affect the management of people.

This chapter will therefore begin with an examination of how national context might impact the nature of HRM policies and practices. We will draw on data from the 'Cranet' survey of international comparative HRM to illustrate this. We will then move on to discuss the different ways in which HR can be organized internationally and to briefly consider the management of global international careers and expatriate assignments.

How does national context affect HRM?

The simplest approach to explaining the relationship between HRM and performance outcomes is in the universalistic paradigm, suggesting that there is a single linear relationship between variables that can be extended to the entire population (Delery and Doty 1996; Martin-Alcazar *et al.* 2005). This claims that HRM practices can be applied in all cases, universally (Dewettinck and Remue 2011). Indeed, some HRM practices and priorities are shared across national contexts, but others are distinctive to particular geographies or countries. Dewettinck and Remue (2011) compare the universal perspective to the contextual approach that emphasizes the 'particularities of all geographical and industrial contexts' (p. 38). According to Brewster and his colleagues (Brewster and Bournois 1991; Brewster 1995, 1999), context both conditions and is conditioned by the HRM strategy, meaning that 'HRM is understood differently, researched differently and is, in practice, conducted in quite distinct ways in different countries and circumstances' (Larsen and Brewster 2000: 12).

Dewettinck and Remue (2011) also explained that, in addition to the distinction between examining universalism and contextualism, scholars in the field of international HRM have also researched convergence and divergence. In convergence, management practices are seen as becoming more alike internationally as a result of competitive pressures (e.g. Levitt 1983; Prentice 1990). In divergence, the influence of the national socio-economic context is emphasized, meaning that management practices remain or become increasingly different across national environments (e.g. Hofstede 1980; Whitley 2000). Differences in HRM policies and practices between countries and continued divergence of policies and practices are usually attributed to one of two factors: national culture or national institutions.

Culture is prominent in the management literature as a source of differences in practice across national contexts (Hofstede 1991; Schwartz 1992; Trompenaars and Hampden-Turner 1998; Budhwar and Sparrow 2002). However, there is little agreement on the actual definition of 'culture'. Alas *et al.* (2008) described culture as 'commonly experienced languages, ideological belief systems (including religion and political belief systems), ethnic heritage and history' (p. 50). One of the most well known academics in this field, Hofstede (1980), defined national culture as 'the collective programming of the mind acquired by growing up in a particular country' (p. 262). On a similar note, House and Javidan (2004), authors of the GLOBE study, defined national culture as the 'shared motives, values, beliefs, identities and interpretations or meanings for significant events that result from common experience of the members of collectives that are transmitted across generations' (p. 15).

Hofstede (1980) found, through an investigation of culture in more than 40 countries, that national culture differed on four dimensions – power distance, uncertainty avoidance, individualism, and masculinity. Hofstede later added long term orientation as a fifth dimension (Yeh and Lawrence 1995). Hofstede's dimensions have been widely used in a range of empirical studies (Kirkman *et al.* 2006), including a number investigating the impact of national culture on HRM (for example, see Newman and Nollen 1996; Schuler and Rogovsky

1998). However, Hofstede's work has been widely criticized for being overly simplistic, using a sample from a single organization, and ignoring heterogeneity within countries (Sivakumar and Nakata 2001; Kirkman *et al.* 2006).

A number of scholars have endorsed the use of clusters rather than individual countries in comparisons of national culture. Ronen and Shenkar (1988) explained that a similar culture may exist across a number of nations, therefore theoretically the unit of analysis should be the culture rather than the nation. As an example of cultural clustering, Schwartz organizes similar country cultures into seven cultural clusters based on three bipolar dimensions (Schwartz 1994, 2006): autonomy (freedom and independence to pursue one's own ideas) versus embeddedness (independence and shared collectivism); mastery (assertive actions to change the world) versus harmony (fitting into the world as it is); and hierarchy (ascribed roles and obligations) versus egalitarianism (individuals as being equal). These seven clusters include Confucian Asia, Eastern Europe, English Speaking, Latin America, Southeast Asia, Sub-Saharan Africa/Middle East, and Western Europe. Similar studies have been conducted by Ronen and Shenkar (1988) who reported eight empirical studies using general work-related attitudinal data to develop eight country clusters; Filella's (1991) European study established three different patterns of HRM within Europe, which echoed that of Hofstede's (2001) general cultural classification; Sparrow *et al.* (1994) developed a worldwide pattern concerning the importance of HRM practices to organizations forming five country clusters which are similar to those reported in Moss-Kanter's worldwide survey concerning HRM issues (see Sparrow and Hiltrop 1997), and, finally, Gupta *et al.* (2002) reported, through the GLOBE research, five clusters involving European countries.

Dewettinck and Remue (2011) noted however that 'contextual influence cannot be reduced to a merely cultural impact' (p. 41) as management practice might also be affected by economic, technological, political, social, legislative, religious, language, policy, environmental, institutional, and historical factors. A broad array of research focusing on institutional determinants of organizational practices has been published. These perspectives share the assumption that formal institutional considerations are important antecedents of management practices because they limit and structure the actions and interactions of managers and employees alike (Brookes *et al.* 2011). Two main approaches to institutional effects on management practices can be identified. The first approach is that of Hall and Gingerich (2004) which focused on broad regime features, based upon the varieties of capitalism concept (Hall and Soskice 2001) (see Chapter 3). Hall and Gingerich demonstrated on the basis of econometric data that key measures of corporate governance and labour relations in an economy can be combined to produce a single factor which captures much of the variance of these elements. The index they developed combines measures of shareholder power, dispersion of firm control, size of stock market, level and degree of wage coordination and labour turnover. The second approach (Botero *et al.* 2004) focuses on national laws.

Botero *et al.* (2004) argued that 'Every country in the world has established a complex system of laws and institutions intended to protect the interests of workers and to help assure a minimum standard of living for its population' (p. 1339). Over and above some basic civil rights protections, they distinguish three bodies of law: employment law, collective relations law, and social security law. Unlike social security laws, both employment laws and collective or industrial relations laws have a direct impact on employer organizations. The more defined and detailed these laws are the less latitude there is for employers and employees to negotiate.

The studies discussed above reflect different aspects of national context through their emphasis of a variety of institutional and cultural concerns (Sparrow and Hiltrop 1997; Brewster *et al.* 2004). A number of studies have demonstrated that HRM practices that are considered appropriate in one national context may be less appropriate in another (Youndt *et al.* 1996; Ferris *et al.* 1999). Ignjatovic and Svetlik (2003) summarized this suggestion in that

> the explicit assumption of a contextual approach is that country-specific factors [such as national culture and institutions] influence the behaviour of individuals and organizations thereby causing differences in HRM institutional settings, strategies and practices. Social policy regimes shape labour markets and employment relations to which organizations then adjust accordingly. They model HRM in line with different social, cultural, political and institutional settings and HRM simultaneously makes its contribution in the adjustment of organizations.
>
> (p. 26)

In line with this suggestion, a large amount of literature has been devoted to examining the impact of both cultural and institutional characteristics of national contexts on HRM policies and practices (e.g. Hofstede 1993; Whitley 2000; Hall and Soskice 2001; Budhwar and Sparrow 2002; Sparrow *et al.* 2004).

Paik *et al.* (2011) provide a useful illustration of how aspects of both institutions and organizational culture (using Hofstede's (1997) cultural dimensions) might affect HRM practices. These are summarized in Table 7.1 below.

We can also illustrate the differences in HRM policies and practices using data from the Cranet survey (see boxed text). For the purpose of this chapter, we have used data from eight countries: Denmark, France, Germany, Italy, the United Kingdom (UK), Japan, the United States of America (USA), and Taiwan. We have selected these eight countries as they are culturally and institutionally different. For example, Japan and Taiwan have relatively low levels of individualism compared to the other six highly individualistic countries; the USA, UK, and Denmark have low levels of uncertainty avoidance compared to the other five countries. In addition, Germany and Denmark are coordinated market economies with high levels of legislative provision compared to the liberal market economies of the UK and USA.

Table 7.1 The impact of cultural and regulatory context on HRM

HRM practices	Impact of cultural context	Impact of government & regulatory context
Recruitment & Selection	For individualistic culture, selection based primarily on individual's potential contribution For high uncertainty avoidance, specific narrow job description	Equal employment opportunity, anti-discrimination laws
Training & Development	For individualistic culture, self-improvement, and autonomy For high uncertainty avoidance, training tends to be task specific, highly structured	Requirements for skill certification and recertification Training cost tax incentives
Performance Management	For individualistic culture, individual accomplishment is measured For low uncertainty avoidance, the setting of challenging goals that involve high risk taking	Due process requirement Arbitration for grievance resolution based on recognized union contract
Compensation	In high uncertainty avoidance cultures, compensation tends to be fixed and seniority based, while in low uncertainty avoidance societies, preference is given to high income variability through performance related pay In collectivistic societies, incentive systems tend to be group based	Legislation in minimum wages, pension, and benefits Laws on unemployment compensation
Employee Relations	For collective cultures, maintain harmony and group cohesion	Level of union support Collective bargaining recognized procedure

Source: Paik *et al.* (2011).

For the purpose of illustrating differences in HRM policies and practices between national contexts, we have chosen three areas of HRM: selection, performance management, and compensation.

Table 7.2 shows some marked differences between the countries in relation to the selection methods used. Indeed, it appears that there are distinctive patterns of selection within the Latin countries (Italy and France) and Confucian countries (Japan and Taiwan) as compared to the others. For example, panel selection interviews are commonly used in Denmark, Germany, and the UK, whereas one-to-one interviews are more common in France, Italy, Japan, and Taiwan. This might be related to the fact that power distance is relatively high in the countries that allow a single individual to make the selection decision.

The Cranet survey

Cranet is a comparative survey of organizational policies and practices across over 40 countries. The unit of analysis for the Cranet survey was the organization and the respondent was the highest ranking corporate officer in charge of HRM. This is in line with Kumar *et al.*'s (1993) use of key informants in research and with Arthur and Boyles' (2007) suggestion that the use of key informants is appropriate in research concerned with HRM.

The questionnaire was developed using an iterative process based on past literature on HRM policies and practices and discussions with the research team. It was conducted in 2008–10 by a business school resident in each of the countries in our study, To ensure comparability, questionnaires are translated from and, as a check, translated back into, English and are piloted locally. Respondents in each country were identified via the use of a database of senior HR managers in public and private sector organizations. Potential respondents were contacted via letter or email and sent a copy of the questionnaire. Non-respondents were later sent a reminder letter to try and encourage response. The response rate for the individual countries varied between 20 and 35 per cent.

The UK, USA, and Denmark are more likely to use references, especially compared to Japan and Taiwan. This might be due to the high emphasis placed on individual performance in these countries.

More similarity between countries can be seen with regard to performance management (Table 7.3). This might be a reflection on a more universal perception of an appraisal process representing good practice in HRM. There are, however, some interesting differences that might be related to national context. For example, Taiwanese countries are less likely to use appraisal data to inform career moves – this might be a reflection of the continued reliance on *guanxi* for making promotion decisions in this context.[1]

Table 7.4 shows a number of differences in the use of compensation practices between our eight countries. In this case, some of the differences might be related to national institutions rather than to national culture. For example, the differences in use of share schemes, profit share, and stock options is likely to be related to national schemes that support these practices.

The tables above demonstrate that HRM policies and practices differ according to national context. A more important question, perhaps, is whether HRM practices are more or less effective depending on the national context in which they are used. Research in this area is somewhat sparse, and the results are mixed, with Gerhart and Fang (2007) and Gerhart (2008) concluding that there was no evidence to date that national culture had any impact on

Table 7.2 Methods used for selection of managers

Country	N	Panel interviews	One-to-one interviews	Application forms	Psychometric tests	Assessment centres	Graphology	References	Ability tests
Denmark	362	84	40	21	71	9	0	82	22
France	157	18	99	61	14	8	12	52	10
Germany	420	77	72	33	14	41	1	69	11
Italy	157	6	95	33	24	21	4	64	15
UK	218	88	71	68	60	33	2	91	54
Japan	389	9	70	61	20	7	0	12	31
USA	1,052	80	93	89	15	14	1	98	14
Taiwan	229	18	85	50	42	10	10	28	39

Note: % organizations responding 'yes' to using each practice

Table 7.3 Performance management methods

Country	N	Appraisals for managers	Appraisals for professionals	Appraisals used for pay	Appraisals used for training	Appraisals used for careers
Denmark	362	60	42	77	90	88
France	157	69	60	66	87	89
Germany	420	79	78	68	88	79
Italy	157	82	76	82	82	80
UK	218	86	85	56	85	74
Japan	389	88	88	95	59	75
USA	1,052	92	96	87	86	79
Taiwan	229	91	93	93	80	52

Note: % organizations responding 'yes' to using each practice

Table 7.4 Compensation practices

Country	N	Share schemes	Profit share	Stock options	Performance related pay	Bonus based on individual performance	Bonus based on team performance
Denmark	362	19	9	13	26	63	43
France	157	21	78	10	32	75	40
Germany	420	17	64	22	61	77	36
Italy	157	24	12	33	80	87	67
UK	218	22	20	20	55	63	58
Japan	389	57	12	13	42	78	42
USA	1,052	12	26	25	77	66	46
Taiwan	229	64	70	44	56	74	47

Note: % organizations responding 'yes' to using each method

the effectiveness of particular HR practices. However, more recent research conducted using Cranet data (e.g. Peretz and Fried 2011) has supported the need to consider the 'fit' between HRM practices and national context when designing HRM systems. For example, Peretz and Fried (2011) found that not only did national culture values explain an organization's approach to performance appraisal, there was also support for an interactive effect between national values and performance appraisal on organizational performance. Peretz and Fried concluded that 'the results support the notion that the level of fit between national values and PA [performance appraisal] practices adopted by organizations in a particular culture is an important contributor to organizational performance' (p. 25). More work is needed in this area, but the prospect of the cultural fit of HRM practices affecting organizational performance emphasizes the need for organizations to consider national context when designing HRM systems.

Having discussed the impact of national context on both the use and effectiveness of HRM policies and practices, we will now go on to consider the implications of these differences for those organizations working across national boundaries. In a nutshell, the lack of a single universal set of effective HRM practices means that organizations working in more than one context must consider the nature of these contexts when creating an HRM strategy. We will examine this issue in more detail in our next section that focuses on international (rather than comparative) HRM.

Implications for HRM practice within a multinational corporation (MNC)

After the Second World War, the numbers and geographical expansion of MNCs increased dramatically, aided by technological advances in transport, communication and information processing, reduced trade barriers, and increased availability to finance foreign ventures (Dickmann and Baruch 2011). This increase in operations across national boundaries leads to questions about HRM in international settings and how the HR function can best structure itself to be effective (Farndale *et al.* 2010). Brewster *et al.* (2007) emphasized the importance for organizations to operate effectively across national borders, but went on to note that this issue was no longer restricted to MNCs but also relevant to small and medium-sized enterprises (SMEs), international joint ventures, and not-for-profit organizations. In addition, micro-multinationals, typically small start-up businesses which are going global, take advantage of new technologies to avoid the start-up costs of setting up businesses in different countries, for example by manufacturing in one, low cost country, and selling at higher prices, for example through agents or online. High-tech companies can also sell services internationally without the costs of expensive offices, by using new computer technology.

Farndale *et al.* (2010) explained that the interdependence, interaction, and standardization across subsidiaries of MNCs become critical in this internationalized context. Taylor *et al.* (1996) referred to the choice of whether to transfer management practices from headquarters to the subsidiaries of an MNC as exportation or adaptation strategies. Edwards and Kuruvilla (2005) call this the 'global-local question': how MNCs balance the pressures to develop globally integrated HR policies on the one hand (exportation), while also trying to adapt and be responsive to local pressures (adaptation). MNCs and their subsidiaries must seek a balance between the implementation of HRM practices that conform to the legitimate expectations of their host environment or the pursuit of more distinctive practices in their foreign subsidiaries based on those employed at home or best practices learned from other sources (Gunnigle *et al.* 2001). This is not a clear-cut decision as both strategies of exportation and adaptation to the local environment have advantages and disadvantages.

Exportation allows the standardization of the distinctive skills learned in corporate headquarters in the subsidiaries, organizational learning through knowledge transfer from headquarters to subsidiaries, and advantages from integration and coordination of activities (Dickmann 2003; Gooderham and Nordhaug 2003; Lertxundi and Landeta 2012). It is often presumed that MNCs should pursue some degree of uniformity in order to ensure that their HR practices across countries are consistent with and contribute to a global business strategy, as well as transferring knowledge and expertise across borders both from the headquarters into subsidiaries and vice versa (Edwards and Kuruvilla 2005). Key reasons for the standardization of HR practices could therefore include economies of scale, higher quality, and increased international coordination (Bartlett and Ghoshal 1989). Internationally operating firms are particularly likely to transfer their home HRM if they regard these personnel approaches as superior. An ethical dimension may also lead to the international standardization of practices that are seen as legitimate in its country of origin or other national jurisdiction the firm operates in. As suggested above, MNCs might also seek to integrate around a specific set of HR policies and practices in order to support their wider business strategy (Schuler and Jackson 1987; Ferner 1997; Dickmann 2003). Indeed, whether deliberate or not, some form of 'country of origin effect' (Edwards and Kuruvilla 2005: 7) is bound to occur.

On the other hand, adaptation (or customization) allows flexibility in shaping management practice to the specific context and therefore minimizing problems caused by political sensitivities. Adaptation also allows companies to learn from subsidiaries as a potential source of innovation and to experience positive business results from being aligned with the country's cultural background (Newman and Nollen 1996; Bird *et al.* 1998; Lertxundi and Landeta 2012). Parry *et al.* (2010) went one stage further than this to argue that there may be coercive forces that actually make it impossible to standardize HR policies across borders or normative barriers to international standardization in the form of the increasing professionalization of occupations via their institutional bodies. Market characteristics or work norms exert normative pressures for local isomorphism if their inherent values are distinct from those held abroad. Adaptation therefore allows organizations to operate effectively in particular countries by being sensitive to the prevailing culture and values in that country and satisfying national level regulations and institutions in the labour market (Edwards and Kuruvilla 2005).

The institutionalization of specific HR practices is impacted by a complex range of factors, not least the nature of the institutional environment in each host location. In fact, subsidiaries of MNCs provide us with a useful illustration of the isomorphic pressures that we have discussed throughout this volume (see Chapter 2). Subsidiaries are subject to the influence of institutional forces from both the corporate headquarters and host country, such as the coercive force of host country legislation, the normative forces of both the owning MNC and host context, and the desire to mimic practice in both other subsidiaries and in other local organizations. Our discussion of the influence of national context on HRM above, informs the idea of how a variety of cultural and institutional factors in both the home and host country might influence the nature of HRM in a subsidiary of an MNC.

Edwards and Kuruvilla (2005) explained how subsidiaries are both embedded in the business system of their 'home' country through country of origin effects and the use of expatriates from the home country to fill managerial positions and transfer knowledge into the subsidiary. Alternatively, legislation and labour market regulations in the host country also influence practices within a subsidiary, especially in coordinated market economies such as Germany. Indeed, Farndale and Paauwe (2007) considered both competitive and institutional drivers for standardization and differentiation of HRM practices in subsidiaries of MNCs. Farndale and Paauwe drew upon DiMaggio and Powell's (1983) distinction between competitive and institutional isomorphism. Competitive isomorphism suggests that similarity in organizational practices are driven by the need for firms to keep up with competitors, whereas institutional isomorphism is based on the three mechanisms of coercive, mimetic, and normative influences as discussed in Chapter 2 of this volume. Finally, Farndale and Paauwe drew on the resource based view (RBV) (Barney 1991), suggesting that firms also strive to differentiate themselves from their competitors in order to develop sustainable competitive advantage. Farndale and Paauwe's empirical findings identified that MNCs are driven by competitive isomorphism and competitive differentiation at a global level and by normative and coercive drivers at a national level.

Edwards and Kuruvilla (2005) went on to suggest that most authors argue for a combination of global and local pressures and the need to adopt a middle way in order to balance these pressures.

Leadership and control in MNCs

A number of typologies have been suggested to categorize the ways in which MNCs respond to the dual pressures to standardize and localize management practices. One of the earliest of these (Perlmutter 1969; Hennan and Perlmutter 1979) suggested four 'types' of leadership in MNCs: first, 'ethnocentric' in which all subsidiaries follow head office policies and practices; second, 'polycentric' in which policies and practices are localized to each individual context; third, 'regiocentric', where policies and practices are developed on a regional (rather than country) basis; and fourth, 'geocentric', a worldwide approach that adapts policies where necessary and coordinates policies when this is beneficial to the company.

Another popular, but now relatively old, typology compared MNCs on the dimensions of operational integration and responsiveness (Bartlett and Ghoshal 1989). The basic premise of Bartlett and Ghoshal's work was that highly integrated firms would find it difficult to be responsive to change, whereas highly responsive firms have a quality advantage but a cost disadvantage. Bartlett and Ghoshal (1989) proposed four configurations: multidomestic, global, international, and transnational.

1. A multidomestic configuration is polycentric, with relatively loose links between the country of origin headquarters and foreign subsidiaries. This means that both integration between subsidiaries and knowledge exchange is low, and HRM is generally conducted at a local level rather than being standardized across the organization. Bartlett and Ghoshal suggest that the advantage of this configuration is that it is locally responsive, but the lack of consistency means that it is inefficient in managing across the global organization.
2. A global organization has high integration across subsidiaries and the headquarters and strong knowledge transfer from the headquarters to subsidiaries. The advantage of this structure is that there are clear control and coordination mechanisms across the organization. However, subsidiaries are offered little autonomy which can have a negative effect on local responsiveness and innovation.
3. Bartlett and Ghoshal describe integration in international organizations as being less defined. People are recruited globally and knowledge flows through a network of foreign affiliates and headquarters. This means that subsidiaries are allowed a reasonable degree of autonomy in order to encourage innovation.
4. The transnational configuration in Bartlett and Ghoshal's typology is seen as the ideal structure for achieving quality, cost, and innovation. This is a networked structure that allows high integration, responsiveness, and knowledge transfer when they are necessary and possible.

Although this typology is now 25 years old, it is still commonly used in the literature on international HRM.

Farndale *et al.* (2010) suggested that there are stages in internationalization for a company and that firms move through Bartlett and Ghoshal's stages from international to multidomestic to global to transnational as they internationalize. This means that coordination complexities increase, emphasizing the dependence of subsidiaries on corporate headquarters and interdependence between subunits and between subunits and headquarters. International HRM strategies and structures evolve over time as the firms and strategies change.

More recently, Dickmann and Müller-Camen (2006) built on Bartlett and Ghosal's typology to develop a model of strategies, structures, and processes specific to international HRM. They identified two key dimensions: standardization (integration / coordination / globalization versus differentiation / responsiveness / localization) and knowledge networking (communication flow including control and coordination). This is summarized in the diagram below (Figure 7.1).

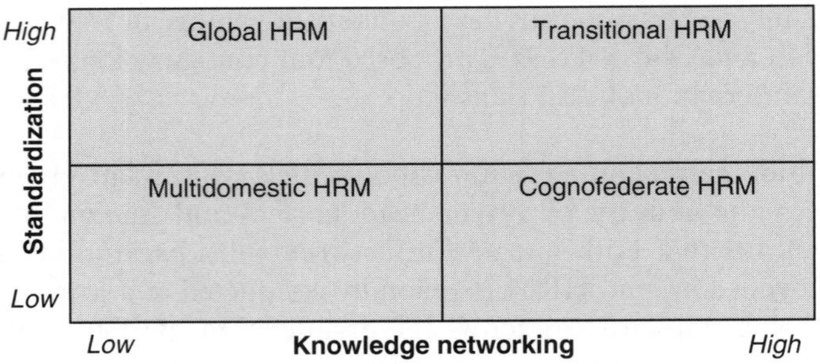

Figure 7.1 IHRM configurations in MNCs
Source: Adapted from Dickmann and Müller-Camen (2006).

The literature has suggested a range of factors that affect the level of central (i.e. corporate HQ) control over HRM policies and practices (Ferner *et al.* 2011). These include: first, the existence of direct reporting relationships between the HR function in subsidiaries and at higher levels at corporate HQ; second, the presence of central bodies for identifying HR requirements and driving HR policy development; third, formal global systems for monitoring HR; fourth, the existence of human resource information systems (HRIS) to monitor specific areas of HRM; fifth, mechanisms for delivering shared HR services across national boundaries; and, sixth, mechanisms for bringing together members of the HR function on a cross national basis (Farndale and Paauwe 2007). The centralization of HRM has also been said to be affected by the home country of the organization (Harzing and Sorge 2003) in that some countries such as the USA tend to be more centralized than others such as Japan (Ferner *et al.* 2011). It has also been suggested that the quality of the headquarters based HRM has an impact on whether or not these practices will be transferred to the subsidiary (Lertxundi and Landeta 2012). Finally, centralization is said to vary by the area of HR under question with areas that are of strategic importance to the MNC such as performance management being more closely controlled (Ferner *et al.* 2011).

Brewster *et al.* (2007) undertook a rare large scale study to examine the drivers and nature of organizational strategies in MNCs. Their analysis produced five categories of organizational drivers: first, 'efficiency' – characterized by high outsourcing of business processes and high centralization of practices; second, 'global provision' – an emphasis on building a global presence and e-enabling management; third, 'information exchange/organizational learning' – organizations with high knowledge transfer and management and who forge strategic partnerships; fourth, 'core business process convergence' – the creation of core processes; and fifth, 'localization' – decentralization of decision making to the subsidiary. In addition to these five drivers, Brewster *et al.* (2007) also identified three enabling factors with regard to these drivers: first, e-enabled HR knowledge transfer; second, HR affordability; and third, a central HR philosophy. From these five drivers and three enabling factors, Brewster *et al.* (2007) concluded that, rather than relying on all of the above drivers and enablers, firms adopt the drivers and enablers in different combinations, suggesting that multiple driving and enabling 'recipes' exist within global HRM.

Caligiuri *et al.* (2010) provided a useful guide to deciding which HR practices should be localized and which should be standardized. They suggested that practices should be localized if something is legislated, a given social norm is particularly strong, or if a given social norm affects a non-strategic practice. Alternatively, practices should be standardized when they are essential for competitive advantage or they affect the key employees in the most critical roles. Farndale *et al.* (2010) agreed that strong dependence of subsidiaries on headquarters is likely to occur when firms are newly internationalized, when the home country has a distinctive HRM approach, when the home and host country are similar, and when the subsidiary is the source of a critical resource. Therefore, subsidiaries are more likely to be independent of HQ when there is a large gap between the home and host country in terms of national characteristics.

The decision of whether to centralize or localize HRM practices undoubtedly has an impact on the role of the HR function within an MNC. Sparrow *et al.* (2011) identified four main roles for the corporate HR function within an MNC: first, as a champion of processes, monitoring, and ensuring the effectiveness of HR processes across the organization; second, as a guardian of culture, overseeing the implementation of global values and systems; third, network leadership and intelligence, to maintain an 'awareness of leading edge trends and developments in the internal and external labour market, the ability to mobilize the appropriate human resources and a sense of timing and context' (p. 43); and fourth, as managers of internal receptivity, to manage the careers of international employees.

Conclusions

Consideration of the impact of national context on HRM provides us with a useful illustration of the wider influence of context on managing people. Comparative and international HRM are not new areas of investigation, hence we have not attempted to cover them in depth here. However, they are increasing in importance as globalization, the number of MNCs, and the need for SMEs, public sector organizations, and not-for-profits to operate across national borders increases. The advent of internet trading is increasingly significant as this avoids some of the difficulties and costs associated with establishing a whole business in a new country. However, there are risks in the lack of control and the potential for fraud, for falling foul of the money laundering regulations and not being able to move profits out.

Past literature, and our own Cranet data, provide irrevocable evidence that there is no one set of HRM policies and practices that are universally appropriate. While some HRM might be seen as universally good practice – the need to recruit, select, and develop high quality employees, and to manage and reward performance, for instance – the detail of these HRM practices should be shaped to both the institutions and culture of the individual country. Firms investing in new geographical locations must be aware of this in order to manage their people effectively.

The importance of the different requirements for HRM across national contexts becomes particularly apparent when we consider MNCs. While managers of MNCs might be tempted to standardize processes across subsidiaries, in order to achieve cost savings, increased control, and the transfer of knowledge from headquarters, the difference in national institutions and culture might make this impossible if the organization is going to work effectively. It is also important to consider the value of knowledge transfer from subsidiaries in order to promote innovation and development within the organization.

The capacity to adapt some practices to the local context is easier than for others. Taking recruitment and selection as an example, actual recruitment and selection methods might be adapted to the local context but company wide competency frameworks on which recruitment and selection are based are less flexible. Similarly, the identification of talent, as part of a talent management system, usually has to be common across the company in order to ensure fairness and comparability. The ease of operating across national borders is also dependent to some extent on industry sector or occupation. Some types of workers, such as those in oil and gas or construction, are used to working around the world on contracts. For service industries, standardization across national contexts might be more difficult due to cultural influences and differing expectations.

It should also not be presumed that good practice flows only from the headquarters of an MNC to the subsidiaries. MNCs might have much to learn from around the world. Indeed, consideration of local practice and ideas can be a source of innovation and competitive advantage. After all, the most important criteria for the selection of HR practices should be how they can help the business as a whole be successful, both in the short and long term.

The lessons to be learned from this overview of the impact of national context on HRM should not be limited to national context alone. As moving into new national contexts requires organizations to modify their HRM structures, policies, and practices in response to normative, coercive, and mimetic isomorphic influences (as well as to competitive pressures), so do the other changing external contexts discussed in this text. In particular, differences in national values (culture) might be reflected in the changing values of new generational cohorts, differences in institutions might be reflected in the development of new employment legislation (such as equality and diversity for instance) and the changing economic environment following the 2008 global economic downturn. The creation of agile and flexible HRM practices so that an MNC can operate across national borders and address change effectively will surely also allow that MNC to adjust to the changing external context within their own country.

Notes

1. *Guanxi* refers to the emphasis on social connections within the Chinese culture.

Part III
The impact of context on HRM

8   Promoting equality and diversity

The United States is like a deck of playing cards. No matter what the sex, suits or ranks of each card are, all are significant in their own way. Without one card, the deck becomes incomplete. America, similar to a deck, is insignificant without diversities. Diversity is what makes the United States complete.

Le (2007)

Despite the above observation, even President Obama has recently been under fire in the USA for an apparent lack of diversity in his Cabinet. It was suggested that, despite the increasing emphasis on diversity within American society, Obama's Cabinet did not reflect the same emphasis – a now infamous photograph of the President with his senior advisors showed that, out of 11 advisors in the photograph, 10 were men, and 8 were white (Hall 2013). We could suggest that this paradox between the increasing diversity in society and that in the senior echelons of organizations, in this case the US government, is reflected across the Western world. Specifically, it could be suggested that this is symptomatic of the failure in many cases of the diversity in society to be reflected in organizations, particularly at senior levels.

In Chapter 2, we discussed the changing nature of the workforce with regard to increasing diversity on a number of levels, including gender, ethnic origin, and age. Indeed, demographic trends such as the ageing workforce, increased immigration, and the growing participation of women in the labour market have increased the diversity of the population and therefore most workplaces. On a societal issue, the increase in diversity, particularly ethnic and religious diversity, has led to widespread concerns about the integration of different minority groups into the societies of countries such as the UK, and has resulted in the impact of a lack of such integration on social cohesion. In addition, it has been suggested that events such as the 9/11 attacks in the USA have led to increased discrimination and hostility towards Muslims (Hudson *et al.* 2007). Coupled with increased media attention and public concern about the level of asylum seekers and immigration generally in the UK, this may have potentially led to increased discrimination against ethnic minorities generally (Hudson *et al.* 2007). A number of racial disturbances in

Northern England in 2001, for example, led to concerns about racial segregation across the UK and an emphasis on the importance of a sense of community in order to address these issues. In the USA, evidence has suggested a negative relationship between societal diversity and social cohesion, although in the UK and Europe income inequality and deprivation in particular areas is likely to be as important in driving a lack of social cohesion as ethnic diversity per se (Migration Observatory 2012).

These events are relevant to HR practitioners who hold the responsibility for creating integration and cohesion within organizations – and therefore also have an impact on the local community. This might be true in public sector organizations in particular. For example, in the UK efforts at social integration are hampered by the fact that important societal roles such as police and judges are still less likely to be held by ethnic minorities. Recruitment of ethnic minorities into the UK Armed Forces remains difficult to achieve, despite considerable effort on the part of recruiters. All of these factors are not only to some degree dependent on a public sector employer such as the police to attract ethnic minorities into these organizations, but also has a profound effect on the ability of other employers to attract, retain, and integrate minorities into their organizations. Generally, a lack of integration and social cohesion in society will be reflected within organizations therefore making it more difficult for HR practitioners to integrate minorities into their workforce. These factors mean that an analysis of the current state of equality, diversity, and inclusion practice is particularly relevant in our investigation of the relationship between external context and HRM activity.

As the composition of the workforce has become more varied, consisting of employees from a variety of nationalities, cultures, ethnic, and religious backgrounds as well as a wider range of ages and both genders, the management of diversity within organizations has become more complex. This increased diversity has had a profound effect on the management of people within organizations and therefore provides a valuable opportunity for us to examine the impact of this contextual trend on HRM. This chapter will therefore examine the different ways in which employers can conceptualize equality and diversity and the role of the HR function in operationalizing this.

Defining diversity

It is important to note here that the definition of diversity has not always been clear. Indeed, Mannix and Neale (2005) suggest that scholars have struggled to clearly define diversity, as it has been applied to such a large number of differences among people. We can distinguish between surface level diversity, as that which includes demographic difference, and deep level diversity as differences in attitudes and beliefs (Harrison *et al.* 2002). Mannix and Neale (2005) develop this two factor approach into one that is more multifaceted and includes several clusters of diversity characteristics (Table 8.1).

Table 8.1 Categories and types of diversity

Category	Type of diversity
Social category differences	Race Ethnicity Gender Age Religion Sexual orientation Physical abilities
Differences in knowledge and skills	Education Functional knowledge Information of expertise Training Experience Abilities
Differences in values or beliefs	Cultural background Ideological beliefs
Personality differences	Cognitive style Affective disposition Motivational factors
Organizational or community status differences	Tenure or length of service Title (including work function, seniority, discipline, etc.)
Differences in social and network ties	Work related ties Friendship ties Community ties In-group memberships

Source: Mannix and Neale (2005).

For the sake of simplicity, we will focus here on the dimensions of diversity that Mannix and Neale (2005) call 'social category differences', as this aligns well with national and organizational approaches to diversity across the Western world.

Equality to diversity and inclusion approaches

It is important to distinguish between equality approaches and diversity management or inclusion approaches at the outset of this chapter, as these represent different management approaches. Historically, organizational responses to diversity have reflected national legislation that focuses on the equality of opportunities for workers. Therefore, at a basic level, Western organizations are required to comply with the raft of employment legislation regarding equality, human rights, and outlawing discrimination on a number of grounds. In the UK, for instance, there has been legislation around equality since the Equal Pay Act in 1970, most recently the Equality Act 2010 that outlaws direct and indirect discrimination at work and in vocational training based on sex, race, age, religion or belief, disability, sexual orientation, marriage or civil partnership, gender reassignment, and pregnancy or maternity. This means that employers have been forced to adopt a range of policies and practices that ensure the equal treatment of employees, in order to comply with this legislation and live by the letter of the law. However, for many organizations, the management of a diverse workforce has moved beyond the promotion of equality to the development of policies and practices that actually value and emphasize the differences between employees. This has also developed into the notion of 'inclusion' – when an organization takes steps to ensure that all employees feel comfortable, included, and valued within the organization, regardless of their race, age, gender, etc.

Ozbilgin and Tatli (2011) suggested that diversity management is 'a management philosophy of recognising and valuing heterogeneity in organizations with a view to improve organizational performance'. They go on to explain that this approach was offered as an alternative to equal opportunities in the UK and was concurrent with significant changes in the political economy towards liberalization and deregulation in the USA and UK. The move towards diversity management and inclusion has been marked by a move away from the emotive and legal case for equality and elimination of group based structural disadvantage towards the individualized and performance driven business case arguments. Subeliani and Tsogas (2005) state that diversity management 'positively values difference and thus provides a radically new approach to the question of difference at work … Managing diversity seems to be a proactive strategy with the aim of maximizing the utilization of employees' potential' (p. 832). Diversity management therefore is focused on a broader and more inclusive definition of diversity to include many visible and invisible characteristics of individuals. Armstrong *et al.* (2010) note that some researchers have suggested that equality and diversity are at opposite ends of the same continuum and merely indicate a progression in developing equality in organizations (McDougall 1998), while others say it is not useful to distinguish between them (Malvin and Girling 2000). However, it is not possible to separate managing diversity in the workplace and providing equal employment opportunities because legislation shapes the way in which diversity is managed (Monks 2007).

The main differences between equality and diversity management might be in the motivation for adopting the approach. Diversity management and inclusion approaches are often driven mainly by the desire to improve organizational performance; while the introduction of equalities legislation has been driven by considerations of equity. These drivers are often presented as the business case and moral case respectively (Urwin *et al.* 2013). It might be that the choice between equality and diversity management is driven to some degree by the context in which an organization operates. For example, Ozbilgin and Tatli (2011) noted that there are some sector differences in the adoption of equality and diversity management approaches. Diversity management is more common in the private sector due to the emphasis on profit and sales while public sector organizations tend to focus on social responsibility, probably due to their more legalistic approach and the influence of trade unions. However, they also observe that the increased emphasis on value for money in the public sector means that there is also a move towards diversity management in this sector.

Having defined equality, diversity management, and inclusion approaches, we will now draw on our own research to examine the implications of such approaches for HRM policies and practices. Our research has focused mainly on one dimension of diversity, that of age diversity. We will first examine how organizations within the UK reacted to the coercive mechanisms of the Employment Equality (Age) Regulations introduced in 2006 to outlaw age discrimination and develop age equality at work. Staying with age as an example of diversity, we will then look at how organizations have reacted to mimetic and normative isomorphic pressures to take a diversity management approach to age differences at work.

Reactions to age equality legislation

While equality approaches to age might also be driven by mimetic and normative forces promoting the moral case for removing discrimination and inequities between individuals in different social categories, by far the most prominent driver of organizations developing policies and practices to encourage equality is the existence of legislation. In this way, demographic changes in the population (and, as such, in the labour market) have an indirect impact on HRM policies and practices. In the first instance, changes in employment legislation are driven by changes in the labour market, and this legislation, in turn, affects the ways in which employers act through their HRM practices. The Employment Equality (Age) Regulations, introduced on 1 October 2006 in the UK (now replaced by the Equality Act 2010) outlawed both direct and indirect age discrimination in employment and vocational training. This legislation was driven primarily by the changes in the age demographics in the population, as discussed in Chapter 2. In addition, it was apparent that, despite the ageing workforce, older workers were underrepresented in the UK workforce (Loretto *et al.* 2005). This was viewed, in part, as the result of employment practices adopted by employers who favoured the recruitment and retention of younger workers (McVittie *et al.* 2003).

The 2006 legislation meant that employers needed to audit their HRM policies and practices in order to remove or to objectively justify policies that were seen as discriminatory according to age, and therefore represented a strong coercive pressure on employers to ensure equality between employees of different ages. It is important to recognize that the pressure to comply with coercive forces is not just due to the legislation itself. There are also social pressures to comply, arising from social norms or values. Compliance with employment legislation (particularly anti-discrimination law) is achieved not only because it is the law, but also because some see a moral or business justification to comply. Indeed, with regard to age equality, some employers might support anti-discrimination activities as a moral duty, while others need a good business reason for compliance or they will have difficulty justifying the costs, and would be tempted to give lip service rather than commitment to anti-discrimination legislation.

We studied employers' reactions to the 2006 age discrimination legislation and the impact of this coercive mechanism on HRM policies and practices (Parry and Tyson 2009). There was a clear coercive pressure to change HR policies and practices in organizations. However, many employers originally saw this legislation as actually damaging to their interests, suggesting that the business case for these changes was not particularly strong. There was some evidence of mimetic pressures, with pressure groups such as the 'Employers Forum on Age' and 'Age Positive' promoting the moral case for age equality. In addition, professional networks such as the CIPD, and employment lawyers, published best practice guidelines and ran seminars on these topics.

Our research, based upon a longitudinal survey of HRM policies and practices and four case studies with UK organizations (see Parry and Tyson 2009 for more details of this methodology), shed some light on the forces driving the introduction of age equality practices by UK organizations. The results clearly showed that the 2006 legislation was the main driver for changes to HR policies on employee age, with a relatively high proportion of organizations introducing policies and practices on age discrimination in the year prior to the legislation. This supports the suggestion of equality practices being driven mainly by coercive mechanisms. However, this research also showed that there were a range of other forces, as opposed to only coercive forces, that affected an employer's choices when introducing age equality policies. This suggested that contextual factors outside of national legislation were also important in shaping an organization's approach to equality. For instance, the nature of the organization itself was important, in that public sector organizations were more likely to have adopted policies at an earlier stage. Preparedness to adopt the legislation was also a function of the values of the organization in question, in that organizations with inclusive values and an ethos of social awareness and responsibility were likely to have taken greater steps to adopt age equality policies in response to the legislation. This might suggest a moral justification for the new law. In addition, the introduction of age discrimination policies was related to the commitment of the board or senior management to eliminating age discrimination, providing further evidence of the impact of the values of the firm on the introduction of HR policies.

Our results therefore suggested that legislation does not always represent a form of coercive change. In many of the organizations studied, there was also a business case for improving age equality or an alignment of interests between what was desired by organizations and what was dictated by the legislation. Many of the organizations surveyed had developed business cases based on the need to reflect a changing society and demographic pressures. We can therefore suggest that coercive forces are sometimes modified or enhanced by moral or utilitarian justification.

Through this analysis of the impact of the 2006 UK age legislation on HRM policies and practices, we can begin to see how changes to the age demographics of the workforce have affected HRM policies and practices by virtue of national legislation. Specifically, in our study, the introduction of legislation had forced organizations to introduce policies and practices such as an age discrimination policy; bans on age related decision making in recruitment, promotion, compensation and benefits, and training; the creation of a task group on age equality; age discrimination training for line managers; and monitoring systems for the age of employees. It can be seen that these policies are generally aimed at removing age discrimination and therefore promoting equality and inclusion for employees of all ages, rather than at recognizing, valuing, and leveraging the differences between employees. The employers' reaction to the age discrimination legislation in 2006 was very much one of compliance, with the promotion of age equality being seen as the means of complying with the law.

Effectiveness of equality approaches

It is worth noting here that, despite the introduction of legislation and the common adoption of an equality management approach towards age, the evidence suggests that in the workplace there continue to be stereotypical attitudes towards individuals based on age. For instance, Loretto and White (2006) found that attitudes based on general stereotypes played a strong role in organizations, with over half of employers feeling that a person's performance decreased from age 50 onwards. They also found evidence that many employers generalized from what was actually limited experience of older workers, with older workers seen as lacking technological skills and being less adaptable to change than younger workers. Our own research (Parry and Tyson 2009) found that stereotypical attitudes about both older and younger workers remained prevalent in HR managers, the very people responsible for designing and implementing age management policies, and that there was little change in these attitudes after the introduction of the Equality (Age) Regulations in 2006.

If we look back at other anti-discrimination legislation in the UK, such as that created for gender, race, and disability, and more recently the Equality Act (2010), we see a similar pattern, with a focus on compliance and therefore equality. We also see that, despite the general compliance with this longer term equality legislation, its success at promoting real equality between demographic groups is unproven. Most campaigners for equality would agree that women and minority groups remain disadvantaged regardless of legislative steps to address this problem.

A useful illustration of this can be found via consideration of the gender pay gap. Despite the UK Equal Pay Act of 1970, inequality between men and women in terms of pay still exists over 40 years later. For example, in

2012 figures from the Office for National Statistics (ONS 2012c) is the suggestion that, while the pay gap between men and women for full time workers in the UK was narrowing due to higher growth in women's pay compared to men's, this gap remained at almost 10 per cent. Evidence in the USA has also suggested a persistent pay gap between men and women. For example, a study released by the American Association of University Women (AAUW) in October 2012 showed that full time working women earn on average 82 per cent of what their male peers earn (USA Today 2012).

Similarly, there remains a lack of women in very senior roles in organizations. While the number of women in senior roles within the EU is rising according to research by Hay Group (Peacock 2013), still only 17 per cent of board positions in Europe were held by women in 2012 (compared to 11 per cent in 2011). This research also showed that the pay gap between men and women in board level roles was 9 per cent in 2012, up from 7 per cent in 2011. Male directors' pay was £83,747 on average while women were paid £73,162. In some countries this pay difference was considerably wider – for example there was a gap of 22 per cent between male and female board members' average pay in Italy.

It is also true to say that legislation regarding discrimination against racial or ethnic minorities has also not been completely successful at removing inequalities in the labour market. Black, Asian, and Minority Ethnic (BAME) individuals have historically been disadvantaged in the labour market. While we see improvements in the job prospects of Indian, Chinese, and Black African groups, Pakistani and Bangladeshi groups have much lower employment prospects.

The above figures suggest that coercive pressures of legislation alone are not sufficient to overcome disadvantages for women and minorities. For women, despite widespread compliance with the law, disadvantages still exist due in part to occupational segregation (women being clustered into stereotypically female jobs that are associated with low pay such as clerical, caring, and catering roles); the need for many women to work part time to address caring responsibilities; and discrimination in pay systems, with women being paid less than men are paid for similar work. It has been suggested that this situation might get worse under the current economic situation in the UK at least, due to the reduction in the size of the public sector. Many women who work within the private sector are at risk of being forced out of the public sector into the private sector where the pay gap is typically higher, therefore leading to an increase in the overall pay gap (Fawcett Society 2012).

Doubts about the effectiveness of equality approaches might be one reason why there has more recently been a move away from a focus on an approach to workforce differences based on equality, to one that not only recognizes and values differences, but also takes advantage of the differences between workers in order to seek to achieve competitive advantage for the organization. We will now move on to examine diversity management and inclusion approaches, using age diversity management and inclusion as an example.

Diversity management and inclusion approaches to age diversity

The need to recognize and manage age diversity, rather than ignore differences in workers based on age (as per an equality approach), has arisen from the growing business need for employers to effectively retain and engage different age groups. The ageing workforce and increasing life expectancy means that older workers are becoming increasingly important as a source of the skills and experience that employers need. This means that it is important for employers to engage with older workers in order to retain them and ensure that they continue to make a significant contribution to the organization. In addition, competition for the fewer younger workers entering the workforce has increased, meaning that employers also need to find a way to attract, retain, and engage with this segment of the workforce.

This is an extension of the idea of market segmentation adopted in marketing in which the needs and preferences of particular segments of the population are identified in order to tailor marketing and selling activity to these preferences (as discussed in Chapter 11). This can only be achieved if employers understand the different things that might be important to these different age groups, i.e. if employers recognize and address age diversity rather than acting as though different age groups have the same preferences, as might be the case in an equality approach. For example, research has suggested that, while financial rewards will still be important to some older workers, for others, extrinsic rewards become less important and the emphasis moves onto having a fulfilling and rewarding job. Armstrong-Stassen (2008) found that older workers were attracted to organizations in which the HR practices were tailored to the needs and desires of older workers. These included flexible working such as compressed working weeks, practices to increase workforce participation, extended career breaks, age limits for shift work, training and development programmes for their age group, job design to accommodate changing physical needs, reduced workloads, performance evaluation, compensation, and recognition and respect (Paul and Townsend 1993; Remery *et al.* 2003; Saba and Guerin 2005; Armstrong-Stassen 2008).

Of course, not all organizations are developing HR practices aimed at older, or indeed younger, workers, and many still use a one-size-fits-all approach when it comes to HRM. A review of the research evidence by Vickerstaff (2010) found that many organizations still have no specific strategies with regard to age management, and Claes and Heymans (2008) found that organizations varied from those that applied ad hoc practices when problems arose to those with a specific retention policy and associated practices for older workers.

As suggested above, the driver for age management practices might be in the business case for attracting and retaining the skills and experience that an organization needs. On a broader note, the potential business benefits of diversity more generally have been often discussed in the academic literature. For example, Cox and Blake (1991) suggested six main business benefits of a diverse workforce based on their review of the early literature. First, a cost argument, that the cost of doing a poor job in integrating workers is increasing so those who manage diversity will gain a cost advantage. Second, the resource acquisition argument, that adopting a diversity management approach will develop reputations of favourability for the organization as prospective employers of, for example, women and ethnic minorities so these organizations will get the best personnel. Third, the marketing argument, that organizations will obtain insight and sensitivity to the needs of different customer groups from having diverse employees and that this will improve marketing. Fourth, the creativity argument, that the presence of a diversity of perspectives and less emphasis on conformity to past norms should improve creativity. Fifth, the problem solving argument, that heterogeneity in decision and problem solving groups potentially produces better decisions through a wider range of perspectives; and, finally, the system flexibility argument, that the system becomes less standardized and therefore more fluid as it becomes more diverse which creates more flexibility to react to environmental changes. Similarly, Subeliani and Tsogas (2005) suggested that increased diversity can lead to a better understanding of local markets and customers, increased ability to attract and retain the best people, greater creativity, better problem solving, and greater flexibility for organizations.

The business case aside, the move towards a diversity management and inclusion approach is also driven by mimetic and normative isomorphic forces. The growth in a diversity management and inclusion approach has been influenced by the commonly held view of professional bodies such as the CIPD and SHRM that this is 'best practice', and also by case studies of organizations successfully using this approach. Despite the espoused business case for increased diversity and diversity management, the evidence for a positive impact of diversity on performance generally is mostly anecdotal and therefore unconvincing (Urwin *et al.* 2013). It can be suggested that the recognition that different segments of the workforce might have different needs and preferences (as described for older workers above) has the potential at least to improve the recruitment, retention, and engagement of these groups. In this way, a business case for a diversity management approach to age differences exists, particularly in light of the growing evidence that employers will be unable to obtain the human capital that they need from the decreasing numbers of younger workers alone. However, a similar lack of evidence exists of the effectiveness of organizational practices in extending working life and engaging older workers. This might be because, despite the large amount of discussion about the HR policies and practices that should be adopted to engage with, for example, older workers, there is little evidence that UK employers at least are actually developing policies and practices to encourage the engagement and retention of older workers (Parry and Harris 2011).

For other areas of diversity such as gender and race, diversity management approaches are perhaps more developed, but evidence that these approaches have a positive impact on organizational performance is still sparse. In one rare empirical study Armstrong *et al.* (2010) used a survey to examine the relationship between high performance work systems and diversity management practices with productivity outcomes. They found that increased use of high performance work systems led to higher performance and that diversity management in addition to high performance work systems led to even more gains. Firms that used diversity management demonstrated high levels of labour productivity, increased workforce innovation, and decreased voluntary turnover. When firms used high performance work systems and diversity management in tandem, the combination explained 13.2 per cent of the variance in labour productivity, 8.8 per cent in workforce innovation, and 8 per cent in voluntary turnover. More research of this type is definitely needed in order to establish the actual value of diversity management approaches for employers, over and above their face validity.

The tension between diversity and equality management approaches

It is important to recognize that equality and diversity management approaches do not necessarily exist easily side by side. While equality is often seen as the baseline approach adopted by organizations in order to comply with anti-discrimination legislation, and diversity management as an advance on this minimum standard, in fact, there are some tensions between the two approaches. Indeed, Kirton and Greene (2009) suggested that the business case and moral case for managing diversity are not always aligned and that an emphasis on diversity management in order to serve a business case might mean that employers are more likely to serve organizational objectives rather than improve working lives. In contrast, Ozbilgin and Tatli (2011) suggested that the legislative focus of equality management might drive away a proactive approach towards diversity. This means that there is a need to focus on the positive aspects of diversity management rather than take a judgemental tone pointing at non-compliance. However, they also emphasized that business case arguments should not preclude ethical and legal cases. Looking again at age diversity, there is some evidence that the adoption of age discrimination legislation has had a deadening effect on employers' proactivity in addressing age related issues on the grounds that to do so would be discriminatory as it would introduce different treatment for different age groups (Parry and Harris 2011). For example, Harris *et al.* (2011) found that infringing age legislation was the reason most frequently provided by employers for not developing policies aimed at older workers. It was viewed as 'risky' to deviate from an equality based approach to address issues arising from the employment of older workers because of creating the potential for litigation and unfairness to other age groups.

Increasing complexity

We have focused above on age diversity to illustrate equality, diversity, and inclusion approaches to managing diversity in organizations. This consideration of a single aspect of diversity does, however, perhaps provide a somewhat simplistic understanding of equality, diversity management, and inclusion. It is important to realize that HR practitioners within organizations are managing multiple characteristics of diversity simultaneously, and each of these has its own complexities. For example, turning again to ethnic diversity, the multi-cultural nature of the population in many countries, including the USA and those in Europe, means that there are now a number of different value systems within a single country. For example, a large number of Muslims reside in the UK and France and 16 per cent of the US population are Hispanic. There is pressure on the HR function within organizations to develop HR systems, rewards, and an organizational culture that accommodates this diversity. At one level this might include allowing time for prayer during the working day or accounting for differences in religious holidays or eating requirements. At a more complex level, this might include examining those rewards or management styles that are most attractive to employees of different ethnic groups, ages, and religions, for example.

Complexity also increases as people might be a member of more than one minority group. For instance, there is evidence that older women are more likely to be discriminated against (Duncan and Loretto 2004; Davis 2005). This increased complexity of diversity means that there are increased challenges for line managers in managing their teams. It falls to the HR department to support line managers in this role, through diversity and cultural awareness training and through the introduction of appropriate systems and support.

The dimensions on which diversity is considered are increasing both within and outside of legislation. In legislation, we have seen not only age but also religion or belief and sexual orientation added to discrimination over recent years. As practice moves away from equality and towards diversity management approaches, employers are also beginning to consider differences between employees that are outside of legal requirements. One area of diversity in which difference has become commonly recognized and accounted for is in generational diversity. While this is basically an approach to addressing age diversity, it is generally treated as being different to chronological age per se.

Generational diversity

A generational approach to age diversity divides people into different age cohorts, or generations. As discussed in Chapter 2, a generation can be defined as 'an identifiable group that shares birth years, age, location and significant life events at critical developmental stages' (Kupperschmidt 2000: 66). In Chapter 2, we detailed the four generations within the workforce: Veterans, Baby Boomers, Generation X, and Generation Y (Strauss and Howe 1991). Individuals in different generations are said to have different characteristics and preferences at work. For example, Veterans are generally characterized as being loyal to employers, believing in hard work, believing in the status quo, and having respect for authority figures. Veterans believe in the intrinsic value of hard work and have a work ethic that hinges on loyalty, dependability, and a 'stick to it' mentality. They obtain job satisfaction from the work itself and from doing a job well, and do not necessarily need the work to have particular meaning (Berl 2006). Zemke *et al.* (2000) describe the core values of Veterans as including: dedication/sacrifice, hard work, conformity, law and order, respect for authority, duty before pleasure, adherence to rules, and honour. Baby Boomers emphasize optimism, team orientation, personal gratification, health and wellness, personal growth, accomplishment, achievement, and social recognition. They are dedicated, in fact they might be seen as workaholics and are willing to put in long hours and use their personal resources to get the job done. They regularly work 50–60 hours per week (Carlson 2004; Berl 2006). Generation X is seen as getting bored quickly, having a short attention span, expecting immediate gratification, and distrusting institutions (Filipczak 1994; Caudron 1997). They are also self-reliant and adaptable to change (Tulgan 1997) and value a sense of belonging and teamwork, the ability to learn new things, autonomy and entrepreneurship, security, and flexibility. Finally, Generation Y is seen as team oriented, cooperative and interdependent, and possessing tighter peer bonds (McCafferty 2003). They are technologically savvy with high personal experience of web 2.0 technology.

It is important to note that the evidence for differences between generations is mixed and fraught with methodological problems (see Parry and Urwin 2011 for details). Despite this, the idea of generations has been adopted widely by practitioners and consultants alike, with many organizations developing different HRM approaches for different generational groups. For example, it has been suggested that the different generations use different channels when job seeking, have different preferences for training delivery, and have different attitudes towards careers, performance management, working patterns, and leadership (Parry and Urwin 2010). For example, Generations X and Y are said to like to learn independently and use computer based training or the Internet, whereas Baby Boomers and Veterans prefer traditional classroom based training. In addition, Generation X is said to need immediate and frequent feedback on their performance and to place particular emphasis on work–life balance and flexible working. Finally, Generation X value autonomy at work rather than authoritarian leadership, while Generation Y wants to have fun and be offered social opportunities (Parry and Urwin 2010). It can be seen therefore that, in the case of generations, employers might take a diversity management approach to generational differences in order to attract, retain, and engage these different groups of employees.

Conclusions

This chapter has discussed the impact of one of the most significant contextual changes – that of increasing diversity – on HRM. The changes in the demographics of the workforce have led both to legislative developments that coercively force employers to change their HRM policies and practices and also to the development of the moral and business cases for equality, diversity management, and inclusion. The taking up of the moral and business case by professional bodies and by other organizations leads to the creation of mimetic and normative forces that also encourage employers to change their HRM practice. While legislation and the moral case have focused mainly on the need for equality or equal opportunities within organizations, the move towards a diversity management approach, particularly in the private sector, has been shaped by the development of a business case for recognizing, valuing, and leveraging differences between employees, and for ensuring that they feel valued within the organization. It is interesting to note here that the empirical evidence for such a business case is sparse, showing that organizations are being led by a general impression of best practice driven by mimetic and normative forces rather than by actual business evidence.

The growing reliance on generational differences as an axis of diversity is similarly driven by mimetic and normative forces, but not in this case by coercive mechanisms. While the evidence for generational differences is mixed and problematic, it is in this area that significant diversity management work has been undertaken over recent years. This again is interesting as it shows how an idea, such as generational diversity, can gain momentum within HRM, without the basis of any real evidence of its utility. This suggests again that employers are basing the adoption of HRM policies and practices on institutional forces rather than taking a more evidence based approach.

The lack of an evidence based approach towards equality, diversity, and inclusion might be one reason why the introduction of legislation to outlaw discrimination has not been completely effective in addressing inequalities in the labour market. Another reason might be the sheer complexity of the external context with regard to diversity. It might be that the coercive mechanism of legislation is not sufficient to address the nuances of diversity and its effects in the labour market. In fact, the external context with regard to diversity becomes ever more complex, not only with increasing diversity but also with the introduction of additional diversity characteristics, such as generational diversity, and the recognition that individuals who fall at the intersection between two or more aspects of diversity might be more at risk. The introduction of multiple value bases within society and the resulting difficulties with integration and social cohesion have all led to an increased emphasis on equality diversity and inclusion, while at the same time making the management of these issues more complex for HR practitioners.

The recent economic downturn potentially adds yet another layer of complexity to the management of equality, diversity, and inclusion. The evidence suggests that different groups are affected differently by the economic downturn. The pay gap between men and women and between BAME minorities and others remains in place regardless of the economic context. Job opportunities that arise for ethnic minorities during economic buoyancy are generally partnered by contractions in such opportunities during an economic downturn. For example, the Chicago United Survey in 2010 found that the growing pipeline of executives 'of colour' had been thinned after the economic downturn due to layoffs (Reuters 2010). In the UK, as black British workers are over-represented in financial services and the Chinese are most likely to work in engineering and financial services, these two groups have been hit harder by the recession as these are the sectors most affected. However, there is also evidence that women in the USA lost fewer jobs than men during the recession so were actually not as affected as men by the economic downturn, meaning that they are likely to bounce back more quickly. In addition, we know that budgets for diversity teams are often cut during a recession, as many companies scale back to focus on their core business. All of these changes add generally to the challenge of managing diversity and equality.

9 Corporate social responsibility

One of the characteristic features of the period since the economic downturn has been a public reaction and challenge to existing institutions. These include, originally, the regulators and the political institutions, and more recently companies, the press, and supra-national organizations such as the European Commission and the central banks. These pressures for scrutiny have come on the back of scandals, failures by the regulators, and failures in economic policy in many southern European countries, with attendant shocks in the Eurozone countries as a whole, as the scale of the financial problems became apparent.

Many additional ethical issues have arisen alongside economic problems. These arose as public perceptions of recognized institutions seeking to cover up individual deception, such as corporate failures, Members of Parliament presenting false claims for expenses, excess rewards being obtained by directors of failing companies, invasions of privacy from telephone hacking by the press, and moral failures revealed by child abuse allegations involving religious communities. People around the world are worried about the institutions that were supposed to be protecting society's interests, but which seem to be engaged in deceit in order to avoid the discovery of their own wrongdoing. There are moral issues at the centre of these concerns, so the wider society needs to be reassured on matters in which those with responsibility in public life are involved, such as their honesty, trustworthiness, and the transparency of their reasons for decisions. This shows how important corporate social responsibility is for society to function normally. Because taken for granted behaviours have not been monitored (for example, in the cases of accurate reporting of the Greek economy to the European community before the recession, or the actual exposure of some banks in the USA and the UK and in Europe to risks or bad debts), reassurance is not just a 'nice to have' check on financial probity, it is essential for public confidence to be restored. At the heart of these debates on topics such as the regulation of financial services, the role of the press, what actions were taken over allegations of child abuse, hospital failures in their treatment of patients, and the myriad of small and large scale failures of those whom the public trusted to monitor these matters, there are ethical and corporate social responsibility (CSR) requirements which have not been addressed.

PRINCIPLES OF SOCIAL RESPONSIBILITY	PROCESSES OF SOCIAL RESPONSIVENESS	OUTCOMES & IMPACTS OF PERFORMANCE
Legitimacy: businesses that abuse the power society grants them will lose that power	**Environmental Scanning:** gather the information needed to understand and analyse the firm's social, political, legal, and ethical environments	Effects on people and organization
Public Responsibility: businesses are responsible for outcomes related to their primary and secondary areas of involvement with society	**Stakeholder Management:** active and constructive engagements in relationships with stakeholders	Effects on the natural and physical environments
Managerial Discretion: managers and other employees are moral actors and have a duty to exercise discretion toward socially responsible, ethical outcomes	**Issues/Public Affairs Management:** a set of processes that allow a company to identify, analyse, and act on the social or political issues that may affect it significantly	Effects on social systems and institutions

Figure 9.1 Corporate social performance
Source: Wood (2010).

How socially responsible private and public sector organizations are in the twenty-first century context is now a matter of widespread concern. In her summary of previous research strands in this field, Wood (2010) referred to her useful model (Figure 9.1) which explains the key principles of corporate social performance (CSP), from the business (or corporate) perspective, the actions which have consequences for stakeholders and society, and the areas of CSP where outcomes and impacts will be found.

In this chapter, we are examining the HRM applications of CSR, and the impact on people and organizations. In Chapter 5, we discussed the extent to which the search for legitimacy had haunted HR specialists. The ostensible legitimacy of the organization is transmitted by the HR function's actions to the employees. The HR function, performed by HR specialists and by line managers, has a critically significant presence in public areas of responsibility, for example in managing diversity, whistle-blowing, health and safety, and issues of social justice, as well as ensuring employee voice and consultation mechanisms are in place, so that there is upward as well as downward communication, and so that employment relations are well managed. As we have argued throughout this book, HR strategy as a part of business strategy has a strong focus on adjusting what happens inside the organization to what happens outside the organization: to the economic, social, technological, and legal contexts. As we have suggested in Chapter 11, there is a relationship between marketing and HRM, which means corporate communications are linked into corporate affairs and into public relations, as well as being embedded in a culture where corporate brands and brand values are expressly linked to corporate values. Those in corporate affairs will also have an understanding of shareholder relationships, and corporate reporting. These linkages are a part of the management of stakeholder relationships.

This chapter will seek to clarify how CSR has developed, and become relevant to the work of the HRM function. We will therefore consider how CSR relates to CSP and the broader business goals, and the application of CSR to changing social institutions. We will then go on to discuss what this means for the HR function at a time of institutional review and challenge to the existing models of capitalism.

The growth of interest in CSR

In his concise description of how CSR developed as both a field of academic study, and as an area of strategic concern for senior managers, Lee (2008) described how the meaning of CSR has evolved with the promulgation of ideas to wider groups of different academic and corporate stakeholders, in his view of how CSR came to be regarded as a mainstream business activity from the late 1990s onwards. CSR has moved on from being a matter for the broader society to consider in macro terms, to being a concept understood at the organization level of analysis, with potential impacts on corporate financial performance due to the high costs of reputational damage. CSR also moved from being considered as largely theoretical, from being 'explicitly normative, ethics driven, to being implicitly normative and performance oriented' (p. 54). By the late 1990s, shareholders were more likely to be convinced that there were performance gains to be achieved since CSR was seen to be related to the economic performance of their investments. He quoted Muirhead *et al.* (2002) who showed that most corporate respondents regarded CSR to be a part of their business with 70 per cent having a corporate foundation for social causes. One consequence of these developments was that directors felt confident in seeking business objectives through CSR, instead of depending on ethical arguments.

In her account of CSP, Wood (2010) set out CSP's conceptual history. Her description showed how definitions and the domains covered by CSP are a function of the social concerns and institutional crises of particular periods. For example, she described how CSP and CSR were 'introduced into management literature to help to solve intransigent social problems' (p. 51). This helps to explain how the private sector was included in attempts at resolving the social and economic problems of the 1960s and 1970s. Following the interest in stakeholder analysis in the 1990s, a more sociological and inclusive view of CSR and CSP emerged, as shown in her own work, so there was more interest in measuring CSP at a time when performance measurement was in vogue, probably because of the growing need for measurement to satisfy the requirements for a business case. This context dependency surfaces important dilemmas; for example, at a time of a major recession, as is currently the position, should corporations privilege social over financial outcomes, or is this a false dichotomy, as CSR through CSP can be seen to serve both ends?

The business case for CSR

From the above description of the path of development of CSR, we can see there has been a growing acceptance of a business case for CSR. Carroll and Shabana (2010) have set out the main features of such a business case for a company, and how this links into HR strategy. The benefits in a business case for CSR are based on the notion that CSR can be a source of competitive advantage. This case can be summarized, drawing on the work of Karucz *et al.* (2008) for companies which can invest in CSR.

1. CSR reduces risk and cost, it is claimed. The risks which can be avoided are the possibility of tighter regulation from the state, and perhaps internationally, by having in place robust corporate CSR policies. Charitable giving reduces tax liabilities. The charities chosen could be those whose interests are close to the company's.
2. Adopting CSR policies strengthens legitimacy and reputation, as the company is seen to be engaged in more ethical and altruistic objectives, rather than profit or self-serving interests. Private companies can work for the public good, to create public value, and still make a reasonable profit, it is argued.
3. CSR is a means to obtaining a competitive advantage. The belief is that to stand out as a worthy trading partner, by investing in the distinctive and inimitable culture of a business supported by the espoused values, the company can take the moral high ground. By being honest, transparent, and environmentally friendly, it may attract customers, for example through the green agenda.
4. If strong CSR approaches are adopted, companies can create win-win situations with their stakeholders. Value creation is seen as not just the province of one company, but rather the outcome of joint efforts, between employees, customers, suppliers, and the community. Business success, it is argued, is more likely to follow from joint efforts of actors working in a common cause to produce wealth and public value, for example from training, education, and apprenticeship schemes. Employees volunteering for community or charity projects exemplify win-win, if they are able to gain new skills from the experience.

The case contains a number of potential contradictions. It would seem strange now to suggest that reducing tax liabilities would be seen as evidence of a sense of CSR by companies. Similarly, attempts to avoid regulation could be perceived by stakeholders as a sign of a lack of legitimacy of the company concerned.

However, perhaps the most important evidence revealed by these typical arguments advanced for corporations to take social responsibility seriously is the reminder this provides of the need felt by companies to establish an accepted relationship with the rest of society in which they have an approved and admired status. This aspect of CSR may explain the concentration on communications with stakeholders, the quality of which determines the extent to which a convincing case can be made. 'Since creating stakeholder awareness of and managing stakeholders' attributions towards a company's CSR activities are key prerequisites for reaping CSR's benefits, it is imperative for managers to have a deeper understanding of key issues related to CSR communications' (Du *et al.* 2010: 9).

To take forward the issues raised by the motives of firms' engagement with stakeholders, Noland and Phillips (2010) sought to disentangle the question of whether there are differences between moral forms of communication with stakeholders and strategic forms by drawing on the ideas of Jurgen Habermas, the German philosopher, and his followers (whom they term 'Habermasians'), and counterpose these arguments with those of the academic commentators they describe as 'ethical strategists' (p. 41). The Habermasians took the same position on language and communications, as a method for negotiating meaning, as is taken by sociologists who regarded reality as socially constructed since the 1960s and 1970s, and that the process of meaning construction should be a central concern for social scientists (Walsh 1972). The view by Habermasians follows Habermas's interests in domination within communications, which leads to the assumption that acting in their own interests will be naturally expressed in the corporation's management communications with their stakeholders. Noland and Phillips (2010) noted that adjudications between stakeholders and the firm would not achieve a morally legitimate outcome, because of the coercive interest underlying the communication. They went on to argue that stakeholder engagement does not automatically mean that the firm has adopted a socially responsible position, that capitalism is not necessarily an end in itself, and that the issue is whether the ends of capitalist businesses are morally justifiable, rather than whether or not the means are justifiable. In this way they argue that while the dangers of a dominant rhetoric from the company should be acknowledged, ethical strategists would re-evaluate the ends of the business in terms of what is corporately responsible for society. We can add to this discussion by recalling that stakeholders themselves are also not necessarily neutral in their desire to influence companies through their discourse, also used in the service of their own interests.

As Noland and Phillips (2010) recognized, Habermas's ideas make a more fundamental contribution to the debate on CSR than in the necessarily simplified version above. The application of the more recent discursive approach of Habermas is discussed by Scherer and Palazzo (2007), who looked at how the concept of deliberative democracy, which incorporates ethical discourse and economic bargaining, could be brought in to resolve the problem that there are often no generally accepted or determined normative or positivist positions for corporations, other than those they decide themselves. For example, there may not be an externally located source of irrefutable scientific data available, leading to accusations that the corporation, tied down by its own duties to shareholders and to its other stakeholders, is establishing norms which are driven by the profit motive, rather than by any ethical code. Instead, what is suggested is a wider public debate, conducted under the aegis of the state in many fora, in a transparent fashion so that the various interest groups can come to a position by the soundness of their arguments, and by bargaining where necessary, over the economic outcome, where there may well be winners and losers. As they put it: 'The aim is to (re)establish a political order where economic rationality is circumscribed by democratic institutions and procedures' (Scherer and Palazzo 2007: 1097).

The impacts of the changing context

Restoring trust is so important and urgent, often political leaders cannot leave the matter to restore its own equilibrium over time, and ultimately politicians feel obliged to respond with advice, and often regulations and new laws. A good example here is the horse meat scandal in Europe in 2013, when horse meat was mislabelled as beef in prepared meals sold by supermarkets all over Europe, with damaging effects on corporate reputations. Governments in Europe were urged to act swiftly, for fear of damaging both consumer confidence and supermarket brands, to root out what was seen as a criminal conspiracy. International collaboration was essential in this instance. In the same vein as Habermas's ideas, governments and European institutions have been trying to introduce a form of deliberative democracy to exercise more controls over financial institutions, with wide ranging debates in the media, and reports on what went wrong and how issues such as the Libor rate setting scandal could be avoided in the future. Very often, because of economic interconnectivity, these debates have to be international in scope. The members of the 'Occupy' movement who were demonstrating on Wall Street as well as on the steps of St Paul's Cathedral in London were also part of the debate, as they asked questions about the financial system itself, arguing that there was a moral case to answer about the failures of the system.

Some academic commentators have taken a cynical view of the HR function's approach to outsourcing and to the use of 'contingent labour': the casual, part time, and temporary work which is growing. Legge (2000) suggested that HR managers are complicit in encouraging a race to the bottom in living standards, through the drive for competitive advantage which will push down wages in the developed economies, as well as prevent pay from growing in the developing world, where many of the suppliers and sub-contractors have their manufacturing facilities.

Sometimes we can see that companies act in anticipation of contextual change. For example, the whole debate on climate change and the need for a 'green' agenda has led firms to review their policies towards energy use, packaging, layout of buildings, facilities such as car parks, and so on. Marks and Spencer's 'Plan A' is a company wide initiative which was launched in January

2007 and initially involved reviews of all policies, from company transport and benefits, distribution, to packaging and product sourcing, as well as of fundamental issues such as product design and marketing. The objectives stated were to work with all stakeholders (including customers, employees, manufacturers, distributers, and suppliers) on 100 commitments to be achieved in five years, which has been extended to 180 commitments to be achieved by 2015.

The achievements are impressive. The company intended to reduce its carbon footprint, and has become a carbon neutral retailer. It planned to reduce waste, and by 2012 it was sending nothing to landfill; it promised to use sustainable raw materials and to trade ethically so it helps small scale farms and smallholders in the developing world through fair trade deals, for example on cotton and on coffee, where it guarantees a stable price, and contributes to local development projects. It promised to help customers to live a healthy lifestyle, which it seeks to achieve with dietary advice, and research projects such as a breakthrough breast cancer study (Marks and Spencer Plan A 2013). We can see how CSR is directly important to a retailer such as Marks and Spencer. Without denying its genuine desire to improve the lives of all it encounters in business, this approach is entirely consistent with the objective of attracting and retaining customers, as it states, having consulted with its stakeholders: 'We're doing this because it's what you want us to do.' CSR is good for business, and the culture and style it projects fits well the types of customers who would favour an environmentally aware business. The HR function thus has the challenge of helping to sustain that culture, and of factoring in the values the company espouses to its treatment of staff, and the employment practices of its suppliers. However, the fact that Marks and Spencer can gain a competitive advantage from its ethical approach implies that there may not be many other similar retailers who have been able to adopt the same strategy. To look at the relationship between HR and CSR we will go on to look at two relevant illustrations: one drawn from employment legislation, and the other from executive pay.

Employment law and CSR

The expansion of employment law has been partly to meet the Habermas type requirement for procedures and for legal regulation where these codes and advice fail, for example in conducting redundancy programmes, in health and safety, and in relations with trade unions, so that in the latter area, there are ways for trade unions to obtain bargaining rights, and there are rights to consultation. In the important field of health and safety, statutes are intentionally restrictive to help to avoid accidents. The expansion of legal constraints and guidance for managers is not just in the European Union. In the USA, there is a constant stream of new State laws and regulations, as well as Federal legislation. Recent examples such as anti-bribery laws and laws which seek to avoid the mistreatment by companies of whistle-blowers can be found on both sides of the Atlantic. Many of these laws in all jurisdictions are concerned with the way employees are treated, and we can see that in this sense, employment law is very much about CSR.

In the UK, the long history of statutes and regulations extends rights and responsibilities beyond what is written in the employment contract, as there are various implied terms to contracts which apply to employees and some to employers, for example the employees' duty to act in good faith towards his/her employer. However, employment law from the time of the early Factory Acts has set down additional requirements for the conduct of the employee, and specific responsibilities on both parties. These have extended to the creation of property rights in the job for the employee (who is able to receive compensation if the circumstances of losing his or her job allow this, for example redundancy payments, unfair dismissal compensation), and codes of behaviour for both the employer and the employee, for example relating to discrimination against employees (see Chapter 8). In recent years, statutes which relate to the conduct of the business have been strengthened, for example, on topics such as stipulating the offence of corporate manslaughter, anti-bribery legislation, and the legislation protecting whistle-blowers which in the UK is the Public Interest Disclosure Act, 1998.

In the USA there are over 47 Federal laws which are concerned with whistle-blowers, including the well known Sarbanes-Oxley Act of 2002. Some of these relate to particular industries, such as the airlines, the nuclear power industry, transportation, defence contractors, health care, and the food industry. Successes have included cases proving that a big drug company knowingly sold contaminated drugs, cases against hospitals for mismanagement, and others in the tobacco industry (Meinert 2011). There is often a personal cost still to the whistle-blower, in spite of legal protection. Meinert quoted research from the US National Bureau of Economic Research, which showed that in 82 per cent of instances where the identity of the whistle-blower was revealed, the person was forced to resign, or was dismissed or demoted. The health and personal lives of whistle-blowers were often affected, with many instances of depression, divorce, and other health problems. Forty-three per cent were denied pay increases, or promotion. In 2009, the US National Business Ethics Report showed 15 per cent of whistle-blowers suffered retaliation, including verbal abuse and ostracism. The latest legislation, the Dodd-Frank Act (2010), applies to publicly quoted companies and their private subsidiaries and affiliates, and may help to prevent some of the difficulties and dangers whistle-blowers face.

The role of HRM is affected by legislation. In an official capacity, the function increasingly has to act as regulator, internally, on behalf of the state. Unofficially, HR managers are just as likely to be asked to find a way around the legislation, so that senior managers can do what they wish, without hindrance. In either case, there are issues of conscience to resolve, and if the intention is to avoid the effects of a statute, this is likely to go to the corporate lawyer to find a way through. Big businesses usually try to buy their way out of trouble by paying off the complaining employee. However, eventually this tactic is expensive, and becomes a tax on managers for their own failings in not managing situations without the disruption caused by the threat of legal action.

This is one way in which HRM and CSR become intertwined. However, one could interpret the role more as one of participation in deliberative democracy, as Habermas described. All employment legislation is elaborated, and its application to particular circumstances is made in judgements through the appeal system, so that definitions of behaviour and meaning are given to the statutes over time. The legal system, including the consultative process, is engaged in a debate to try to match and to regulate expectations of different stakeholders, to decide which social responsibilities there are for corporations. Nevertheless, the Habermas process for dealing with conflict does seem to rely on there being two parties who want to come to an amicable settlement. We have seen from the US examples quoted above that the resolution of injustices and wrongdoing by corporations often depends on brave individuals, with few resources, being prepared to fight for what they believe in, challenging a powerful organization in spite of the consequences. This is where the HR manager must make a decision. If there is a complaint it must be investigated thoroughly before HR management commits to a course of action. Ultimately, more damage can be done to the corporation in covering up mistakes, however painful that is for existing senior management, than investigating complaints properly at the outset.

There are tribunals and opportunities for due process, to decide if the company has obeyed the relevant statute. If we apply Wood's model, therefore, the legitimacy of a company's actions depends upon the corporation applying the law correctly. In preparing the corporation to deal with new laws, HR management must undertake the activities described, such as environmental scanning, and engage with stakeholders, such as trade unions and customers as well as senior management, so that the effects of new laws are brought into the corporation through training and development activities. The arrows in Wood's model (Figure 9.1) are a little misleading, since, as the model shows, 'businesses that abuse the power society grants them will lose that power' (Wood 2010: 54). The intention of the model is to show that the legitimacy of the organization in the eyes of society, and of employees, depends on the extent to which the external context has been understood and correctly analysed by managers. The model does show clearly that the effects on people and organizations are a consequence of the legitimacy, the public responsibility, and the managerial discretion exercised.

Executive pay and CSR

In the second illustration of HRM and CSR, concerning executive rewards, we need first to understand the economic and the legal context. The banking crisis has exacerbated the already long-standing, widespread belief that senior executives in FTSE 100 companies, those with high market capitalization such as one would find in the Fortune 500 list, and market traders in Financial Services are overpaid, and have been too often given absurdly high bonuses, with little accountability for failure. There is also a perception that the standards of fairness which are typically applied to these executives' rewards are not the same as those applied to more junior employees. The particular interest of the public, in the UK, USA, and in the European Community following the banking crisis, derives from accusations that reward systems in Financial Services encouraged excessive risk taking. It is with this in mind that in 2013 there were EU proposals to cap market traders' bonuses. The proposal is to limit the bonus element to a maximum of twice base pay. This may have the effect therefore of increasing base pay amounts. The collapse of several banks and, in the UK, the fact that these banks were bailed out at the expense of the public purse, partly because they were seen as 'too big to fail', also produced negative public reactions about the conduct of executives who were still paid bonuses, instead of being sacked.

From the legal perspective, the regulators have long been trying to catch up with the reality of a very dynamic market place. Although there were some regulations about the payments to directors, these were typically only concerned with process, as it remains unpopular with managers and shareholders to place arbitrary limits on the amount an individual can earn. Successive governments in the UK, USA, and in Europe in the 1990s sought to bring some controls over director-level rewards, because of the public outcry expressed in the press and other media. There have been periodic expressions of public outrage, usually as a consequence of discoveries of massive bonus payments, or termination deals, and concern over rising levels of senior executive pay and benefits, which had long outstripped the relativities found at other levels in companies (Tyson 2005). There were questions about the roles and the responsibilities of board members, directors, and the corporate governance arrangements in publicly quoted companies. These concerns were expressed and investigated through a series of reports in the UK from the Cadbury Committee, the Greenbury Committee, and the Hampel Committee, all in the 1990s.

The control mechanism of the London Stock Exchange was the Combined Code (1998), which was introduced following the Cadbury and Greenbury Reports, and which stipulated in the broadest terms the expected actions of boards in setting director-level remuneration ('companies should pay what is necessary to attract and retain Directors to run the company, but should avoid paying more than is necessary'), without going into detail, or mentioning amounts or providing a sound regulatory system. Instead, the intention was for self-regulation, and the system would be run by the board. There were requirements to disclose in the annual reports the amounts paid to the highest paid director, normally the CEO, and that rewards should be related to performance. The Code also describes the role and functions of a remuneration committee, which should be set up, with the non-executive directors' involvement, to oversee the rewards for the board members.

After more scandals, the government of the day established a more regulated regime, through the Directors Remuneration Report Regulations of 2002, later incorporated into the Combined Code. These regulations set out the role of the remuneration committee, the requirement to publish details of the pay received by the directors, including details of comparisons (a comparative graph showing the total shareholder return for the company for the previous five years compared to an equity market index), and of the incentive schemes, stock options, and benefits paid. Perhaps the most important requirement was that shareholders have to be given the opportunity to vote on the remuneration report every year, at the Annual General Meeting of the shareholders. However, the results of the vote were not binding on the corporation, and at least theoretically could be ignored. There were similar attempts to review the problems of executive pay, and similar corporate governance issues in other countries, for example in France, the Vienot Reports I and II 1995 and 1999, the Hellebuyck Report 1998 and 2001, and the OECD Principles of Corporate Governance 1999, and in Germany the German Corporate Governance code, (Cromme) 2002. There has been a remarkable degree of convergence on these issues (Point 2005).

In spite of all the effort, there were continuing scandals, and reward surprises. These were increasingly about rewards for failure, perhaps because it seemed incredible that, at a time of recession and austerity, individuals were able to take away vast amounts of money when their company failed, as happened in the case of the Royal Bank of Scotland. A 'High Pay Commission' was established in November 2011 by The Rowntree Trust and the 'think tank' Compass. The government has decided to make the results of the shareholder vote on the annual remuneration committee report mandatory on company boards. The areas for concern were not just the absolute amounts of executive pay, but also the relative amounts, compared to lower level employees.

One question which could be raised is, leaving aside the clamour of the popular press, why should governments be involved at all in the determination of pay levels for directors? The difficulty in answering that question may be why successive governments in capitalist economies have been slow to become involved, preferring instead to seek voluntary agreements, and to leave the matter as far as possible to the shareholders and the companies themselves. In fact, governments have avoided making official statements for the most part about pay levels, but have sought to ensure there are adequate and efficient processes in place. It is really the failure of shareholders to be sufficiently active in protecting corporate interests, where there are relatively small amounts of money involved, which has resulted in the state making any interventions at all. The pattern of voluntary codes followed by outline processes, monitored by associations of companies, as in employers' associations, or in this case companies listed on the London Stock Exchange, before initially loose regulation, which then has to be tightened up to have the desired effect, is repeated in many similar instances of government and industry relations, for example, the gradual shift to federal law on whistle-blowers, as discussed above. Government does have some influence through its ownership of companies, including those banks taken over by the state at the time of the financial crash, where it has influence as the major shareholder. The UK's finance minister (Chancellor of the Exchequer) ultimately has to sign off any new public appointment where the salary proposed is more than the Prime Minister's. This could of course be more a consequence of the problems with the UK's public finances than an attempt to reduce top level pay rates to reasonable levels, although in other public sector related industries, such as the BBC and the Post Office, pay at the top has been publicly questioned.

Three responses are usually found to the question of the involvement of the State with private sector pay. First, massive disparities in pay between the top and the bottom of society damage social cohesion. Pay packages at the top include base pay, short term incentives, usually annual bonuses, long term incentives (either paid in shares or deferred bonuses, or both), benefits, generous pension schemes, and life insurance, sometimes private health care and other similar schemes, and 'perks' such as company cars, company accommodation, free lunches, concierge services, and the like. As an indication of the differences between the levels, FTSE 100 directors received average increases in their total earnings of 49 per cent compared to average employee increases of around 3 per cent in the year 2010–11 (IDS 2012b; Trevor 2012). The FTSE 100 median CEO total earnings were £2,711,238 in the same year, with some CEOs being paid over 100 times average pay (High Pay Commission 2011). When the State raises taxes on those with only average earnings, communications that 'we are all in it together' are likely to be met with cynicism. The various anti-capitalist movements are able to show what they will argue is 'unfairness' in the relative earnings of the different groups in our society. There are advantages to society as a whole if the State tries to reduce unfairness.

Second, is the argument that the amounts paid to directors reflect the need to have efficient industries and high quality decision making in our corporations. The State's involvement in the process of deciding rewards (rather than the amounts of rewards) has been to ensure the effective working of capital markets and industry, as a part of the national interest; the main institutional shareholders were consulted widely over the changes to corporate governance that have been introduced, and have welcomed them. The separation of ownership from control (the 'agency' issue) requires there to be sufficient direction of companies and monitoring of their activities, without interfering in the day to day management of corporations (Jensen and Meckling 1976).

The third explanation is the pragmatic point that if governments take actions which might result in a CEO resigning, this could cause damage to the business, and put jobs and prosperity at risk. Decisions about individual rewards should not be made without a considerable knowledge of the performance and the contribution of the CEO to the business, which non-executive directors are in the best position to understand.

If we take Wood's model, we have discussed the principles of legitimacy, public responsibility, and managerial discretion. We can see that the role of the HR specialist ostensibly is very much involved in managing the process and the decision making will be made by other non-executive board members. However, the HR function helps to create and direct the culture, to ensure fairness, and to represent standards of decision making in the company. There will be the professionalism of the support given to the remuneration committee, especially to its chair, and the provision, either directly, or through consultants, on comparators, and on job sizing as well as how the rewards at the top interface with the direct reports to the board. Similarly, the evidence upon which performance is judged may be from organization wide systems, such as the balanced scorecard, which contain sections on the corporation's contribution to the wider society.

For those who are deciding about director-level pay, for example CEO rewards, the three categories in Wood's model fit exactly the areas which will have to be covered with any analysis. There is a need for comparisons and for a wider understanding of the social and the political context which is necessary in order to make the correct judgement. Much of the important work will occur behind the scenes in managing the stakeholders who will include the chair of the board, the institutional shareholders, and may include the other non-executives that are not on the committee, and other figures who may have an interest – business partners, government ministers, etc. The most senior public affairs individual in the company might be involved after the decision, to ensure the message about any significant decision is well managed in the financial press. The other important person in a reward decision is the recipient. The chair may well decide to sound out reactions to any proposed significant changes with the CEO, maybe in a general way, beforehand.

Conclusions

In this chapter we have described a number of important linkages between HR and CSR. From Wood's (2010) model we can see that HR is closely involved in conducting the processes of social responsiveness, and in establishing and maintaining the legal legitimacy of the corporation and its public responsibility. It is directly accountable for many people management outcomes, as our illustrations reveal.

CSR is itself an outcome of corporate values, which help to support corporate cultures. The ways of behaving which cultures inculcate cannot be quickly adapted or changed. Similarly, ethical ways of working and a sense of corporate responsibility cannot be put on like a suit of clothes in the morning. Corporate values and CSR have to be really believed and to be believable to succeed. This is why CSR has to be an aspect of HR strategy, as it would need to be an aspect of marketing strategy and financial strategy, and be brought to life in the everyday transactions between people within corporations, and when dealing with people outside the corporation through the processes in which HR plays a significant role. An HR policy on 'hotlines' for whistle-blowers to use, for example, may be helpful, but of itself would not create the openness, trust, or the degree of security whistle-blowers need, unless the HR function is prepared to defend their right to blow the whistle on malpractices, and to make that clear in all their interactions.

CSR requires a joint effort across the business – drawing as it does on marketing and public affairs as well as HRM and all other major functions. There is one aspect where HR can make a significant contribution. This is in process work which we have seen is essential to obtain corporation wide commitment to CSR and which involves what could be described as a form of discourse ethics, which is concerned to provide a process which enhances consensus, allows potential conflicts of interest to be resolved, and is a mechanism for understanding different positions (Winstanley and Woodall 2000). This is, of course, consistent with Habermas's ideas about a 'deliberative democracy' as a valuable way for corporations to engage in a genuine and trusting way with stakeholders.

10 Talent management

Back in 2008, research from Hewitt Associates found that half of employers felt that they were missing crucial business opportunities as a result of short-comings in managing talent (Woods 2008). Indeed, the concept of talent man-agement has become central to the management of people in many organiza-tions. It would certainly be unusual to read any HR magazine or attend any HR conference without some mention of talent management practice. Given the relatively recent emergence of talent management as a concept, in the late 1990s, it is surprising perhaps that it has already taken such a prominent role in the HRM repertoire.

In Chapter 5, we discussed the change in the role of the HR function. An important shift in the role for HRM has been the increased focus on the man-agement of talent within organizations. In this chapter we will therefore focus on talent management, looking at the nature and meaning of 'talent man-agement' as an approach and examining its roots and evolution. Specifically, we will discuss the changing context within which talent management has evolved and the impact of this environment on the current issues and pri-orities for managing talent within organizations. In order to inform this dis-cussion, we have interviewed five academic and practitioner experts in talent management, as well as drawing on published resources.

Defining talent management

First of all we must be clear on what we mean by 'talent management', although this is not as simple as it sounds. An examination of the literature on talent management fails to find a single definition of this concept (Aston and Morton 2005). Lewis and Heckmann (2006) concluded that there was a 'disturbing lack of clarity regarding definition, scope, and overall goals of talent management' (p. 141), while Scullion and Collings (2010) commented that one of the key challenges for talent management (or more specifically global talent management) was to come up with a common definition for the concept. Much of the debate around the definition of talent management has focused on the question of whether it is actually any different from HRM. Indeed, Scullion and Collings went on to say of global talent management that a second challenge for this field was to distinguish itself clearly from international HRM.

Lewis and Heckmann (2006) attempted to categorize the available definitions of talent management and suggested three streams: first, that talent management is merely a new label for HRM; second, that talent management emphasizes the development of talent pools by predicting talent needs and managing the succession of employees into key positions; and third, that talent management is about the management of talented people. Collings and Mellahi (2009) added a fourth stream, that talent management is about identifying key positions within the organization that could affect the competitive advantage of the firm. Whether talent management is actually different from HRM is still open to debate. Indeed, McDonnell *et al.* (2010: 150) suggested that: 'The extent to which talent management represents a new and discrete management activity as opposed to the latest human resource management (HRM) exhortation remains largely unknown.' This might actually vary between organizations. Adding to the confusion is the fact that talent management is sometimes referred to as a policy objective, emphasizing that the organization intends to develop those it believes have talent for the work in their roles; whereas other references to talent management might be shorthand for the talent management system, i.e. the method by which the organization intends to develop talented people (for example, the assessment, management, development, and career management systems) in order to meet policy objectives. In our experience, there are some organizations that have relabelled their practice 'talent management' while continuing to use the same traditional HRM practices. In other organizations, however, talent management might encompass a number of HRM practices but represents a different type of system of these practices. In line with this idea, McDonnell *et al.* (2010) noted that several authors had suggested that talent management 'involves integrated HR practices designed to attract and retain the right people in the right jobs at the right time' (p. 151). Other authors have gone as far as to name the groups of practices included in talent management as consisting of three sets of practices: recruitment, staffing, and succession planning; training and development; and retention management (Stahl *et al.* 2007). In some organizations, according to other authors, talent management might represent a different mindset. Creelman (2004) for instance described talent management as a mindset that puts talent at the forefront of organizational success. Similarly, Cappelli (2008b: 74) suggested that talent management 'is simply a matter of anticipating the need for human capital and then setting out a plan to meet it'.

In essence, it seems that talent management is about having the right people at the right time; about putting in place (HRM) systems and practices that allow an organization to identify, attract, develop, retain, and reward talented people in such a way that the organization can fill key and critical roles effectively. In this definition we combine the practice based definitions of talent management with Lewis and Heckmann's suggestions that talent management is about succession planning and managing talented people. Talent management can be all of these things, and it can involve a change of mindset on the part of the organization in order to achieve this. In this way, there is no 'right' definition. We suggest here that the exact definition and nature of talent management is dependent on the organizational context. For some organizations, talent management will be about developing and retaining talented employees, for others it will be designed to create a competitive advantage by attracting the 'best' employees. The definition of talent management will be dependent on an organization's business strategy, culture, and ethos as well as the nature of the work that an organization does. In this suggestion we immediately see the importance of context in the evolution of talent management, at least at the level of individual organizations. Later in this chapter, we will examine the wider impact of context on the nature of talent management.

The definition of talent

There is also significant confusion regarding what actually constitutes 'talent', and yet it is essential that organizations define what they mean by 'talent', if any attempt at a talent management system is going to be successful. Mellahi and Collings (2010) suggested that talent could be seen as a source of competitive advantage for organizations but that talent was of little strategic value unless it is 'identified, nurtured and used effectively' (p. 144). McDonnell *et al.* (2010) explained that there is some debate as to whether everyone should be included as talented, but went on to suggest that: 'While the "everyone counts" mantra is both appealing and admirable, if this is what talent management means then defining the term may be akin to the "emperor's new clothes"; that is giving an existing concept a new name' (p. 151). McDonnell *et al.* (2010) used Lepak and Snell's (1998a) HR architecture as a framework for talent management, suggesting that talent management systems should focus mostly on specialist functional staff with a high level of critical knowledge or skills and also on high potential employees that are likely to succeed into leadership roles. Those in contractual work or alliances and partnerships are likely to receive minimal investment as their skills are more easily purchased on the labour market. It can be proposed again that the precise definition of talent will be specific to the individual organization or even department.

Our own research (Parry and Tyson 2007) suggested that the definition of talent varied greatly between organizations. Most large organizations concentrate much of their talent management effort on the 'talent pipeline' for senior management or strategic leadership roles. While some others do use the term talent to cover the entire workforce, we have found that most of their actual talent management activity focuses on those with top leadership potential. Garrow and Hirsch (2008) suggested that a talent management strategy should start by clarifying its focus through addressing three questions: first, for what part of the organization and what kinds of job roles;

second, where in the organization might employers find the right kinds of people for target roles and how far ahead (when) employers need to start developing them so they will be good candidates for the target roles? Third, what development outcomes are employers looking for to overcome potential resourcing difficulties? It is obvious that the answers to these three questions will differ across organizations so the definition of talent and the way that it is subsequently treated is also dependent on the organizational context. In fact, the understanding of what constitutes talent might differ within a single organization, between different departments, levels, and individuals. Despite this, some organizations have developed talent management systems based upon mimetic and normative isomorphic forces so that their talent management systems imitate those used by other organizations or those suggested as best practice by professional bodies such as the CIPD. In order to be effective in ensuring that an organization has employees with the skills and capabilities to fill key roles, talent should be defined with reference to the organization's business and HR strategy and a talent management system should be tailored to an organization's specific talent needs and the context in which they operate.

Our discussion of the definition of talent management and talent itself has shown clearly that the context in which an organization is operating is vital in the evolution and design of a talent management strategy. On a broader level, we can suggest that the nature of talent management as an approach is also shaped by the external environment in which the organization exists. In our discussion below, we will move on to consider the context in which talent management emerged and the changes to that context that might have affected the evolution of this approach, but first we must understand the general characteristics of a talent management system.

The talent management system

While the exact nature of talent and talent management varies by organization, the broad components of a talent management system are generally similar across organizations. These are represented in Figure 10.1 below, based on our research.

In summary, we suggest that a talent management system begins with an analysis of the needs of the business in terms of 'talent'. This analysis should be based on an HR strategy that is fully aligned with the business strategy and aims to establish what the definition of talent for that organization should be. What talent is needed to ensure the successful achievement of operational goals? This might be addressed by answering Garrow and Hirsch's questions above. Out of this analysis, a set of competency frameworks for the business can be established and those people that may be defined as 'high potential' or 'high performers' (i.e. as talent) can be identified. This allows an organization to plan which employees may be able to succeed into management or other important roles. Based upon this competency framework, these

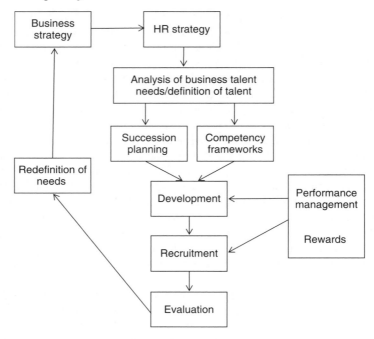

Figure 10.1 The talent management system

individuals can be developed and any skills gaps can be identified by reference to the planned requirement in order to establish the recruitment needs
of the organization. Performance management and rewards systems can be
installed in order to retain and develop both current and new employees.
This process should then be evaluated and the information from the evaluation used in order to redefine the organizational needs in light of changing
market conditions or business strategy. Evaluation in this case could include
assessments of the return on investment (ROI) of talent management activities, the availability of talent for organizational needs, or the effectiveness
of succession planning and the existence (or not) of hard to fill vacancies. In
our experience, talent management systems in most organizations follow this
basic framework.

   To some degree, the adoption of practices within the framework, to attract,
identify, develop, reward, and retain talented employees, will also be similar,
as they are subject to isomorphic forces (DiMaggio and Powell 1983). Indeed,
Stahl *et al.* (2007) suggested that the adoption of talent management practices
was affected by mimetic forces. Specifically, Stahl *et al.* (2007) suggested that
talent management practices were adopted partially because they were associated with best practice organizations so other firms tried to imitate them.
We suggest here that the adoption of talent management is also driven by
normative forces as professional bodies such as the CIPD and consultancies

promote the use of such practices. However, there is still room for variation within the boundaries of isomorphism, and the adoption of particular talent management practices by organizations will also be affected by the specific internal and external contexts in which they operate. In support of this suggestion, McDonnell *et al.* (2010) found that the nature of talent management practices by multinational enterprises (MNEs) was impacted by the contextual factors of organization size, the standardization of products regionally or globally, and if the MNE had a global HR policy formation body on the use of talent management practices. Garrow and Hirsch (2008) emphasized the importance of 'fit' between a talent management system and the organization and went on to suggest that 'fit' was needed at a number of levels: first, fit with the strategic objectives of the talent management system; second, with the culture of the organization; third, with the workforce and the psychological contract; fourth, with other HR practices and policies; and finally with management roles and capabilities.

Talent management practices will also vary according to the country in which an organization is located. Schuler and Tarique (2012) explained these differences with regard to coercive isomorphism. They suggested that coercive isomorphism can be used to examine the forces or drivers external to the firm that are beyond management control such as national culture, economic conditions, political system, legal environment, and workforce characteristics as opposed to mimetic isomorphism that is used to examine forces that are internal to the firm such as business strategy. Schuler and Tarique went on to explain that firms need to balance external and internal forces in order to develop appropriate talent management.

Research therefore supports the proposition that talent management differs according to the external context. We therefore adhere to this point of view but go one step further, to suggest that changes in the external context also have an isomorphic effect on talent management as a whole, outside of the more stable contextual differences between countries or between organizations. We will now move on to discuss how changes in the external environment influence the development of talent management.

The talent management context

Cappelli (2008a) traces the origins of talent management to the improved economic landscape after the Second World War, but most scholars relate this concept to the late 1990s and the idea of a 'war for talent' developed by McKinsey and Company in 1997 (see Axelrod *et al.* 2002; Mellahi and Collings 2010). Either way it can be related to economic improvement and increased competition for labour. In 2001, McKinsey and Company noted that 'the market for talent is the most competitive it's been in decades' (Axelrod *et al.* 2002: 2). In addition, Schuler *et al.* (2011) described the late 1990s as a time when there was 'a demand for talented employees that far surpassed the supply, thus creating a global talent shortage' (p. 506).

The creation of talent management as an approach can therefore be related to a context of economic buoyancy, a competitive labour market, and increased competition for labour. As we all know, the economic landscape of the late 1990s bears little resemblance to the current situation in the United Kingdom and across much of the world. For instance, in 2013, the UK is recovering from a prolonged double dip recession and suffering from relatively high unemployment (particularly youth unemployment). In fact most of Europe and the USA are still trying to recover from the 2008 economic downturn and are currently experiencing relatively high unemployment. Can we therefore really expect organizations' needs for talent management to be the same as they were 20 years ago? Indeed, the recent financial crisis has led to increased volatility and uncertainty, with around 95 per cent of organizations freezing or decreasing their HR budget and around a quarter forced to change their approach to talent management (26 per cent) or cut their talent management budget (24 per cent) (CIPD 2009). There is also some evidence that organizations are changing the practices that they use to retain talent, with Sweet *et al.* (forthcoming) finding that organizations were less accepting of, and extended fewer opportunities for, flexible work during a time of economic downturn (2009) than in a time of economic buoyancy (2006).

In contrast, a number of our interviewees felt that the economic downturn had not changed their approach to talent management dramatically as their talent management mindset or philosophy remained the same. It was felt that talent management was not necessarily resource hungry and that formal development programmes that were expensive could be replaced with cheaper ways of developing people such as experience based assignments and job rotation. One of our interviewees, however, did mention an interesting indirect effect of the economic downturn on talent management. She suggested that people were not really moving organizations at present due to the level of uncertainty in the job market. This is a dual challenge for employers: first they need to think about how to hold onto people if the economy improves and people start moving; and second, they need to develop ideas to deal with the lack of opportunities as a result of people not moving by, for instance, creating project work to keep people engaged. There is also a probability that pressure on costs means that narrower definitions of talent are used, perhaps focused on just a few strategically important roles.

The economy is not the only aspect of the talent context which is changing. Indeed, Schuler *et al.* (2011) suggested that while the global talent shortage remains a pressing challenge for many businesses, there are a number of new talent challenges that have emerged. These challenges are shaped by globalization, changing demographics, demand for workers with particular competencies and motivation, and the supply of people with those competencies and motivation. Hatum (2010) agreed that the external context has changed and went on to suggest that the role of talent within organizations has also changed along with the context. Hatum (2010) proposed that, since the 1990s, a new business context has emerged characterized by macro environmental changes, changes in the way firms are organized, and demographic changes. Tarique and Schuler (2010) agreed that talent management challenges are driven by a number of exogenous drivers that are out of management's control, including globalization (the migration of individuals between countries), demographic changes, and a gap between the demand for talented individuals and supply.

Specifically, according to Hatum (2010) macro environmental changes have been shaped by acceleration in the rate of change in the economic, social, technological, and political worlds; increased global linkages; information technology growth; knowledge based competition (the use of knowledge as a primary base of competitive advantage); and political uncertainty. This has led to intensified competition, shorter product lifecycles, and technological innovation, meaning that organizations and the talent within them also needs to change. Organizations have therefore changed the ways in which they organize through an increase in agile and virtual organizations. Economic difficulties have led firms to take steps to ensure their survival such as outsourcing, downsizing, de-layering, etc., resulting in flatter structures. In addition, the world is experiencing demographic changes such as the ageing workforce and economic changes. Against this backdrop, Hatum suggests a need for 'next generation talent management' (p. 7). Whysall (2012) agreed that the external context was changing dramatically and questioned the shelf life of talent management strategies given the pace of change. Whysall proposed that future demands require different skills to those that are needed now in that talented people will need to be able to stretch and adapt. This means that flexibility and agility are important in talented individuals and that a future characteristic of how talent is defined is likely to be the capacity to learn. Schuler *et al.* (2011) supported this idea of a need for agility and suggested that organizations need to engage not only in workforce and human resource planning but also in scenario planning so that they can undertake HR planning for a number of different potential scenarios.

The experts interviewed for this chapter agreed that talent management as an approach was still evolving and was being shaped to some degree by the external context. One of our interviewees, a Talent Manager from a large retail chain, suggested that talent management is not yet completely embedded within organizations as it is still changing and new ideas are arising all the time. She felt that this was exciting but that it was difficult to keep up with something that is constantly changing. This comment paints an interesting picture of the talent management situation within organizations – that employers are constantly playing 'catch up' as new ideas and demands emerge in the talent environment – and supports the ideas of Schuler *et al.* (2011) and Whysall (2012) that organizations need to create agile talent management systems in order to cope with constant flux.

In order to examine the impact of contextual changes on talent we will now focus on two areas of change from Hatum's (2010) work – macro economic and demographic changes. As Chapter 4 has already looked in some detail at changes in organizations' ways of organizing, we will not discuss this again here.

Macro environmental changes

Hatum splits macro environmental changes into globalization and technology. We have discussed the impact of technology on HRM in some detail in Chapter 6. As mentioned in Chapter 3, macro economically, we see that the global economic map is changing through the rise of the BRIC countries, and the nature of work is changing with a shift to knowledge intensive industries and a resulting shortage of high quality knowledge workers. Another long term trend is the general increase in globalization through the expansion of world trade, the ability to reach customers around the world, and the global labour market. As discussed in Chapter 3, in the UK alone net immigration in the year up to June 2011 was 250,000 people, including the increased mobility from Eastern European countries, up from 5,000 in 2009 to 40,000 in 2010 (ONS 2012b).

Globalization has been seen as particularly important in shaping talent management approaches. The shortage of global managerial talent has the capacity to constrain the implementation of global strategies for multinational corporations (MNCs), meaning that the adoption of effective global (rather than just local) talent management approaches is increasingly important. Scullion and Collings (2010) discussed the factors driving the emergence of global talent management as a key strategic issue for MNCs: first, the role played by globally competent managers is increasingly critical due to growing global competition; second, competition for talent has moved from within countries to across countries; third, there is a general shortage of managerial and professional talent in MNCs; fourth, the shortage of global managerial talent constrains the implementation of global strategies for MNCs; and finally, the growth of emerging markets means that a particular sort of managerial talent is needed that can operate within these complex and distant markets. Tarique and Schuler (2010) also noted that the global environment has changed the way that business is conducted and created the need for organizations to manage their workforces in a global context. Tarique and Schuler suggested that organizations need to find people who 'can effectively manage through the complex, challenging, changing and often ambiguous global environment' (p. 123).

The Chartered Institute of Personnel and Development (CIPD) (2011) provided a useful list of the current global trends and challenges in talent management, based upon their experience:

- The move to relocate work close to sources of plentiful and often cheaper labour (constantly moving target);
- How to attract global talent (particularly challenging if you do not have a big brand name);
- Developing leaders with a global mindset to drive growth;
- Getting the global consistency/local relevance balance right;
- Understanding and navigating the political, legal, social, and economic climates of emerging markets and the Far East and understanding differences in cultural values;

- Developing cultural sensitivity and awareness;
- Managing diversity, inclusion, and respect in increasingly multicultural workplaces;
- Gathering insight about current talent and their aspirations across all businesses, geographies, and languages and using this to differentiate the organization;
- Recognizing and clearly articulating the financial value of global talent to the business.

It can be seen that this list represents some difficult challenges for employers to consider in developing a global, rather than just a local, talent management strategy and system. Generally these challenges are ones that did not exist to the same degree in the late 1990s when the idea of talent management first emerged and was focused only on the local context. In fact one of our interviewees, an academic expert in talent management, questioned whether talent management was even a valid concept in non-Western countries as it is generally seen as primarily an Anglo Saxon activity. This is an important consideration for firms expanding into non-Western territories. We have discussed the impact of globalization on HRM more broadly in Chapter 7.

Changing workforce demographics

Changing workforce demographics have become a particularly pressing problem with regard to identifying, locating, and managing talent. In particular, the ageing workforce means that employers are being forced to consider how their talent management practices address the needs of different age groups, particularly those at the oldest and youngest ends of the workforce. In the UK alone there will be around 19 million people over 65 by 2050 (around a quarter of the population) and life expectancy in the UK is now at an average of 80.17 years. The result of this and changing legislation, such as increases to the state pension age and removal of the default retirement age, means that the average age at which people leave the workforce is rising. The ageing workforce is described in more detail in Chapter 2, but let us focus here on the impact of this trend on talent management. One question is whether people are engaged by different factors as they get older? Research has suggested that the answer to this question is 'yes', with older workers placing less emphasis on financial rewards and hierarchical achievement and more on intrinsic rewards such as job satisfaction (see, for example, Sturges 1999). Age diversity within the workforce can also lead to challenges. The ageing workforce means that there are now up to four generations in the workforce (see Chapter 2) leading to a range of different employee needs and preferences to be accounted for with the potential for inter-generational conflict. We discussed increasing workforce diversity and its implications for HRM in more detail in Chapter 8; however, it is important here to consider it as a dimension of the changing context for talent management. In addition to the challenges posed by increased age diversity and a higher number of older workers, the forth-coming retirement of a large segment of the workforce (the 'Baby Boomers') means that organizations will need to set up systems to address the transfer of knowledge from these older workers before their retirement.

Calo (2008) has provided a detailed discussion of the impact of the ageing workforce on talent management. More specifically, Calo described the convergence of three 'demographic related realities' (p. 405) that would affect the management of talent: the loss of knowledge from the retirement of Baby Boomers, a projected shortage of workers, and an overall ageing workforce. Calo suggested that those organizations that relied on recruitment to replace the knowledge lost through turnover would find this strategy increasingly ineffective. Therefore organizations need to create systems whereby knowledge can be transferred down through the organization. Calo suggested that such a system would include:

1. Demographic inventory and profile: gathering information about who holds knowledge and when they will be retiring;
2. Knowledge risk profile: identifying at-risk positions and developing a plan to develop the successor to these positions;
3. Policy assessment: assessment of the impact of existing policies on retirement patterns and knowledge transfer;
4. Job and career redesign: to retain older workers and promote mentoring of younger workers;
5. HR competencies: in managing an ageing workforce and knowledge transfer.

Despite Calo and others' urging, recent research from the Sloan Center of Aging and Work at Boston College (Pitt-Catsouphes *et al.* 2009), showed that over two-thirds of organizations (68 per cent) in the USA had not analysed the demographics of their own workforce with regard to talent management and around three-quarters of organizations (77 per cent) had not looked at when their employees were going to retire.

While the ageing workforce means that employers will need to consider how employees' needs and preferences differ by age, there is also some evidence that employee attitudes are also changing more broadly. In Chapter 2 we discussed the changing nature of careers and the psychological contract. These changes also have a profound effect on the nature of talent management. Talent management systems that focus on lifelong careers are now out of date. In fact, Whysall (2012) suggested that the biggest problem with regard to effective talent management was 'the continued perception of talent management as synonymous with traditional, linear career progression. As a result, a disparity has emerged between employees' expectations and employers' options' (p. 3). Whysall goes on to explain that despite the fact that organizations are becoming flatter and the opportunities for linear career progression fewer, employees still need to feel that they can develop their careers within an organization. She describes this as a need to 'move from a career ladder to a career lattice' (p. 6) by facilitating lateral as well as vertical job moves. This will allow people to shape their own career pathways, therefore also supporting the move towards more protean careers.

Conclusions

Considering the above changes in the context, and the resulting impact on organizations and employees, we can indeed question the relevance of talent management as it was conceived in the late 1990s. Research from the Sloan Center of Aging and Work at Boston College has suggested, however, that most organizations are not taking the steps to examine how their talent needs and the appropriateness of their talent management systems might have changed as a result of the economic and demographic contextual changes. Their survey of employers within the USA showed that more than half of the organizations surveyed (56 per cent) had not assessed the skills that they needed and exactly half (50 per cent) had not assessed the competency sets of their employees. This suggests a lack of planning despite the fact that a large proportion of employers felt under pressure with regard to talent management because of the economic downturn (64 per cent) or the ageing workforce (40 per cent).

Employers need to consider the external environment and develop agile talent management systems that address this changing context. Organizations that maintain the talent management processes that were appropriate 15 years ago will find that these become increasingly ineffective as they do not account for changes in the nature and expectations of the workforce or in the external environment in which the organization is operating. However, talent management is still of importance for organizations: there is evidence that employers still have difficulty finding high quality applicants therefore providing an incentive for them to focus on talent management. Organizations therefore need to review their talent management systems in the light of environmental changes in order to ensure that they have the talent that they require and maintain the competitive advantage that this brings.

11 The intersection between the HR and marketing functions

This chapter will examine the relationship between activity in human resource management (HRM) and in another organizational function, marketing. Over recent years we have seen the HR and marketing functions become increasingly intertwined. From an HRM perspective, a growing number of concepts from marketing are being 'borrowed' by HRM. Most notable is the fact that the HR function is increasingly being required to develop and promote the brand of the organization as an employer. In order to achieve this, HR is adopting the broader principles of brand management in order to develop an employer value proposition and employer brand that can be communicated both internally and to potential new employees. In conjunction with this development, organizations are now beginning to use another principle from marketing, that of market segmentation, in their design of HR policies and practices, particularly in rewards and retention. From a marketing perspective, market oriented organizations are being encouraged to use the organization's human capital to promote the organization's brand both internally and externally.

This chapter will examine the intersection between the HR and marketing functions in some detail. Specifically, we will examine developments in both HRM and marketing practice that have occurred independently but are in fact overlapping in order to emphasize the need for the two functions to work more closely together. Indeed, Hathcock (1996: 243) noted that 'a strategic marketing perspective drives the new breed approach to human resources'. First we will examine the increasing importance of a company's human resources to its marketing, through an examination of the literature on 'internal marketing'. We will then look at how attention in the HR literature has built on the concept of internal marketing, to discuss the use of marketing principles in HRM, through a focus on employer branding. Finally, we will discuss the relationship of internal marketing and employer branding with a concept that has recently become popular in HRM, employee engagement. Throughout the chapter we will discuss how these trends have been affected by the external context.

Internal marketing

From a marketing perspective, it has been suggested that employees must be motivated to align their behaviour with the organization's identity or brand and to act as ambassadors for the corporate brand (Hulberg 2006; Henkel *et al.* 2007). This means that employees must be motivated to 'personify and deliver the brand promise' (Schultz and de Chernatony 2002). Employees who identify with an organization's brand are more likely to act consistently in ways supporting how the organization wants to be perceived by its customers (Aurand *et al.* 2005).

This means that, increasingly, organizations are being urged to undertake a multidisciplinary, cross functional approach to corporate marketing (King 1991; Balmer 1995; Brexendorf and Kernstock 2007) and to integrate the marketing and HR functions in order to recruit, train, and develop employees in ways that are accordant with the corporate brand (Hulberg 2006). The process of developing employees that understand the brand promise and their part in delivering this promise is known as 'internal marketing' (Berry 1980; Mosley 2007). Fiske *et al.* (1993) suggested that internal marketing was based upon the idea that everyone in the organization has a customer and that employees must believe in the service and be happy in their jobs before they can satisfy the external customer. This means that an employer must attract, select, and retain the best employees who recognize and value their role in delivering excellent service to external customers (Berry and Parsuraman 1991). Internal branding therefore seeks to develop and reinforce a common value based ethos according to the corporate vision or mission (Mosley 2007).

The idea of internal marketing is linked to the idea of an internal market orientation within organizations, in which employees drive services (Gummesson 1990) and works on the assumption that the attitudes of employees influence customers' perceptions of the service they receive (Foster and Cadogan 2000). This idea is related to the service–profit chain (Heskett *et al.* 1994). Mosley (2007) suggested that engaged and satisfied employees are more likely to deliver a consistently positive service experience and went on to propose that employees are key in developing sustainable service brand differentiation. We have discussed the impact of the employee-customer-profit chain within Sears (Rucci *et al.* 1998) in some detail in Chapter 4. Indeed, research has shown that employee satisfaction is strongly and directly related to customer satisfaction (Piercy 1996) and the level of perceived service delivery (Pantouvakis 2012). Reza *et al.* (2012) showed that internal marketing could indirectly positively affect service quality through the mediator of organizational citizenship behaviour. Similarly, Sanchez-Hernandez and Miranda (2011) showed that HRM activity supported by the marketing function and an internal market orientation is related to increased service quality.

Pantouvakis (2012) suggested that it is the relationship between employee attitudes and customer outcomes that has led to the development of the internal marketing concept in which organizations should apply marketing programmes and tools to the internal market (employees) in a way that parallels those used externally. Therefore, internal marketing has been defined as using 'a marketing perspective for managing an organization's human resources' (Bak *et al.* 1994: 38) and as 'the process of creating market conditions within the organization to ensure that internal customers' wants and needs are met' (Lings 2000: 28).

Pitt and Foreman (1998) discussed the rise of interest in internal marketing and noted that at least one major marketing text at that time (Kotler 1991) emphasized that an organization must carry out both internal and external marketing in order to be successful. Pitt and Foreman suggested that it 'makes no sense to promise excellent service before the company staff is ready to provide it' (p. 25). Pantouvakis (2012) suggested however that very little empirical research had been conducted into internal marketing approaches and, as a result, only a few organizations have applied this approach in practice. Indeed, there have recently been calls for increased efforts in internal marketing (Yoon *et al.* 2007).

The relationship of the concept of internal marketing to HRM is obvious. The marketing literature has debated whether internal marketing is actually simply good HRM (Pitt and Foreman 1998) and therefore part of the role of the HR function (Bateson 1991). In fact, Pantouvakis (2012) suggested that all approaches to internal marketing support the idea that HRM forms the basis for the internal marketing concept. Pantouvakis (2012) went on to suggest that internal marketing should cross the boundaries between marketing and HRM, in that employee satisfaction should become the responsibility of both the marketing and HR functions. Indeed, Mosley (2007) noted the potentially important role played by the HR function in embedding the desired brand ethos and culture, but also noted that this role had historically often been limited to communication support rather than to shaping management practice. Martin and Beaumont (2003) also suggested that HR's role in internal marketing was limited by being restricted to communicating rather than driving and developing brand values.

Collins and Payne (1991) went on to discuss internal marketing in some detail as a 'new perspective for HRM' (p. 261). Collins and Payne suggested two aspects of internal marketing: first, that every department and person within the organization is both a supplier and a customer; second, that staff must work together in a manner supporting the company strategy and goals. Collins and Payne (1991) suggested that people who buy goods and services are in a similar kind of exchange process as to people who seek employment that is satisfying and interesting. An HR manager with a market orientation would have good knowledge of the needs and wants of the groups (of employees) served and develop a coordinated approach to servicing those requirements. Collins and Payne also described a series of marketing activities for the

HR department that are similar to those undertaken by the marketing department. These included: market research in order to understand the needs of the client group; the development of a mission and some clear objectives for the HR department; and market segmentation in deciding which groups should be emphasized. Market segmentation allows the HR department to satisfy the needs of particular groups more effectively but can cost more – high customization of HRM means an increased demand for resources from the HR department. Finally, the HR department must develop and implement the marketing mix in terms of designing the product or service and communicating this product or service to the internal customers (employees) through advertising, indirect publicity, and face-to-face selling in order to influence employees to behave in a particular way.

The application of marketing principles to HRM was eventually picked up by HR scholars and practitioners in around the mid 1990s. The last 15 years have seen HRM adopt both the theory and language of marketing, most notably through the growth in the use of 'employer branding' as an approach to attracting and retaining employees (Panczuk and Point 2008).

Employer branding

The increase in competition for human resources towards the end of the twentieth century meant that employers needed to find ways in which they could distinguish themselves from their competitors in the battle to attract and retain talented employees. The adoption of marketing principles by the HR function can be directly related to this need to be competitive in the labour market, in the same way as the reliance on employees to promote organizational values through internal marketing in the 1980s and beyond was driven by the need for an organization to compete for customers. We can suggest that the adoption of marketing principles by the HR function has been driven by the external context, specifically by the need for an employer to attract and retain talented employees. In this way, the attention on employer branding has been driven by similar contextual factors to those driving the emphasis on talent management (see Chapter 10 of this text).

Kim *et al.* (2012) noted that marketing strategies, defined as 'the overriding principle a firm used to organize and allocate its resources to generate profit from customers' (p. 1612) could also be used to engage with future and existing employees. Recruitment efforts are similar in many ways to an organization's efforts to attract customers (Cable and Turban 2003), as both customers and potential employees develop positive and negative impressions of an organization based upon the messages that it communicates (Collins and Stevens 2002; Kim *et al.* 2012). It was based upon this principle, and against the background of the increased competition for labour, that the idea of employer branding as a focus for the HR function was developed.

It is interesting to note here that, in a time when competition for labour had increased and many employers were struggling to attract and retain talented employees, the HR function turned to expertise from a different function – marketing – in order to find a solution to these problems. We can suggest that this is a form of normative isomorphism, in that the HR function is drawing on good practice in the same way as it might adopt activities that are seen as good practice in HRM. However, in this case, where existing good HRM practices for attracting and retaining talented employees have failed to prove effective, the HR function has been forced to seek solutions elsewhere. Therefore, finding synergies between the attraction and retention of employees and the attraction and retention of customers, the HR function has drawn on good practice in another field, marketing.

Employer branding therefore applies the well established principles of marketing, specifically consumer branding, to the practice of HR management (Backhaus and Tikoo 2004) to create a unique and attractive employer brand image that exists only in the minds of current and potential employees. Ambler and Barrow (1996) were among the first to suggest that principles of consumer branding were applicable to the development of an employer brand. They defined an employer brand as 'the package of functional, economic and psychological benefits provided by employment and identified with the employing company' (p. 187).

Given that the purpose of employer branding is not only to attract and retain employees but also to promote positive employee attitudes such as employee satisfaction, motivation, and commitment, its alignment with the concept of internal marketing is apparent. Martin *et al.* (2011) defined an employer brand as 'a generalized recognition for being known among key stakeholders for providing a high quality employment experience and a distinctive organizational identity which employees value, engage with and feel confident and happy to promote to others' (p. 3618). They go on to describe employer branding as the 'process by which branding concepts and marketing, communications and HR techniques are applied to create an employer brand' (p. 3619). Similarly, Moroko and Uncles (2008) described employer branding as a strategic framework that incorporates both marketing and HR so that a company can attract, retain, and motivate those employees who can deliver on the company's brand promise. Through these two definitions, employer branding can be seen as the development of the internal branding approach into one that is owned and taken forward by the HR function.

However, in the HR literature, employer branding does not however necessarily focus on the need to develop employees who will live the organizational brand and therefore market the organization to customers through their behaviour, but rather on the need to recruit and retain motivated employees in order to achieve a competitive advantage. In this way, employer branding has been commonly aligned with the resource based view of the firm (Penrose 1959; Barney *et al.* 2001). Despite the subtle differences in the motivation behind internal marketing and employer branding, it can be seen that, in practice, these two approaches are very similar. Indeed, Edwards (2010: 5) commented that employer branding involved a 'very obvious mix or coming together of the fields of marketing and HR', while Martin *et al.* (2005) noted that the employer branding concept came first from marketing and then was eventually discussed also by HR scholars.

Employer branding therefore represents a direct application of marketing to HRM. Employer branding theory uses a set of principles that can be seen to be closely related to the general branding literature. First, employer branding includes the development of an 'employer value proposition' (EVP) that specifies the benefits of employment with a particular organization and everything that an employee receives from that organization (Michaels *et al.* 2001). The EVP should explain why 'a smart, energetic, ambitious individual would want to come and work with you rather than with the team next door' (Chambers *et al.* 1998). We will discuss the potential content of the EVP in our chapter on total rewards (Chapter 12). The EVP is a brand concept developed by managers that needs to be communicated to current and potential employees via a suitable 'marketing mix' (Maxwell 2010). Again, an idea obviously taken from the marketing literature, this refers to all of the channels that a manager can use to communicate the EVP to current and potential employees. This might include recruitment advertisements, websites, job interviews and job previews for potential employees, and company newsletters, the intranet, and other internal materials for existing employees (Miles and Mangold 2004). Edwards (2010) emphasized the importance of communicating the employer brand and Ruch (2000) suggested that 'businesses should think of recruitment as marketing: the right message, right product, right price, right customer, right channel' (p. 42). A number of companies have paid much attention to communicating their employer brand. For example, Starbucks has made considerable use of web 2.0 to communicate its 'Employee First' brand through online forums (www.morillas.com).

In the same way that marketing has moved away from short term customer attraction and towards long term relationship building, so HR has moved towards creating long term relationships with employees so that they can retain them for longer. Of course, employees are not exactly the same as external customers, and it is important for both scholars and HR practitioners to remember this. The relationship that employees have with their employer constitutes a much larger part of an individual's life than that between a customer and product or service provider, and has the capacity to have a much more significant impact on an individual's life. This means that the direct application of marketing techniques, without consideration of the unique relationship between an employer and employee, is probably not appropriate – marketing principles can provide a useful basis for the attraction and retention of talented employees but should be adapted and tailored as appropriate into tools and techniques that are appropriate for use with potential and existing employees. Miles and Mangold (2004) suggested that the key to effective employer branding was understanding the relationship between an organization and its employees. This is related to the idea of the psychological contract (Backhaus and Tikoo 2004) discussed later in this chapter.

Employer branding therefore is about identifying the unique employment experience by considering all of the tangible and intangible rewards that the organization offers, as well as the character of the organization itself, such as the organization's key values and guiding principles (Edwards 2010). Ambler and Barrow (1996) suggested that a strong employer brand needed to be relevant to both current and potential future employees and deliver benefits that are considered important and cannot be obtained from a different employer. The employer brand is said to be linked to a range of outcomes. From a marketing perspective, employer branding aims to enhance the firm's corporate and consumer brands, first by attracting potential employees who are capable of consistently representing the organization and, second, by motivating employees to behave in particular ways that will promote the desired brand image (Ambler and Barrow 1996; Miles and Mangold 2004). In this way, employer branding is closely aligned to the concept of internal marketing, discussed above. From an HR perspective, employer branding can enhance the value of an organization's human capital therefore allowing them (in the terms of the resource based view) to provide a source of sustained competitive advantage.

In the HR literature, employer branding has been most commonly linked to effective recruitment. The occupational psychology literature has examined the factors which make an organization attractive to potential employees in some depth (Edwards 2010) and emphasized the importance of both the employer brand and the more general reputation of a firm. This literature has found that job seekers are more likely to apply to an organization which already has a positive reputation (Cable and Graham 2000), as well as an attractive employer brand. Cable and Turban (2003) found that corporate reputation was important in increasing the likelihood of potential applicants applying to an organization. Cable and Turban found that both the degree of familiarity with an organization and external ratings of corporate reputation could affect job seekers' perceptions of an employer. Cable and Turban therefore suggested a brand equity perspective whereby perceptions of an organization's reputation act as a form of employer brand.

Kim *et al.* (2011) emphasized the fact that functional areas of organizations other than marketing, including HRM, also benefit from marketing activity. For example, evidence has shown that a strong corporate or product brand can be central to attracting future employees (Hieronimus *et al.* 2005; DelVecchio *et al.* 2007). Similarly, Ruch (2000) suggested that the successful companies are those who transfer their brand equity in the market place to brand equity in recruiting and retaining the best employees. Ruch went on to explain that Generation X is made up of savvy consumers who are brand sensitive rather than brand loyal so companies must apply brand management and marketing thinking to the employment experience by understanding, managing, and valuing young employees with the same care and coherence used in consumer marketing practices (Ruch 2000). The increase in the use of marketing approaches in HRM can also be linked to the changing attitudes of the workforce. We can see also that HR and marketing are intertwined here and reliant on each other in order both to attract employees and to be competitive in the attraction of customers. Google is a good example of an organization that has used employer branding successfully. This organization has developed a strong brand image both as an internet search provider and as an employer – generally perceived as somewhere that is fun to work. This has helped Google to attract and retain the talent that it needs in order to maintain its competitive advantage.

Returning to our interest in the external context, not only has the emphasis on employer branding arisen as a result of a particular external context, but the use and nature of employer branding continues to be shaped by the external context. As we have already discussed in our chapter on talent management (Chapter 10), the 2008 economic downturn has led to changes in the labour market so that the highly competitive environment that led to an emphasis on both talent management and employer branding is not necessarily still the same. Based on this assumption, there has been some suggestion that the changing external context has led to a change in the focus of employer branding. For instance, Martin *et al.* (2011) related a change in the emphasis of employer branding to the changing economic context. Until recently, employer branding was mainly related to the attraction of new talent in relation to the 'war for talent' and the tight labour market in the 1990s, as discussed above. In this context, employer branding was about the communication to, and attraction of, talented employees. It is important to note that, despite the global recession and currently poor employment outlook, employers are still facing talent shortages and hard-to-fill vacancies, therefore employer branding is still important in the attraction and recruitment of potential employees. In particular, positions in the skilled trades, sales, technical work, and engineering remain difficult to fill globally, according to research from the Manpower Group (2009) that found that 30 per cent of employers were still having difficulty in filling key roles at the height of the recession. However, since the global economic downturn of 2008–9 the emphasis of employer branding has moved to some extent onto the engagement of existing employees (Balain and Sparrow 2009; Sparrow and Balain 2009; Scullion and Collings 2011). In the next section of this chapter we will focus on the potential impact of the employer brand on existing (rather than potential) employees, through an examination of its relationship to the psychological contract and employee engagement.

Employee engagement and the psychological contract

Employer branding can be linked to the concept of the psychological contract (Backhaus and Tikoo 2004; Miles and Mangold 2004; Martin 2008; Edwards 2010). The employment offering is made up not only of the contractual terms and conditions but also of the more implicit aspects of the employment relationship – these factors comprise the psychological contract: 'an individual's beliefs regarding the terms and conditions of a reciprocal exchange agreement between the focal person and another party' (Rousseau 1989). As we mentioned in Chapter 2, Rousseau (1989) distinguished between transactional and relational psychological contracts in which transactional contracts rely on a 'quid pro quo' relationship based on economic rewards, and relational contracts rely on longer term relationships based on trust and fairness. These two types of psychological contract have been related directly to employer branding, in that an employer brand will contain features that are transactional (e.g. pay for performance) and relational (socio-economic) (Martin and Hetrick 2006). Martin and Hetrick also add a third type of psychological contract – an ideological contract – that relates to the commitment of an employee and employer to a particular ideological cause. It is important to note that, while there has been a long term trend in employers attempting to develop relational psychological contracts with employees, the recent economic downturn has led to a return to more transactional psychological contracts in many companies. This has accompanied the changes to formal employment contracts, such as the increase in part time and temporary/casual work, in order to develop a more flexible workforce that does not involve the long term expense for employers that is not as acceptable in less volatile and unstable economic times (see Chapter 2).

The relationship between the employer brand and psychological contract has been conceptualized in two ways: first that the employer brand, as perceived during recruitment, forms the basis of the psychological contract (Backhaus and Tikoo 2004); and second, that the psychological contract forms the basis of the employer brand which is communicated to current and potential employees (Miles and Mangold 2004). Edwards (2010) suggests that actually these two perspectives are complementary in that the content of the employer brand and psychological contract probably inform each other.

The reality of communicating the employer brand is very different for existing as opposed to potential employees. While most of the literature has focused on employer branding as a recruitment tool, it is just as important to communicate an attractive employer brand to existing employees. Indeed, the literature on internal marketing emphasizes the importance of motivating and retaining employees so that they provide a high level of service and communicate the organization's brand to customers. It is in this area that the notion of employer branding can be related to employee engagement.

The notion of internal marketing can also be associated with employee engagement. Rafiq and Ahmed (2000) described the evolution of internal marketing into an approach used as a vehicle for strategy implementation or organizational change. For example, Varey and Lewis (1999) proposed that by including concepts such as 'internal relationship marketing' or 'internal relationship management' in internal marketing, the organization recognizes differing views held by management and employees and can use internal marketing to overcome employee resistance and facilitate organizational change (Snell and White 2009).

Varey (1995) proposed the use of internal marketing to ensure that members of the organization act to create competitive advantage for the firm. Harrison (1987), also in relation to internal marketing, emphasized the importance of aligning parts of the organization to a common purpose. The idea of a market oriented organization suggests a firm in which employees and management are all oriented towards promoting and developing the same organizational brand. Varey (1995) emphasized the importance of two way communication in establishing mutual understanding and trust between the employer and employees. In this way, we can propose a relationship between internal marketing and the concept of employee engagement.

Employee engagement has emerged relatively recently as a concept within HRM and therefore has, so far, been subject to only a small amount of empirical research. Despite this, the idea of employee engagement appears to have resonated with employers so has already become prominent in the world of HRM practice (Vance 2006). Employee engagement can be defined as 'the extent to which an employee is psychologically present in a particular organizational role' (Saks 2006: 604). Robinson *et al.* (2004) suggested that engagement is a positive attitude that an employee has towards their organization and its values. The parallel between the concept of employee engagement and a market oriented organization is obvious. To refer to Harrison's (1987) work on internal marketing above, if employees are aligned towards a common organizational purpose, they might also be described as 'engaged'. Employee engagement is related to some extent to the notion of organizational citizenship behaviour (OCB). OCB has generally been defined in relation to three characteristics: first that OCB is discretionary so is not part of the formal job description; second, it goes above and beyond what is seen as part of the job description; and third, that it contributes positively to overall organizational effectiveness (Organ 1988). It can be suggested therefore that employees who are 'engaged' are more likely to display OCB.

Khan (1990) was one of the first scholars to discuss the notion of engagement in relation to employees and HRM. Khan suggested that people have various degrees of engagement or disengagement at work. The consequence of this is that people use various amounts of their personal selves (cognitively, emotionally, and physically) in their working lives and roles. High employee engagement is characterized by high levels of activation and identification with the organization and employer. The idea of employee identification with the organization is also adopted by the marketing literature. For example, Brexendorf and Kernstock (2007) noted that employees who identify with their organization are more likely to have a positive attitude towards it, to accept the values of that organization, and to align their behaviours with the organizational values.

Engagement has been adopted by HR practitioners as a characteristic of employees that is related to high productivity. Specifically, recent research in the UK suggested that high levels of engagement can lead to lower sickness absence, higher customer service, and better retention, as well as higher innovation and better overall performance (McLeod and Clarke 2009). From a marketing perspective, it can be suggested that engaged employees are more likely to deliver a 'unique and distinguishing brand promise at each and every customer touch point' (Henkel *et al.* 2007: 311).

Research on the antecedents of employee engagement has suggested that high employee engagement might be driven by effective performance management systems (Gardner *et al.* 2001), work climate (Greenberg 1990; Macky and Boxall 2007), and communication (Cartwright and Holmes 2006; Lockwood 2007). Parallels can again be found here between the HR literature on employee engagement and the literature on internal marketing. For instance, Henkel *et al.* (2007) found that employees could be encouraged to act in a way that was consistent with the brand through both formal control activities such as performance management systems and informal systems such as two way communication between managers and employees and employee empowerment.

Conclusions

This chapter has demonstrated the increasing link between the HR and marketing functions. Not only has the marketing function become somewhat reliant on the human resources of the firm to market the organization by internalizing organizational values and therefore living the corporate brand, but over the past 15 years the HR function has increasingly adopted marketing theory and approaches in order to attract, retain, and engage with potential and existing employees. We can see that the overlap between marketing and HRM is most apparent in the alignment of the concepts of internal marketing and employer branding. In many ways these two concepts can be seen as similar, particularly in their espoused outcomes – in producing satisfied employees who deliver on the brand promise and provide competitive advantage for the organization.

Turning to the external context, we can see that the reliance of the HR function on marketing principles could be linked to the increased competition for labour during a time of economic buoyancy. Similarly, the emphasis within employer branding is changing as a result of the economic downturn to one that focuses more on the retention of existing employees, rather than the attraction of new staff. The fact that both HR and marketing have drawn good practice from different, but perhaps parallel, functions within the organization in order to improve their practice is interesting. Might this be a growing trend in HR practice? In the academic world at least we already see that HRM has drawn on a number of other disciplines – for instance, HR scholars regularly use frameworks such as the resource based view (taken from economics). In practice, we have recently seen the adoption of the idea of 'human capital', which relies heavily on economics, and (as discussed in

Chapter 6) we have seen the HR function being forced to work more closely with the IT function in order to obtain the expertise needed for the development of e-HRM systems. The HR function therefore continues to gather good practice from a number of different disciplines in order to enable it to attract and retain talented employees against a changing external context. In this way, normative isomorphism operates across the boundaries of organizational function.

Despite the overlap in activity between HRM and marketing, the literature suggests that to a great extent both scholars and practitioners from marketing and HRM remain separate. Marketers in market oriented firms might be reliant on employees as a way of promoting the organizational brand, and the HR function might increasingly borrow concepts from marketing theory, but in the academic literature at least there is no real evidence of these functions working more closely together. The fact that internal marketing, an approach undoubtedly within the remit of the marketing function, took 15 years to be translated into employer branding within the HR literature, might be taken as evidence of this suggestion.

Within organizations themselves, we could suggest that the relationship between marketing and HR should be one approaching co-dependence. The potential reliance of an organization on engaged employees to promote the corporate brand and on marketing approaches to recruit and retain staff, suggests a need for these two functions to work closely together; whether this is happening within organizations remains to be seen. Certainly, in our own experience some organizations are beginning to appoint employer branding experts who are positioned between the HR and marketing functions, allowing them to draw on both marketing and HRM knowledge. However, these organizations are the exception rather than the rule. More work is needed both to build links between the HR and marketing functions in organizations and to establish the impact of such a relationship on the competitive advantage of an organization within different external contexts.

12 Total rewards

Reward policies and practices are an important part of human resources (HR) strategy. HR strategy in its entirety seeks to give effect to the business strategy, to conduct the mission, and to achieve the corporate vision. 'Rewards' is a term which goes further than the basic policies on pay and benefits, and encompasses all those policies which are designed to attract, retain, and motivate employees to achieve objectives as the corporate response to competition. The significance of rewards is that policies in this area determine costs and performance, and as we will explore in this chapter, the concept of 'total rewards' is coming to mean the processes on engagement and involvement, and those issues related to the management of relationships which affect the hearts and minds of employees, in the search for competitive advantage.

This chapter examines how the changing context described in this book impacts rewards. Since reward policies are interconnected with all the other major human resource management (HRM) policy areas, we can expect that the effects of changes on business and the supporting HR strategy means employers look to rewards as one of the policy levers that can be pulled to reposition the organization in the new reality which is emerging. 'Total rewards' is an approach which emerged in a different economic, technological, and social context, and hence there is strong argument for exploring the field of total reward at this time. Total rewards encompasses all the parts of the reward package (base pay, variable pay, benefits, perquisites), the style of working (management style, organization culture, flexibility, autonomy, work pace), the quality of work (challenges and interest in the work, levels of skill, recognition of achievements), the working environment, and the promises for learning and development (career management, employability, performance management).

The effort–reward bargain, the psychological contract, and motivation

How the effort–reward bargain is structured is central to understanding the motivation and performance of employees. Typically, the effort–reward bargain covers the areas shown in Table 12.1.

Table 12.1 The effort–reward bargain

Rewards	Effort
Basic pay	Physical measurable effort
Incentive bonus	Mental effort
Benefits	Willingness to do extra hours
Time off	Good attendance
Autonomy	Cooperation with change
Satisfying work	Commitment
Power and influence	Using initiative
Relationship with colleagues	Cooperation with others
Sense of achievement	Enthusiasm
Self-evaluation	Flexibility

Source: Adapted from Bowey and Thorpe (1986).

One can see that rewards range across pay and benefits to psychological satisfactions and personal development, and that 'effort' includes the attitudinal characteristics required from the employee.

The psychological contract (as discussed in Chapter 11) is the tacit and sometimes explicit deal each of the two parties expects of the other in the employment relationship, which encapsulates what the employee expects the role to require, and what the employer will require in return, together with their expectations of all the terms and conditions, the employer's HR policies which affect the role, and the physical working conditions. In addition, the employer might have expectations about the employee's attitude to work, the willingness to learn, and any other expectations each has of the other which may be understood as a result of what is said or written or even implied during the recruitment process, and is discussed and adjusted during the ongoing relationship between the employer and the employee (Schein 1978; Rousseau and Ho 2000).

Most motivation theories are concerned with the factors which produce motivation to act and, for those directed at management interests, with how to motivate employees to work in the way desired by management. These theories take the psychological factors to be completely separate from formal contracts, pay, or terms and conditions of service. Herzberg famously labelled pay and the physical conditions of work together as 'hygiene factors' not as motivators, which he saw as the more developmental processes and those factors which would encourage good performance, such as recognition and the sense of fulfilment in the work itself (Herzberg *et al.* 1959). In spite of the time that has passed, the ideas of Herzberg still have high face validity and a hold on managers' thinking. These ideas fed into a similar interest in job satisfaction studies. Another, more dynamic, theory of motivation which is often useful to managers is Victor Vroom's (1964) expectancy theory. So popular has it become, that there are a number of variants. Expectancy theory is based on the assumption of a rational approach, where the motivation

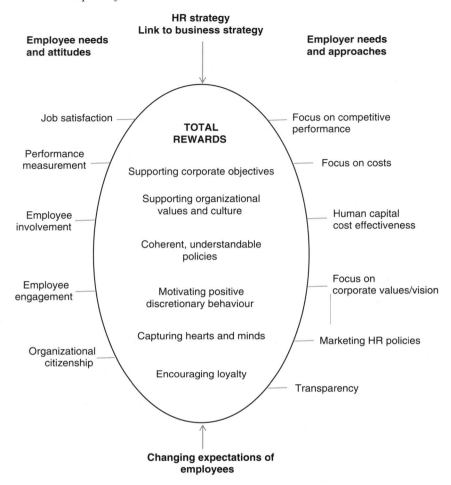

Figure 12.1 Framework of the link provided by total rewards to employee and employer needs

to do something is contingent upon both the expectation and probability of a valued reward, such expectations being influenced by the knowledge the person has of what is required to fulfil the task, their experience of previously performing similar tasks, and understanding of the task (Vroom 1964). The advantage of this theory is that it shows motivation arises not just from the desires of the individual employee, but also from the actions of management, in the way the task is made valuable for the employee, and in the training the employee receives to accomplish that kind of task.

These early ideas on motivation have been taken forward in a number of directions, but one of the most fruitful is in the study of job satisfaction. This suggests that jobs should be designed to be intrinsically motivating, so that the extrinsic rewards of pay and benefits are matched with the intrinsic satisfactions and systematic improvement processes which were believed should be built into the nature of the work itself. Elements of jobs which are 'satisficers' include: feedback on performance (the person should know from the employer whether their work needs improving, or is good, without waiting to be told); a degree of autonomy; task variety; job enrichment (which might come from including some elements of the supervisor's/manager's work in the job); and the potential for enlargement (where the job has scope for a wider range of tasks at the same level).

In Figure 12.1 we seek to explain how managers can shape the various elements in the psychological contract, which are brought together to form what has been variously described as the 'deal', or if we take the employer's perspective, the 'offer' which in the parlance of the marketing of HRM is called the 'employee value proposition' (see Chapter 11) or EVP for short. On the left hand side of the figure are the employee needs from the perspective of motivation and what the employer would want the employee to experience in their relationship with the company, and on the right hand side are the various objectives and behaviours which the employer should adopt to make the business successful, along with the relevant employer demands and obligations in the relationship. Unlike the effort–reward bargain outlined earlier, this is very much an 'employer centred' model, therefore. That is because total rewards (TR) is intended to support the achievement of the organization's goals, and is a particular HR strategy adopted for this end. In the next few pages we describe these elements, before looking at the tactical aspects of TR in responding to the recession and change, followed by an examination of the strategic aspects of TR emerging from the recession.

Employee needs and attitudes

Employee involvement and employee engagement (see Chapter 11) are similar terms, both being aspects of empowering employees to do a good job. 'Employee voice and involvement have a key role in creating engaged employees' (Torrington *et al.* 2011: 256). There are subtle shades of meaning, which suggest that engagement is more about policies and processes for gaining the trust and loyalty of employees collectively, and so using their feedback from surveys and focus groups. The approaches to motivation and job satisfaction described above have progressed to the development of various types of high performance work teams. Here, the intention is to build the motivational characteristics of job satisfaction into systems and processes of work that engage the work team, so that the team operates as a cohesive unit dedicated to achieving its targets to improve performance. These practices often require team reviews of errors, and suggestions for improvements which must be considered by supervisors and senior management, as, for example, in what were called 'quality circles'. These were a response to the productivity and quality problems encountered in the 1970s and 1980s, when there was recognition of the value of some of the Japanese working methods. However, it is not clear how far these approaches were successful, compared to the improvements achieved by robots and new technology applications in manufacturing, where a large part of the human element has been removed. There is less evidence of high involvement work practices in the service sector, and different industries and occupations are likely to adopt their own versions (Boxall and Purcell 2011). Employee involvement is also very dependent for its form on the degree of collectivism, and, in this way, there are contextual differences, where for example there is a tradition of joint consultation, and worker cooperatives. For example, there are different types of co-determination in the Netherlands and Germany where there is a less managerial focus, whereas in the USA, upward communication and individual contribution to work solutions may be more the norm (Paauwe 2004: 172).

These management processes for empowering employees are ways of enlisting the employee relations climate in the cause of management interests in seeking to place the employees' side of the psychological contract in a close alignment with management. At times, and in the joint work of the enterprise, there may well be an identity of interests between management and work people, akin to what Fox (1966) described as a unitary rather than a pluralist frame of reference. The more pluralist frame of reference of managers in the public sector, where for example managers were used to communicating with their staff through trade unions, may explain why trade union membership in the public sector is holding up, and where certain management communications may be covered by collective agreements.

Originating from a more individualist agenda, the concept of 'organizational citizenship' has been developed in the USA (Organ 1988). Organizational citizenship behaviour (OCB) is characterized by the loyalty and willingness of the employee to help beyond his or her role, so that the employee adopts positive discretionary actions which anticipate and forestall problems, and where employees recommend their employer to others, and act as ambassadors for the company. Snape and Redman (2010) reviewed how HRM practices influence OCB and the impact of HR systems and policies on OCB. Taking bundles of HR policies which are associated with high performance work systems – integrated recruitment, development, performance management, and performance based rewards – they show how these connect to performance, and indirectly to OCB. They argue that OCB which shows loyalty and enthusiastic helping behaviours, occurs in reciprocity for the supportive HR practices employees have experienced, and that 'rewards and internal labour market dimensions were positively associated with perceived organizational support' (p. 1241). OCB may be seen as an individual and as a collective or 'group' form (GOCB) of helping behaviour, where there were supportive managers, transformative top management, and competence in group members (Choi 2009). Mossholder *et al.* (2011) reported that HR systems which are collaborative reinforce mutuality in employment relationships and encourage GOCB.

Employer needs and approaches

The employer needs listed are ongoing, and are not just a function of the changed conditions following the recession. The focus on competitive performance is itself a reason for a focus on costs. Payroll costs are a high proportion of total costs in the labour intensive rather than the capital intensive industries, but how much leverage is achieved by the quality of the workforce is a topic for all employers. The desire to improve efficiency pushes employers to adopt well known systems and standards, such as Six Sigma, the Balanced Scorecard, and Total Quality Management movement, as part of organization wide improvement programmes. There is a need for employee engagement and methods to draw on the energies of their staff in order to sustain competitive advantage through continuous improvement. TR can be seen in this context, therefore. The recent focus on costs directs companies to look at pension schemes, to move out of defined benefit schemes, and in the USA examine expensive health insurance schemes, where costs rose dramatically in the years running up to the recession.

A further reason to look at the reward package is to keep a constant watch on the efficiency of any performance related elements, such as performance related pay (PRP), and bonus schemes. Paying for performance has grown in popularity, as there is the promise that, if successful, any financial layout on such schemes is recovered and more, from output or productivity improvements. There can always be an element of managerial discretion on the renewal of any scheme introduced to make sure only the successful PRP methods survive. PRP has grown in popularity. The systems are typically linked to performance formally, often through appraisal policies. For example, McDonald's (the restaurant chain), in a case study published in 2008, described how individual performance drove pay progression through annual measurable objectives, performance being reviewed annually against four ratings – exceptional performance, significant performance, and so on, and appraisers made a judgement on the base pay increase to award from a scale according to each rating. In addition there were bonus schemes such as the Target Incentive Plan, targeting such factors as company performance, team performance, as well as individual performance. There is also a 'Restaurant Bonus Scheme', based on customer service, sales, profit, staff turnover, and customer satisfaction results. McDonald's has worked hard on its 'EVP' and there is a wide range of benefits, which are communicated via a Personal Benefits Report, showing the value of the whole package (IDS 2008a: 11).

This is very much an accepted approach, although sometimes one finds in other organizations the appraisal of performance compared to objectives influencing promotion and bonus results rather than base pay, perhaps reflecting caution about the efficacy of appraisal systems (Murphy and Cleveland 1995), and the possibility of unintended consequences from the objective or output measure driven pay system (Roy 1955; Kerr 1975). As base pay is normally regarded as rigid, downwards, using it to reward performance carries the problem of what happens if and when performance declines, but the enhanced base pay is still in effect? Although there is much evidence that suggests PRP can be effective: 'there is very strong evidence that individual incentives can generate substantial increases in performance' (Gerhart and Rynes 2003: 192), there are many different types of scheme and performance management systems, so success is very dependent upon the design features of the scheme, and how it is applied. TR approaches help to place incentives in the broader context of the employee's relationship with the company, and make it clear that there are other ways in which the company invests in its employees, besides PRP, so that there is a more comprehensive message, of which PRP is only a part.

The cost-effective retention and development of human capital is an important purpose for private sector reward policies. The question here is what is the company getting in return for its investment? TR performs two functions here. First, by bringing all the elements together into a coherent package, the management of total cost is facilitated, and the balance of the different elements in the package is made more explicit. Second, human capital has two elements: firm-specific human capital and general human capital. General human capital represents the value of the education, training, and experience which people bring to their work. In the case of firm-specific human capital, here there is a contribution to productivity in the individual firm where (as in the RBV theory) there are particular routines, highly specialized knowledge areas, and processes which are inimitable and a source of competitive advantage (Topel 1991; Slaughter *et al.* 2007). These matters are part of the debate, for example, about whether senior managers in the UK Civil Service or the top managers (Chief Constables) in the police service could be brought in from outside the organization to perform at a high level? It is argued in response that only people with experience of dealing with the type of work, the organizational context, its history, and fellow employees, and of the industry, will have the competencies to perform well at a senior level, or in a specialized occupation. TR has the benefit of bringing into play the whole career and development package, so there is some accrual of much sought after competencies in management. For some organizations, where there is no career promise, the opportunities within the package offer employability in similar roles elsewhere, and perhaps in the industry, because of the experience, formal training, and development received.

We proposed earlier that corporate values and vision have an important role to play in directing employee effort, and in creating strong cultures. We have also supported the view that organizational agility depends upon such cultures and the shared values they inculcate. The purpose of the total reward philosophy is to harness reward packages to reinforce the values and culture of the organization. By articulating and communicating such a vision, focusing on shared values, the management intention is to encourage a unity of purpose and effort for the achievement of organizational objectives. Rewards are a visible and tangible symbol of what the company values most, in terms of achievements and behaviours of employees. TR therefore seek to ensure an alignment of interests, between management and employees, by a coherent system of objective setting, appraisal, rewards, work style, lifestyle, and the type of working environment.

TR involves the packaging of pay and benefit policies in such a way that they are convincing to employees. TR requires the marketing of HR policies, together, as a coherent package, so that employees can understand the logics and the connections between the elements. The presentation is important, as a way to transmit more than just the basic facts about pay and benefits. The intention is to put the company's value proposition to the workforce. There is thus a message within the package about what it means to work for the company, the kind of lifestyle and work style that is presented, and the future support and prospects which are available. For TR to be effective there would seem to be a need for a marketing effort to be made (see Chapter 11).

The pressure for transparency is also connected to the need to market TR. In this aspect, there is an important need to be explicit about policies and the reasons for their adoption, as a part of the company's narrative on trust. If the employer expects staff to be good organizational citizens, to be loyal and supportive of organizational goals, then a high level of trust is necessary in employees which can only exist if it is reciprocated. Performance based pay can only be successfully introduced if there is a history of trust, as well as objectivity in the criteria used to measure performance. Hope Hailey *et al.* (2012), in reporting their CIPD sponsored research on trust, suggest that there are different approaches to building trust, which employees differentiate, such as the trust in leaders, in the organization, and in their line managers.

Annual Total Reward statements have been produced by major companies such as BP and, as we described earlier, McDonald's, for many years. These statements provide employees with information on the value of all the different elements in the reward package, typically including pension, life insurance, health care, and other benefit costs. This is also the kind of information which is essential if the company is intending to set up a cafeteria type scheme, where employees can choose the benefits they want for their own particular needs from a list of what is available, since reward statements are individualized, showing the total cost of their employment. Cafeteria and salary sacrifice schemes do not usually allow complete freedom of choice by the employee; some benefits such as pension and a minimum holiday entitlement are usually protected, so that a decision is not made by the employee which is likely to be against their own long term interests.

The new pay and total rewards

In Figure 12.1 we show HR strategy linking to business strategy at the top, and the changing expectations of employees at the bottom of the figure. Both of these needs have encouraged companies to think in terms of TR. The characteristics of total rewards shown in the centre of the figure explain how a total rewards philosophy seeks to link the position of employees with that of management. The function of TR is to bring together all the appropriate tangible and intangible aspects of the EVP to encourage the behaviours described in the interests of the organization, including those related to maximizing the value of human capital for the future as well as the present. There are many external trends which encourage employers to review their rewards policies, and which mean employers are driven to think about how the elements in the package fit together (Chapman and Kelliher 2011), and how they can encapsulate the corporate objectives within the rewards. Five main reasons external to the firm can be discerned, as listed below.

- The social, economic, and demographic trends described in the first part of this book showed an ageing population in the West and in Japan, with reduced financial resources to pay for elder care, or to pay pensions. We have also described how generational differences can be addressed by market segmentation policies in the rewards field with packages to suit different groups of people. One of the advantages of cafeteria type rewards is that employees can make their own choices at different life stages.
- In spite of the recession, and unemployment for some employee groups, there is still reported to be a shortage of talented people, so that attraction and retention are still important goals for reward policy. TR is central to any thinking on the EVP. Competitive pressures between firms for the best people may be exacerbated by industry concentration (for example, motor manufacturing, finance, etc. in particular areas), which heightens awareness of what is on offer in the industry. TR becomes therefore an important differentiator.
- The activities of reward consultants may also be a factor, spreading TR practices. During the 1990s reward consultancies expanded their activities. Actuaries pension consultancies, and financial consultancies moved into rewards in a more general way, and sought to move up the value chain in order to enhance profits, moving into HR strategy as a new field. There was an incentive for them to offer new products, such as 'total reward', as a new way for their clients to look at reward (Armstrong and Brown 2005).
- The changes to occupation structures, with the growth of many types of specialism, and of what are 'middle income' occupations, partly driven by new technology, and the expansions of the professions, have also likely produced pressure to find reward solutions which incorporate lifestyle and work style choices. The growing incidence of new working

arrangements of part time, teleworking, and remote working as part of desires for more flexible working and a better work–life balance, have changed the nature of the workforce (Kelliher and Richardson 2012). These kinds of developments are naturally going to lead to reviews of rewards, with these choices in mind, and encourage employers to offer packages with these features.

• During the last decade, the number of elements in the reward package has increased. Variable pay has become a standard part of most reward packages, and is often further disaggregated into annual, long term incentives, team and group bonuses. Base pay has similarly split up into many variants, such as competency based pay, contribution based pay, pay for performance, and similar descriptions where base pay increments are also dependent on performance. Whether such approaches would survive a return of high inflation rates is not clear.

In our comments about the role of reward consultants, we noted their influence in creating what is a new perspective on rewards. Some academics have suggested these changes are 'fads' (Giancola 2009). The interests of consultants are well served by repackaging ideas in a variety of new ways, but these ideas are not just fashionable. There is a ready market for new thinking from reward specialists of all kinds inside organizations, who do need to refresh and to reposition reward systems periodically in order to maintain the motivational power of the system, and to have a narrative which meets the approval of employees and of senior management, in support of the emerging organization strategies.

The 'New Pay' was a term adopted in the 1990s to reflect a sea change in the way companies were dealing with rewards. Instead of pay being confined to a matter of precedent, based on tenure in the job, relativities, and a lengthy pay scale, periodically adjusted for inflation, there was a strategic orientation to rewards. 'Rewards' rather than pay or compensation and benefits entered mainstream discussions around the topic of what do we, the company, need to emphasize in the reward package in order to meet our strategic objectives, and what value is added in return for all the costs of pay and benefits? Companies have moved towards market related pay, with a more flexible approach, and have introduced pay policies which more closely reflect performance. Broad banding has been introduced, reducing the number of pay bands in the hierarchy which resulted in flatter pay structures, and with more flexibility on where to place individuals according to market rates. This meant there was a greater sharing of the risks between employer and employee (for employees, a higher proportion of their pay was at risk), and in the interests of mutuality, productivity gains were shared with employees (Schuster and Zingheim 1996).

These elements persisted into the new millennium, and by a decade later, the 'New Pay' did not seem so new any more. Instead, there has been a move towards TR as described in this chapter. Beyond the base pay and the variable pay elements, TR is about the 'hearts and minds' of employees. In Zingheim and Schuster's (2000) follow-up, they described TR as comprising four components: 'Individual Growth', 'Compelling Future', 'Total Pay', and a 'Positive Workplace'. These elements are good examples of how the whole set of ideas can be marketed, and are a succinct summary of employee needs. The importance of these employee components at that time was that they represented a positive and future oriented leitmotiv. The question this raises is how well can this broad concept of TR survive and remain relevant in the changed circumstances companies now face?

The immediate effects of the recession on reward policy

Throughout this book we have emphasized that HR policies are constantly evolving, in different contexts. In that sense, the changes we have outlined are impacting on a moving target. Some elements of TR are as relevant now as they were at the start of this century: market oriented pay, and the need to reflect organizational performance, with more flexibility, and an accent on employability rather than job security are likely to remain significant planks in policies into the future. Some of these features of the 'New Pay' are consistent with the over-arching corporate need to reduce costs, and the acceptance of the new reality, that job security can no longer be a part of employment arrangements, forms part of the 'new normal' narrative which is emerging.

One aspect which may be changing is the notion that employees should share some of the risk taken by employers in their pay packets. The recession has brought about a degree of risk aversion, as evidenced by retail banks which are more cautious about loans; similarly, companies are reluctant to see employees take risks on the corporation's behalf, and would not wish to see bonus or commission schemes which encouraged more risk taking. Bonuses paid in the UK seem to remain at around the same level according to the ONS (about £35 billion across the whole economy in 2010–11, and 2011–12), although these are down in real terms if inflation is taken into account. It is worth noting that Financial Services accounts for around 40 per cent of the amount paid out (IDS 2012a: 25). One could say that the risks in holding on to continuous employment are enough. However, there are more schemes to encourage share holding and the notion that bonuses can be paid in the company's shares could be interpreted as ensuring employees take on more of the company risk in a direct sense, by becoming shareholders.

At the early stages of the recession, many organizations introduced pay freezes. Some of these were continued, including in the UK public sector, where there were plans to reduce the pay of some groups, for example by reducing the starting rate of police constables in the UK, and by moving in some government bodies towards regional pay, based on the opinion that public sector workers in some regions of the UK were paid more than private sector workers. However, at the same time, some companies, such as HSBC and Tesco, were moving away from regional based rewards in the UK. According to IDS (2012a), pay increases were stable in 2012 with median settlements at around 2.5–2.75 per cent; pay freezes accounted for 12 per cent of settlements. As inflation was also running at around 2.5–3 per cent, most wage earners were not experiencing any income growth. Fewer long term pay deals were being agreed, reflecting the uncertainty in the economy. This shrinkage in earnings power, combined with fewer promotion opportunities because of low growth, indicated the reality of an end to the doctrine of progress for many families.

We can turn to tournament theory for some of the likely effects of a reduction in promotion opportunities. Tournament theory examines and posits a relationship between promotion and incentive which is likened to a tournament, with promotion as the prize (Lazear and Rosen 1981; Gerhart and Rynes 2003). Usually, the number of roles available at senior levels diminishes as one moves up the organization hierarchy, so only a few people, and a diminishing number as they move up, can be promoted. This leads to larger pay differentials as people move up the hierarchy, to offset the diminishing probability of being promoted further. Efficiencies are achieved in the incentives to be promoted, which, it is argued, enhances performance and ensures higher quality people are promoted. Tournament theory therefore seeks to explain pay differentials in a hierarchy (Conyon *et al.* 2001) and is helpful in turning our attention to those who do not get promoted. With the advent of pay freezes, lower pay increases, and fewer promotions, one might expect a reduced incentive effect, and major dissatisfaction among junior staff, since this hiatus in their careers will have a negative effect now and later. This may mean a mass of frustrated people at lower levels, exacerbated if the organization brings in new people from outside, rather than promotes from within. As there are few opportunities elsewhere, locking these demotivated people in a situation where their employer expects them to cover a wider range of work due to downsizing is not likely to be motivational.

The deadening effect of the recession may also influence views of what rewards should be paid. Social comparison theory suggests people are as interested in pay differentials as they are in absolute amounts of pay, and in the way management judge different performance levels. Thus if an individual who is generally known to the staff to be a below average performer is given the same reward as others in the same unit, this undermines all the motivational effect of the rewards 'correctly' awarded to the other employees, since it is clear to the staff that management do not make accurate judgements of performance, and hence the award to them is meaningless. Even at a time when pay systems are disrupted by the recession, the failure to reward good performance accurately is likely to be demotivating.

There are practical pay policy problems for the reward manager. The introduction of a pay freeze is akin to a game of musical chairs – an employee's financial future depends where people are on the pay scales when the incremental system is frozen. If some special cases are allowed, this reduces trust. A scenario where the freeze does not apply to directors, who continue to receive bonuses, produces cynicism. Appointing new starts on higher pay than existing staff because of recruitment difficulties also is demotivating to the remaining employees, and line managers, desperate to keep critically important people, may be tempted to invent new roles to justify promotions and pay increases. All these scenarios potentially undermine the total reward philosophy, for example in relation to OCB. These negative consequences remind us that reward specialists must be prepared with an acceptable narrative to explain policy, to answer questions about equity, fairness, and the impartiality of job evaluation rules and procedures.

Recessionary pressures on reward strategy

The fundamental shift in the business context across the globe has more than a tactical impact on rewards. There are three major strategic areas where rewards are in the spotlight. First, the recession has forced organizations to review all their costs, their business models, and the value they are creating, as part of their drive for competitiveness. Second, organization culture and the engagement of employees is critical for change, and for the organization to adapt and be agile. Arguably, the tactical solutions described above would only be possible with an accommodating culture in which there were high levels of trust, and employee commitment such as would be elicited through a TR approach. Third, the need to be able to survive in the long run depends upon the quality of employees. There is still a shortage, in most countries, of talented people, as we describe in Chapter 10. The recruitment, retention, and reward of the talent necessary to survive and thrive in the future requires a linkage in policies between rewards and talent management – TR provides a means to establish this link.

As we showed in Figure 12.1, employee engagement and involvement is a part of the EVP. The TR philosophy treats these relationships, and training and development, as critical for human capital/cost effectiveness. The TR way of working seeks to ensure the support of organizational culture and objectives. On the one hand, this is expected to encourage productivity improvements through high performance work groups, and on the other, to lead to employees adopting positive discretionary behaviours as good corporate citizens. However, one of the problems facing employers is how to implant employee engagement during the recession, in the midst of redundancies and firm closures, pay freezes, and reduced prospects. The public sector in many countries has been badly affected, as countries try to reduce public debt.

The redundancies, limitations in real terms of earnings improvements, and reduced prospects, may be perceived by employees as a breach of the implicit and explicit promises contained in the psychological contract. Restubog *et al.* (2008) use social exchange theory and the group value model to argue that employee perceptions of a unilateral change for the worst could be seen as a breach of trust, which could reduce employee identification with their employer's interests, with consequences for OCB.

The group value model suggests that how employees are treated sends a symbolic message which picks up relational contract breaches, because procedural injustices, perceptions of unfairness in process, are likely to have 'stronger negative consequences than distributive injustices' which relate to the outcomes received (p. 1381). They go on to separate out two different types of breach of the psychological contract, the transactional – concerned with tangible rewards – and the relational, which covers the longer term issues such as career and development. In their research, using samples drawn from a large public sector organization, they found that perceived contract breaches eroded trust in the organization, but that there was evidence that the transactional breaches were treated as less fundamental than the relational contract breaches as far as OCB is concerned. From this we may conclude that reductions in pay increases and fewer promotion opportunities would be less likely to affect OCB, if they are handled sensitively, fairly, and respectfully. However, there will be individuals who take a different view.

One area where we might expect to see transactional and relationship aspects of a breach of the psychological contract coalescing is top executive pay. We examined the issue in detail in Chapter 9, when we looked at questions of corporate governance and social responsibility. We may note that one of the arguments company management use, that 'we are all in it together', must be authentic to employees. Top pay attracts such strong feelings that we should comment here on some of the pay issues (Walsh 2009). In practice, apart from in Financial Services, the large pay packets are usually found only in the larger publicly quoted companies (those with the largest market capitalization), mostly those in the FTSE 100 and Fortune 500. One of the problems in perceptions is that the variable elements in their packages often contain the biggest amounts paid out each year, but the contracts upon which these are based will cover stock options and deferred bonuses as part of long term incentive plans (LTIPs), which could have been earned many years before (Tyson and Bournois 2005). If the context changes quickly, it could happen that a large payout coincides with a dip in the company's fortune. The other major problem occurs when there is a high payout to an executive who leaves behind a failing business. 'Rewards for failure' has attracted much adverse comment. Perhaps the biggest fallout from the high payouts is a degree of cynicism, encouraging the belief that managers act only in their own interests.

Evidence on levels of employee engagement indicates that engagement has suffered in the course of the recession. The SHRM (2012a) Report in the USA showed employees only moderately engaged. The top five factors which contributed to employee engagement were: (1) opportunities to use skills and capabilities (63 per cent); (2) job security (61 per cent); (3) compensation/pay (60 per cent); (4) communication with senior management (57 per cent); and (5) relationships with supervisors (54 per cent). It is interesting to note that the opportunities to use skills and capabilities and job security came high on the list of priorities for employees, no doubt reflecting the fears of unemployment, and all the problems of loss of identity, of income, and the feelings of self-worth that accompany such a loss. Paradoxically, there is also some evidence in voluntary turnover data, that employees will 'jump' rather than wait to be pushed out, presumably securing their new jobs quickly when these are available (Trevor and Nyberg 2008). Batt and Colvin (2011) found in their study that call centre staff working in high involvement work systems, with internal promotion opportunities, higher pay rates with full time jobs and pensions were less likely to leave. However, where there were short term performance pressures, including commission type pay, there were higher turnover rates.

Talent management is discussed in detail in Chapter 10, as one of the cornerstones of HRM. There are three ways that make talent management and TR important interlinked policy areas. One of the reasons TR is so significant is because it supports talent management as an integrated system which gives effect to the management of the company's capabilities. Competency frameworks are often linked through variable pay systems, supporting the performance management activity of performance appraisal, and acting as the bedrock of any development work, since common competencies, researched for the company, offer the availability for development specialists of a gap analysis to determine learning needs. The achievement by employees of the different set performance levels brings them rewards, and opportunities for development and perhaps promotion and career moves.

Second, talent management involves the differentiation between varying talent levels, and types of talent. TR policies also depend upon market segmentation, and the linkage of types of talent to promotion, and therefore to increments and pay increases, as well as to variations in conditions of service in support of the talent management decisions. A good example of this is Yahoo! in Europe, where the location of an individual in one of the three defined talent pools was reflected in their position in the pay ranges (IDS 2008b). TR approaches are entirely consistent with the market segmentation of talent management, since reward packages including work style and lifestyle choices, together with incentive systems, can be designed to fit the range of work for the group in question. There is also the possibility of introducing cafeteria style benefits, whereby the individual can choose from a range of options. There is some evidence that companies which have segmented their workforce, and have customized EVPs, have higher levels of employee engagement, and if they have focused on critical workforce segments, have better financial performance than their peer group (Towers Watson 2012a).

Third, TR establishes, alongside the talent management system, the behaviours and competencies the firm values and wishes to encourage, and which are consistent with the desired organization culture. This means in addition to performance objectives, there may be specified behaviours, so that two sets of standards are rewarded, the balance between them being a policy decision revealed in the design of the bonus system. This is exemplified in KPMG's performance ratings matrix, which combines behaviours with objectives to be achieved, and is the basis for rewarding staff in an annual assessment (IDS 2008c).

Conclusions

In this chapter we have sought to describe how TR approaches are both supportive of the range of HR policies, including recruitment and retention through the EVP and talent management, and are also drivers of motivation and OCB by creating work style and lifestyle choices, producing high performance cultures, improving work performance and productivity. There are both tactical and strategic challenges in the current context. The need for companies to use their dynamic capabilities in pursuit of competitive advantage means there is a need to concentrate on the routines and the ways of working which are inimitable (following the resource based view). TR is a useful mechanism for succeeding in this critical endeavour. However, we have also demonstrated the significance of coherent HR policy frameworks, applied in an atmosphere of trust, in which transparency, employee engagement, fairness and equity in rewards, and an open management style will help to overcome some of the difficulties facing Western corporations.

13 Employee well-being

The extent to which the individual employee experiences a sense of well-being while at work has long been a central issue for those companies which understood the significance of people management for organizational success. Since the last quarter of the nineteenth century, with the influence of the great Quaker companies in the UK, there has always been a strand of management philosophy which believed that recognizing the interests of employees and incorporating a duty of care towards them are not only morally desirable policies, but are also likely to inculcate commitment and a reciprocal sense of duty in return. The question 'what is work for?' is at the heart of much of the current debate about capitalism and the role of the state, in which attempts are being made to look for new solutions following the financial crash. It would seem that every economic crisis is only a crisis because it is also a crisis of conscience.

In this chapter, we look at how the concept of 'well-being' applies to employees in their organizational context. We explore the sources of well-being, the models of how the various factors interact, the effects of the recession, and work intensification. Finally we comment on a way forward to cope with the stresses and strains of organizational life, presenting a framework to look at the depth of any interventions, the policy responses, and examples of the types of interventions which can be used to improve employees' sense of well-being.

The sources and consequences of employee well-being

The research on this topic covers a continuum from those studies which take a physical and psychological interpretation of health, including mental health, to those which see 'well-being' as associated with happiness and contentment in life generally. Definitions have changed with the changing work context, for example due to new types of work, and the shifting economic and social environment. In its most general sense, therefore, health is seen as encompassing both physical and mental health, and the human need to live a satisfying life, where self-fulfilment is a human need. The World Health Organization defined good health in the preamble to its constitution, in the following way: 'Health is a state of complete physical, mental and social well-being and not merely the absence of disease or infirmity' (1948).

In early definitions of personnel management activities, 'well-being' was captured under the generic headings of 'health, safety, and welfare'. Even now, the duty of care placed on companies includes an over-arching responsibility for the mental and physical health of employees, as well as protecting them from any potential harm arising from exposure to undue risk. This state backed responsibility has its origins in the UK in the Factories Acts, and the subsequent legislation. Even pioneers such as Sir Thomas Legge, who was the first Medical Inspector of Factories and Workshops in the UK, in the early part of the twentieth century, understood that the psychology of workers and industrial relations were important issues for medical practitioners to understand when acting in the field of occupational health. This is demonstrated in his comment that 'psychoneurotic symptoms such as the fear of the loss of work, wages and sight' were factors which could lead to more compensation claims (Carter 1998: 34).

As time has passed, there has come a greater awareness of the importance of the way the working environment can have both positive and negative impacts on employees' mental health. Danna and Griffin (1999) reviewed the literature on health and well-being, and presented a model to show how the various research strands on the topic are related. They acknowledge there are many definitions of health and well-being, all of which cover emotional and mental health properties, as well as physical health. They define the concept as: 'Comprising the various life/work/non work satisfactions enjoyed by individuals' (p. 359). This includes social and family life satisfactions and, in the work area, satisfactions and/or dissatisfactions with pay, promotion opportunities, the nature of the work, relations with co-workers, and their general health. They include 'health' as a sub-component of well-being, including psychological indicators, such as frustration and anxiety. The framework they proposed suggests there are three main antecedents to well-being at work: work setting (health and safety hazards), an individual's personality traits (including type A tendencies, and locus of control), and occupational stress (covering intrinsic job factors, organizational role, relationships, career, organizational structure and climate, and the home/work interface). The consequences of the state of well-being are shown as individual (physical and psychological) and organizational (productivity, health insurance costs, law suits, and absenteeism).

Daniels (2000) rejected those definitions of psychological well-being which equate the concept with job satisfaction. He argued that measures of affective well-being are the best indicators of psychological well-being. 'Affective well-being' is concerned with the experience of positive and negative affects, and is a multidimensional concept which captures the experience of subtle changes in work environments and relationships. Daniels went on to describe five constructs, which each have two poles that are the different dimensions of affective well-being:

> Anxiety – comfort
> Depression – pleasure
> Vigour – tiredness
> Bored – enthusiastic
> Angry – placid

The factor analysis performed showed that these five constructs were within the two super-ordinate constructs of 'positive' and 'negative' affect.

Cox and Ferguson (1994) published a model of how the work environment influences occupational health which is mediated through two pathways. These are the 'physico-chemical pathway' and the 'cognitive-psycho-physical pathway'. These pathways mediate the effects of both physical and mental hazards; that is, there are psychological affects from physical and from cognitive and social and psychological hazards, and there are physical affects from the cognitive, psychological hazards.

There has been a shift away from the concentration on physical well-being, and a greater interest in mental well-being, perhaps because the most obvious physical risks have been subject to legal constraints for a longer period of time, and factory inspection has enforced the laws. The nature of service sector work, where employment growth has typically come in Western economies, seems more likely to have an impact on mental health because physical activity is often subordinate to intellectual activity and interpersonal relationships. There is also now improved diagnosis of mental ill-health than hitherto, and a growing awareness that mental ill-health can have identifiable and significant effects on costs and on organizational performance.

The problems of mental ill-health are often described by managers as forms of 'stress'. Although widely used, the term can be confusing. Roden and Williams (2002) distinguished between 'pressure' and stress. Pressure is a stimulus, which can take various forms, is necessary to initiate action on the part of the individual, and is part of the normal challenges of everyday life. Pressure is described as an 'input', while 'stress' is an outcome. 'Stress occurs when the perceived demands placed on the individual exceed that individual's ability to cope' (p. 47).

Well-being as an organizational phenomenon

Employee well-being is both an individual state of physical and mental health, and also an organizational objective. For management, the question of how to create and to sustain a 'healthy' work organization is answered by policies and actions, and is engendered by a climate of working relationships which are intended to foster the appropriate organization culture. There are a number of factors, frequently quoted, which are thought to be associated

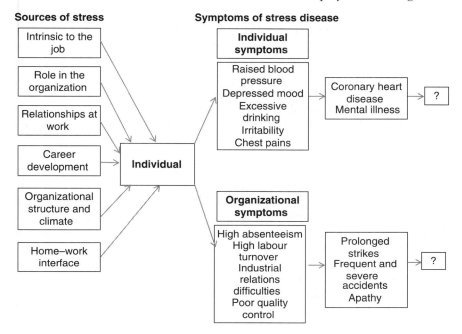

Figure 13.1 Stress – a research model
Source: Cooper and Cartwright (1994).

with a work place where people are encouraged to perform well, which is attractive to join, and a worthwhile and enjoyable place to work. Cooper and Cartwright (1994) identified five factors which are potentially linked to stress in any type of job, and seek to show how these factors, which affect the mental health of the individual, could produce organizational symptoms of stress. These factors are:

•   Those intrinsic to the job (for example, working conditions, work overload or work underload, and new technology).
•   Factors which are related to roles in the organization (role ambiguity, role conflict, and personality issues related to the role).
•   Relationships at work, especially those with supervisors, with subordinates, and with colleagues.
•   Career prospects and development (job security and performance and development).
•   Organization structure and organization culture.

A sixth factor was also identified, which relates to the interface between home and work and could be a potential source of stress, where demands from family and partners might become additional pressures, producing an overload of worry when there are also demands from work. This factor is acknowledged in the Cooper and Cartwright (1994) model (Figure 13.1), which looks at the sources of stress on the individual, and the symptoms of stress, showing the individual health problems associated with severe stress and the possible organizational difficulties which ensue.

This model is useful in reminding us that well-being is not purely a matter for the individual. Together with other models which examine the causes and the consequences of employee well-being, organizational work factors are seen as having a direct impact on employees' sense of well-being, both positively and negatively.

In Baker *et al.*'s (1996) integrated model, psycho-social conditions from within or from outside the organization are described as being modified by perceptions according to the individual's characteristics (including education and age levels), by the degree of control the person can exert, and the support from co-workers and supervisors. This leads us to look at what constitutes a healthy work organization.

An initial test and validation process was proposed by Wilson *et al.* (2004). By work organization they referred to the way work processes are structured and managed. Their attempt to go beyond the individual and into the organizational wide context of relationships followed from Cox *et al.* (1990) and DeJoy and Southern (1993), where work demands and the social, organizational, and physical environments were all seen as being significant in creating the organization climate, and therefore capable of being tested. From the literature review by Wilson *et al.* (2004), there was a conclusion that the basic content domains associated with the studies on healthy organizations are: organizational climate, which informs job design, and job future which leads to 'psychological work adjustment', from which various behavioural and health outcomes derive. The outcomes included labour turnover intentions, absenteeism, psychological health (covering depression, somatic stress, and anger), as well as behaviours such as smoking and alcohol consumption. Their definition of job design perceptions is how employees perceive their immediate tasks, and organizational climate covers perceptions of social and interpersonal relationships, while 'job future' describes the sense of equity, job security, and career prospects. To test their hypotheses, they broke down the overall constructs of climate, job design, job future, and psychological work adjustments into more specific factors, each of which was included within the topics for questions in their survey.

The results from the study confirmed the hypothesized factors, and the clusters in the content domains, so that all of the associations between the factors were supported. These showed that, as organizations improved their policies in the following areas: employee involvement, safety, health, communications, and values about their employees, so employee perceptions of organizational climate improved. This leads to an associated increase in the way employees relate to job design, and a more positive view of their future in the organization. This implies that improving job design (increasing positive attributes such as autonomy, and decreasing negative attributes such as workload) strengthens psychological work adjustments (improving job satisfaction and reducing job stress). Improving scores on job future attributes is associated with strengthening work adjustment, which in turn has positive health outcomes in regard to alcohol and tobacco use, reducing intentions to leave, and improving health and perceptions of general health. This study was limited due to its reliance on responses from 1,130 employees in one US national retailer. However, this limitation is mitigated by the growing consensus among researchers on the factors which have a positive and negative effect on well-being. The other weakness of this study is the failure to include the impact of home life conflicting with work demands as a source of negative effect on employee well-being.

Most of the factors involved in employee well-being are within the broad remit of human resources. But how do the new economic, social, technological, and economic contexts impacting employee well-being lead to changes to people management? The list of organizational factors described in the Wilson *et al.* (2004) model showed that some factors are more important than others in driving the creation of a particular climate: those concerning social and interpersonal relationships, for example, link into organizational support, co-worker support, participation and employee involvement, communication, and the culture around health and safety. The organizational climate also has its basis in organizational beliefs and values, as espoused by its founders and their successors, and is acted out in the policies they adopt towards people management. Although job design is influenced by climate, it is very much subject to the technical systems, the tasks, and the current business model. Hence, line management has a major say in aspects such as workload, the degree of autonomy, role clarity, working conditions, and work scheduling. Job future issues, on the other hand, such as pay, promotion, equity, learning opportunities, and some aspects of job security, are more a function of the viability of the enterprise and the HR policies and practices required to deliver the business strategy. Good examples of attractive organization cultures are often found in SMEs, such as Innocent Drinks, a small manufacturer of 'smoothie' drinks in the UK where all employees whatever their status help out at times of high demand, irrespective of their formal roles, in order to get the products to their customers. Similarly, flat structures in creative companies such as Pixar, which makes computer animated films (having won 40 Academy awards since 1995, and employed 1,250 people) and believed in 'giving people freedom to do their innovative best work, and to manage themselves', meant highly sought after professionals wanted to continue in their teams and to accept tough peer level critiques in order to produce the best quality they could, and remain with a successful business (Mirza 2011: 34).

Some work, although producing pressure and even stress, can be satisfying. Hewlett and Luce (2006) coined the phrase 'extreme jobs' to describe the work performed by some highly paid professionals and managers. They argued that these 'extreme jobs' were found where people worked 60 or more hours per week, were high earners, and held a position with five or more of the following characteristics: unpredictable work flow, tight deadlines and fast paced work, wide scope of responsibility, after hours work events, availability to clients 24/7, responsibility for profit and loss, responsibility for recruiting and mentoring, frequent travel which is often international, a large number of direct reports, and their physical presence required at work for at least 10 hours a day. The notion of extreme jobs is particularly interesting for our discussion here, as Hewlett and Luce also found that, rather than complaining about the nature of their jobs, those in extreme jobs enjoyed their work and felt fulfilled by it. They appeared to be motivated by factors such as: an adrenalin rush, great colleagues, high pay, recognition, status, and power. In other words, these highly paid professionals were challenged and motivated by this mode of working. Nevertheless, long term exposure to the conditions described may well be deleterious to the health of some of those concerned in the long run, through, for example, hypertension, and heart problems.

While Hewlett and Luce's research was limited to employees in professional services and consulting, a recent study by Parry has also found evidence of extreme jobs within public sector health care in the UK (Buchanan *et al.* 2013). These health care managers experienced many of the characteristics described above – long hours, unpredictable work flows, tight deadlines, inordinate scope of responsibility, plus additional health care specific factors such as facing life and death decisions, resulting in both increased stress and increased motivation as in Hewlett and Luce's study.

The psychological adjustments of employees to the demands and pressures they perceive at work, depends on their job satisfaction, organizational commitment, psychological empowerment, and perceptions of stress. These aspects are largely areas for senior managers, supervisors, employees, and their co-workers to tackle, with the help of the specialist HR function as necessary.

What are the impacts of the new context on employee well-being?

The financial crash and the recession that followed have created a context where low growth and debt, with now low levels of demand in the economy, have produced problems beyond the scope of the particular enterprise to resolve. As we have argued earlier in this book, many of these difficulties arose from the overheating economies of the early part of the twentieth century, and the growing lack of competitiveness of the West compared to the BRIC countries, so there is an element of inevitability in what followed. Companies tried to cope with the consequences through strategies of growth by acquisition, greater leveraging, and risk taking. To cope with these, employees were put under increasing strain, due to work intensification, increasing complexity, shortages of talented people, and pressure for more profit to satisfy shareholders and to maintain the share price. The recession which has followed has added new problems, including the shrinking public sector.

Particular segments of the working population seem to have been badly affected. Those aged 16–24 years in Europe, the USA, and Russia are still experiencing high levels of unemployment (see Chapter 2) and, for college graduates, disappointment at the absence of career opportunities. People who would hitherto have sought full time work are now in the part time market, squeezing out older people who wanted to augment their low pensions, and mothers returning to the labour market who cannot afford child care and would normally seek part time work. The number of people working part time but seeking full time work grew in the UK by half a million in the period 2009–12 to 1.4 million (Aldridge *et al.* 2012).

In the 2012 Autumn Statement by the UK's Finance Minister (Chancellor of the Exchequer), he announced that slow growth and austerity will continue in the UK until at least 2018. Across Europe and the USA, many state benefits were being reduced, or increased at less than the inflation rate. There have been extensive public sector job losses. Business closures added to the general level of uncertainty experienced by employees. Many retail businesses have closed or cut back. There was a predicted fall in job creation in the City of London according to the agency Astbury Marsden (2012), anticipating a difficult business environment for agencies, and there were redundancies in motor manufacturing at Ford UK, and Vauxhall, and in the steel industry, where Tata announced 9,000 job losses in South Wales. There has of course also been job creation, but that in itself does not produce confidence or remove uncertainty; many of the new jobs being in small businesses, some of them part time work and some of this, seasonal.

Absenteeism and 'presenteeism' have been reported to be extensive, probably because of the worsening organizational climates recently created. Although the number of staff absent due to sickness fell, from an average of 7.7 days in 2011 to 6.8 days per annum in 2012, according to the UK's CIPD annual pan European Absence survey, there has been an increase in presenteeism, with one-third of people reporting in to work although sick, presumably because they fear losing their jobs. The CIPD survey showed that one in ten people take time off for depression (putting the UK in the top three countries where depressive illness is so extensive). Stress was given as the most frequently cited reason for sick leave in 2011 and 2012.

Stress is reaching record levels in a number of countries and industries according to survey data. Towers Watson, in its 2012 Global Talent Management survey, stated that one-third of UK employers thought there were growing levels of stress. Kivimaki *et al.* (2012) found in their analysis of 13 European studies covering 200,000 people across Europe, that job strain was linked to a 23 per cent increase in heart attacks, and to deaths from coronary heart disease. They concluded that where workers have little or no control over decision making, there is an increased risk of heart attacks.

Work intensification and 'burnout' are identified by researchers as main causes of stress. In the Towers Watson survey (2012b), one in three employees felt they were threatened by 'burnout', were working longer hours, and under excessive pressure. Fifty-eight per cent of British respondents said they had been working for more hours than normal for the past three years. Less than one-third of respondents said that their employers supported health and well-being policies. Thirty-six per cent said their organizations were under-resourced, and 30 per cent felt their work amount was unreasonable. In a separate study by 'Docusign', quoted by the CIPD (2012), 32 per cent of staff (mostly 25–39 year olds) in the UK stated they were expecting to work at home over the 2012 Christmas holidays due to the demands of their work and because new technology enabled the practice.

In the USA, the SHRM Work-Place Bullying survey (2012b) showed that 51 per cent of the companies contacted reported bullying incidents at work. Twenty-seven per cent of HR professionals had been the victims of bullying. In recessions, suicides are sometimes cited as extreme cases where, due to depression or anxiety, individual employees feel there is no way out of their situation, and no future (Doherty and Tyson 1993). SHRM (2012c) reported high rates of suicide in some particular companies in Europe and the Far East (24 suicides in one year in one company, for example). The report suggests that some organization cultures may provoke this type of extreme reaction, probably as a result of a mixture of a vulnerable person highly stressed, with mental health difficulties working in an organization which has a rigid disciplinary approach, long working shifts, work overload, and a lack of recognition.

The impact of the recession on pay has reinforced the difficulties for employees. Aldridge *et al.* (2012) showed that, in the UK, 6.1 million people live in working households whose income is below the poverty line. More than 5.1 million people live in poverty in workless households. There are 4.4 million people in jobs paying less than £7 per hour, and the number of people receiving benefits from the State to top up wages (known as working tax credits) has risen by 50 per cent since 2003, with 3.3 million people receiving them. The researchers conclude by pointing to the large number of people in the UK who are defined as poor, who are moving in and out of insecure, short term, poorly paid jobs.

In the USA, according to research by Career Builder (2012), 40 per cent of non-governmental workers above the age of 18 have trouble managing their personal budgets between pay checks, 53 per cent have found themselves struggling financially, and did not experience this problem until 2008. The Pew Research Center study (July 2012) found that 85 per cent who described themselves as middle class, said it was more difficult than ten years ago to maintain their standard of living. Overall wage growth in the USA between 2008 and 2010 has been at its weakest since the 1960s although there are wide variations between states, with workers hard hit in Arizona, California,

Florida, Michigan, and Nevada, due to the effects on industries such as construction and manufacturing (Conference Board 2012).

What is the HR role in creating a sense of well-being among employees?

There are good business reasons as well as powerful moral and social arguments for giving employees a sense of well-being as an important aspect of HR policies and practices, and a part of the corporate values and governance of the organization. We have discussed overall organizational climate or culture as a significant variable influencing the extent to which employees experience a sense of well-being. We have also argued that organizations need to be agile in the face of change, which requires a powerful core culture, as the 'glue' which holds the whole organization together. The business case centres on both this aspect of HR strategy and the importance of well-being for sustainable long term performance in modern societies where there are wider social obligations on employers than in the past.

Doherty (2002) set out the business case in terms of costs – in particular, the costs of absenteeism, of possible litigation by employees (since in most Western jurisdictions employers have some responsibility to ensure their working conditions do not cause physical or mental health problems), and the organizational performance benefits which derive from good health. In a Guide produced by the UK's CIPD and Mind, mental ill health was reported as costing UK employers £26 billion per year, including £8.4 billion sickness absence, and £15.1 billion in reduced productivity (Chynoweth 2012). It is often claimed that the benefits from health promotion programmes include improved staff retention, higher levels of productivity and output, and contribute to the creation of a positive corporate image, helping to build the brand as a good employer. There are problems in establishing the direct and causal relationships between these programmes and performance. Some studies have sought to show measurable benefits, for example the Towers Watson (2012a) research in which it is claimed that companies with low engagement of employees produced a margin of 10 per cent, whereas organizations with high levels of employee engagement had operating margins of 27 per cent. Employee well-being interventions such as Employee Assistance Programmes (EAPs provide help and advice to employees confidentially on issues that are of concern to them) and good working conditions may well be found in those organizations with higher engagement levels, but this does not, of course, prove a causal relationship. There is also the ever present problem of reverse causality – better off companies can afford more expensive HR policies, for example.

Much has been written concerning organizational and individual resilience as a way to cope with crises positively (Heifetz and Bennis 2003). We have examined organizational agility in Chapter 5, and there is no doubt that many companies have sought the individual competencies associated with resilience, including the capacity to improvise, and to be courageous and optimistic. The resolution to the issues of well-being must commence with an understanding by managers of how to create a sense of well-being among employees. Techniques for coping with stressful environments have also been described, such as programmes on skills, for example mediation techniques, time management, and relaxation approaches, meditation, and muscle relaxation (Sidle 2008). Organizations also sometimes provide 'quiet rooms', where people can go to 'de-stress' (MacLachlan 2011).

In recent years, there has developed a wider interest in the happiness of the population as a whole in countries such as the UK, USA, France, and one of the first to take a State interest – Bhutan. The national surveys of populations in these countries are often intended as some kind of 'audit' as in the French Social Audit, and in the UK where Prime Minister David Cameron is interested in research on what the people of the UK think about economic and social changes and their reactions to government policies. In her review of research into happiness at work, Fisher (2010) analysed the concept at three levels: the transient level (task enjoyment, emotion at work, intrinsic motivation, momentary affect), the person level (job satisfaction, dispositional affect, affective organizational commitment, engagement), and at the unit level (morale, group affective tone, group task satisfaction).

Fisher went on to describe from the literature the causes of happiness in organizations, which include job design and work design processes, such as work scheduling, the degree of autonomy, task significance and task variety, feedback from the job itself, and opportunities for personal control, skill use, physical security, supportive supervision, career outlook, and equity. It is interesting to note that many researchers in the field can see that employee well-being is best understood at a number of levels. In all cases as described in the models of stress, the individual level is always from the perceptions of the individual, and there are also perceptions at the organization level, where the HR function has policies, and the work group level, where supervisors and line managers have considerable influence. At the wider organization level, Fisher described the actions which could be taken to increase happiness, in what we have defined as the organizational climate or culture, which she suggested should, according to the literature, aim to be healthy, respectful, and supportive of the culture, with competent leadership, fair treatment, and jobs designed to give the incumbents autonomy, feedback as a part of the job, and which provide challenging and interesting work.

In order to understand how HR management can decide on the most appropriate level for managers to make interventions for improving mental well-being at work, Doherty and Tyson (1998) constructed a framework which is focused on the depth of intervention, rather than on the levels in the organization structure so often found in the literature. The purpose of the framework is to develop managers in order that they can make the depth of response to mental well-being issues which will produce the desired outcomes. The levels start with the official policies which represent the

APPROACH	DESCRIPTION	LEVEL OF RESPONSE	DEPTH OF RESPONSE
An HR Policy Approach	Espoused policies, formal documented instructions	At cognitive level	M E N T A L
A Problem Centred Approach	Deeper interpersonal perceptions based on knowledge values and beliefs	At pragmatic behavioural level	
A Positive Attitude Approach	Overall philosophy of proactive mental health improvement, accent on preventative policies	At broad organizational level of organizational culture and ideology	W E L L
An Employee Centred Approach	Empathetic understanding of employee's personal condition and reasons for their attitudes and emotions	At emotional level and at level of personal identity	B E I N G

Figure 13.2 A framework for development of an educational approach to managers

company policies that impact on work behaviours, and then progress deeper to produce more sustained effects across the organization, until managers are able to take an employee centred approach. The view taken was that individual issues of well-being are frequently a sign of wider organizational problems, and although there may be pragmatic solutions to immediate issues, to ensure the problems do not continue to emerge at a later time, it is often necessary to go beyond the individual, that is to a wider and deeper solution.

The framework in Figure 13.2 shows four types of approach to helping employees to improve their sense of well-being at work, which produce different levels of response, addressing different needs and situations, and which have an additive effect.

The HR policy level approach is the level where existing official policies are invoked, such as Employee Assistance Programmes, anti-bullying policies, and whistle-blowing policies as a normal part of the employment terms, which are designed to appeal at the reasoned, cognitive level. The logical solution and preset response from the policy will determine the behaviour adopted, it is thought. These include those policies which influence the working environment, on health and safety, and on physical well-being.

The problem centred approach applies pragmatic problem solving to people issues, designed to influence behaviour. Here, managers need a deep understanding of interpersonal behaviour, including the capacity to understand and to interpret employees' behaviours and attitudes, as well as being able to analyse the problem sufficiently to be able to provide a solution, for example, through job redesign or through training to improve performance. The accent is on seeking to enhance problem solving skills of both employees and supervisors, and to ensure managers are able to counsel individuals, using non-directive counselling and similar techniques which help people to solve their own problems, by helping them to discover what their own part is in the problem, and how to change their perception of the problem in order to resolve the issue.

A positive attitude approach sets out an overall philosophy of management, and takes an active role to improve employee well-being. The accent is on 'wellness', in an active way, through programmes designed to overcome health problems such as smoking, high blood pressure, high cholesterol – consistent with the overall philosophy of proactive mental health improvements, supporting the values and the employer brand, which these programmes reinforce. A good example here is the rise in outcome based incentives to encourage participation and the achievement of improved health outcomes in the USA. These programmes were encouraged by the Patient Protection and Affordable Care Act (2010). Financial incentives are given for specific health outcomes, such as reduced blood pressure, or lower cholesterol, with average incentive values of $460. In 2012, 59 per cent of employers used monetary incentives to promote participation, an increase from 37 per cent of employees in 2011 (SHRM 2012d).

The employee centred approach views work from the perspective of the employee, rather than purely from the perspective of management. Management's task is to develop their staff, through coaching and mentoring, and to build on the positive attitude approach so that employees can possess a sense of self-efficacy, and the confidence to be innovative and fully engaged. This is seen as an accepted aspect of managerial work, directly connected to corporate success. An example of this type of approach is cognitive behavioural training (CBT), which was used by a large insurance company to improve employee well-being, job satisfaction, productivity, and labour turnover (Proudfoot *et al.* 2009). 'The program was designed to help employees evaluate and, where indicated, change their work-related thoughts, attitudes and behaviours, and specifically to assess the accuracy and functionality of attributions they made for work-related events' (p. 147). Through a rigorous evaluation, considerable improvements were seen against a waiting list control group, in attribution style, psychological distress, self-esteem, job satisfaction, and intention to quit, as well as productivity improvements.

Conclusions

We have considered both the main factors which affect employee well-being, and the causes and the likely consequences. This led us to outline evidence of the impact of the twin forces of failing competitiveness and recession, which have combined in a mixture which is too strong for many employees, who have found themselves losing their sense of well-being and perhaps their future prosperity as individuals and families, in the midst of unemployment, uncertainty, work intensification, falling real wages, and changed circumstances.

All of the models which affect employee well-being have common factors, such as job design, psychological adjustment, and a belief in work futures. These are employee perceptions of these factors, on which attitudes and actions are formed. These are as insubstantial as the projected values and beliefs of private sector and public sector organizations unless they are turned into actions and events. Hence, to create organizational cultures, policies have to be acted upon, and managers need to reveal in actions the corporate beliefs for these to be put into effect. The necessary pre-condition for health and well-being to be brought into play as a positive lever for achievement for employees and for organizations comes from decisive management action to make it happen.

However, the important and necessary first step is to show companies and public sector organizations the productivity and agility benefits found from improving employees' sense of well-being. We have proposed a four level approach to deciding the appropriate interventions managers, including HR managers, can make. The four level framework, including the employee centred approach, can be applied to all levels of employees, all occupational groups, and all sizes of organizations. These approaches are intended to build a strong resilient workforce, as a pre-condition to high organizational performance. Building self-awareness and adaptability are mutually dependent; these attributes stem from mutual respect, and clarity of personal and corporate identity. The organization climate or culture and the basic policies do need to be in place, and managers and supervisors need to be developed and able to use the policies and to understand their part in achieving the mission through their staff. We described in earlier chapters the significance of a strong organizational culture when we outlined how agility allows organizations to adjust to changes in market conditions rapidly and with least disruption, so that they can remain competitive in the changed scenarios they face. In this chapter we have shown how well-being should be a part of that cause.

14 Conclusions

Evolution, devolution, or revolution?

> Companies need to rethink the critical characteristics and competencies of their future leaders to create a pipeline to lead successfully in a very different world.
>
> Towers Watson's *Global Workforce Study* (2012b)

We were driven to write this book by the unique nature of the period in which we are all living and working. Over the past 30 years, the working world has changed dramatically due to technological, social, economic, and institutional trends that have affected both employees' and employers' values and lives. More recently, the global economic downturn and resulting impacts on business and the labour market have added to this shifting context. This means that we have experienced change on an unprecedented scale. Our purpose in this book was to examine the impact of this dramatically changing context on human resource management (HRM). We have undertaken this by identifying a number of contemporary trends in HRM (for example, talent management) and by examining the relationship of the evolution of such trends to the external context in which organizations are operating. In addition, we have examined how particular aspects of the working context, namely the need to work across international borders and the increased diversity within the workforce, have affected people management. We saw this as an exceptional opportunity to examine HRM at a distinctive time in its history that is both exciting, but also characterized by uncertainty as HR practitioners struggle to keep up with the changing context and prove their value within organizations and societies that are also trying to adapt to the evolving environment.

We started this journey by examining in some detail the changing characteristics of the context in which HR operates. This has provided us with a basis on which to investigate how social, institutional, and economic forces shape HRM. In this analysis we have drawn on both the resource based view (Penrose 1959; Barney 1991) and on institutionalism and neo-institutionalism (DiMaggio and Powell 1983). Research linking HRM to the RBV (see for example Wright *et al.* 2001) has suggested that the adoption of people management practices is linked primarily to the need to create competitive advantage for the firm. However, other authors (for example Paauwe and Boselie 2003) proposed that the context in which an organization operates is actually more important. We have adopted a combination of these views, suggesting that, in order to develop HR systems and processes that promote competitive advantage for the firm, it is important for HR practitioners and line managers to shape their activities to the contextual environment. As discussed in the introduction to this text, organizational effectiveness and competitive advantage are dependent on organizational agility and capacity to change, through the development of dynamic capabilities.

Throughout this text we have discussed the three institutional forces proposed by DiMaggio and Powell (1983) as affecting the adoption of organizational practices, these being mimetic, normative, and coercive mechanisms. We have followed this approach in suggesting that legal institutions and laws, societal norms, demographic trends, religious institutions, and cultural traditions exert influence on organizational agents to adopt particular HRM and other management practices, for example, CSR, talent management, and total rewards. This view has been used extensively in comparing HRM across countries as discussed in Chapter 7 and also in looking at the diffusion of new organizational practices, such as new technologies. However, we suggest that the development of HRM over time is also dependent on these factors. We have shown that all of the factors suggested above have changed dramatically, in the Western world at least, over recent years, and that this in turn has influenced the nature of HRM.

It is against the context of both economic changes and changes to the social landscape in relation to technology, demographics, and individuals' values that HR practitioners are operating. In this environment, people must be managed in such a way to ensure that organizations maintain the skills and capabilities to function effectively, to be competitive, or to provide public services efficiently. Those in the HR function are required to address and take advantage of longer term and dynamic changes in technology, such as the move towards web 2.0, social media, and mobile technology. Technology can often be used to manage people effectively across international borders as well as managing diversity within their own organization, and to operate within the limitations of an increasing amount of employment legislation. All of these changes have made the environment in which HR has to work more complicated and therefore resulted in increased complexity in the nature of the HR role itself.

There have also been economic changes that have a significant impact on an organization's needs for HRM. At the societal level the economic crisis, the failure of public institutions, and the problems of how to deal with these have led to an increased emphasis on areas such as CSR. We have seen the EU and banking regulators worldwide struggle to stabilize the Euro and deal with debt. In the UK, the public sector has been restructured, businesses have closed, and there have been attempts to revitalize manufacturing. In both the UK and USA, governments have attempted to reduce public expenditure. The economic downturn has had an enormous effect on organizations worldwide and has led to increased uncertainty in both the private and public sectors and a reduction in perceived job security. This is a sudden change from the booming economy experienced by most of the Western world in the first few years of the twenty-first century and is therefore a shock to both employers and to employees. The consequences for employees such as redundancy and uncertainty, on top of existing trends towards work intensification, has led to increased stress levels, feelings of isolation, and low levels of employee engagement (as discussed in our chapter on employee well-being). One strategy that employers can adopt to respond to this environment is by attempting to encourage employee engagement and the adoption of organizational citizenship type behaviours. Approaches to achieving this have included the use of total rewards, market segmentation of reward policies, talent management, and the use of the employer value proposition to attract and retain employees.

The nature of the economic changes and of the emergence of high performing economies in the Far East, coinciding with the weakness of Western economies, is a game changer. Organizations are also challenged by the longer term economic changes due to the rise of the BRIC countries and other emerging economies. Chapter 3 highlighted the need for companies in Europe and the USA to compete against these emerging economies and to be responsive to changes in the external environment, particularly to these dramatic changes in the economy. This means that the HR function is now at the forefront in helping the company to develop the dynamic capabilities, particularly leadership and change management competencies, that improve the company's competitive posture. In the current climate, the key to growth for companies might come from international development and collaboration. The emphasis is therefore on enhancing organizational capability that can cope with uncertainty, for example learning capability and enhancing organization development.

Against this backdrop, the structure of organizations is also changing in order to deal with the more complex environment and the need to be flexible and agile. We have seen the emergence of matrix structures, boundaryless organizations, networked structures, outsourcing, and generally an increased complexity and looseness of the way in which firms are organized. These changes also present challenges for the HR function in dealing with new ways of working, and creating an organizational culture that promotes innovation and flexibility.

In reaction to this context of constant and ongoing change, we have seen the management of people morph in a number of ways. We call these evolution, devolution, and revolution.

Evolution

Change within the HR function is nothing new. We have previously seen HRM develop from industrial relations, employee relations, and personnel management. In this way, HRM has always been evolving. In Chapter 5 we discussed the evolution of the HR role in some detail. We suggested that the emergence of HRM as opposed to personnel management in the 1980s was in itself a reaction to the organizational context. This change accompanied an increased emphasis on the strategic management of people within organizations in order to drive competitive advantage for the firm. This represented a change from different foci in early conceptualizations of HRM: on trade unions in industrial relations and on employee relationships in employee relations.

We could suggest that the evolution of HRM has continued with the current emphasis on 'talent management' and by adopting the concept of human capital. These two concepts can also be said to emerge from the changing environment and priorities within organizations: we have discussed for instance how talent management arose from an environment in which employers needed to address the scarcity of high quality skilled employees in the 1990s. Indeed, as we discussed in Chapter 10, some authors have suggested that talent management is merely another iteration of HRM rather than representing a completely unique approach to managing people. Human capital emerged from a focus, particularly in the USA, on the financial and economic outcomes of HRM. Over the past ten years, the emphasis has been on strategic HRM – an approach that involves the integration of the HR function into strategic decision making and an emphasis on managing people in a way that supports long term business goals (see, for example, Tichy *et al.* 1984; Purcell 1995; Schuler and Jackson 2005; Lepak and Shaw 2008).

We can therefore suggest that some of the changes that we see in HRM are a continued evolution of the HR function and role. Certainly, the longer term contextual trends that we have discussed, such as increased diversity within the workforce and technological advancements such as web 2.0, mobile, and Cloud technology could be said to drive the evolution of HRM practice in the long term. We have discussed in some detail in this text the impact of technological advancements, the need to work across national borders, increased diversity, and pressure for organizations to be socially responsible on HRM. All of these represent significant long term changes within the external environment that have had resulting permanent and ongoing impacts on managing people. We have seen from our earlier discussion that the HR function has been forced to change the way in which it works in response to these contextual trends. Employers have widely adopted e-HRM and are using social media and mobile technology in areas such as recruitment, communication and collaboration, and training and development. We have seen that organizational responses to increased diversity within the workforce have themselves evolved from equality approaches to diversity management and inclusion. Finally, we have discussed the need to address differences in cultural and institutional characteristics when operating across national contexts, and for multinational corporations to consider sometimes complicated organizational structures in order to balance global standardization with the need to adapt to the local context. These requirements for HRM are all relatively new and will continue to change as technological advancement and globalization themselves evolve. These underlying trends will continue irrespective of the more immediate changes to the economy.

Technological advancement and globalization might actually be said to increase the speed of evolution and change in HRM by facilitating the spread of new ideas and techniques. Technology and globalization therefore support the impact of mimetic and normative isomorphic influences moving more quickly.

Devolution

We have mentioned above that one of the evolving trends in HRM is the perceived need for the HR function to be strategic. Indeed, much attention in recent years has focused on the need for the HR function to have some involvement in the development and delivery of business strategy and to act as a strategic partner to the business (Ulrich 1997). The increased involvement of the HR function in strategic decision making has often been associated with the removal of operational or transactional HR activity from the HR function onto others, usually line managers (Kirkpatrick *et al.* 1992; Hales 2005; Francis and Keegan 2006; Morley *et al.* 2006). The proposal is that the freeing up of HR specialists from transactional or administrative activity allows them time to focus on more strategic activity. We therefore see the evolution of the HR function's role as associated with the devolution of HR activity to actors other than HR practitioners. Line managers are responsible for activities such as employee engagement and training and development as part of their role. One of the reasons that devolution is a growing trend is that organizations have become more aware of the need to create cultures that support organizational change and agility – line managers have an important role in this development. For instance, employee engagement and identifying the needs for training and development are two ways in which this role is discharged. It is important that employees learn new skills in order to facilitate organizational change – this means that line managers also have an important role in wider organizational development.

We have suggested in this text that, in addition to line managers, transactional HR activity might also be removed from a specialist HR function via the use of HR outsourcing (see Chapter 5) or via the use of e-HRM (see Chapter 6). Indeed, our analysis in Chapter 6 suggests that e-HRM might be used as an alternative to the devolution of HR activity to line managers.

The assumption in the strategic HRM literature is that such devolution allows HR specialists to focus on more strategic activity and therefore to move into a business partner role. Whether this is the case is an important question. Our investigation in Chapter 6 suggests that the use of e-HRM, at least, might enable the HR function to become more efficient, effective, and to play a more strategic role in the organization. However, we have also demonstrated that this is not necessarily the case – whether e-HRM can facilitate a change in the orientation of the HR function is dependent on other factors such as the existing role of the HR function and the skills and engagement of both HR and non-HR employees.

Revolution

Our chief conclusion from this discussion is that the shift in HRM resulting from the changing external context is not limited only to the evolution and devolution described above. In fact, we suggest that there has been a more fundamental change in the basis of HRM, a revolution if you like. The demands placed on the HR function as a result of the changing external context have meant that the HR function has been forced to change the way in which it works. There is evidence that the HR function has struggled to keep up with the changing context, since HR practitioners within individual organizations are potentially reliant on mimetic and normative isomorphic influences in order to design and develop their policies and practices, rather than taking a more evidence based approach to developing HR policies and practices.

HR no longer has the opportunity to evolve over time as it has done historically from industrial relations to personnel management and employee relations, to HRM. Rather, the HR function is 'dragged' along by the need to keep up with the context. We have seen for instance that technology is advancing at a pace that is faster than HR can absorb. As the HR function and HR consultancies develop effective ways to utilize web 2.0, social media, and mobile technology, the technology itself moves beyond these platforms. Even those organizations that might be described as pioneering in the use of technology for recruitment, training and development, communication, and other HR activities, are being forced to play 'catch-up'. We have also seen in Chapter 10 that HR practitioners feel that they do not have the opportunity to embed talent management systems fully before they need to be changed in order to keep up with changing talent needs and advances in talent management practice. This is a symptom of the external environment evolving more quickly than HRM practice can manage. As a result of this, we see that many HR departments are constantly undergoing transformation exercises in order to keep up with best practice and with competitors.

We have also shown that a recent trend in HRM practice is its reliance on expertise from other disciplines. In Chapter 11, we discussed the increasing overlap between the HR and marketing functions. The fact that HRM has adopted marketing concepts in order to attract, engage, and retain employees can be seen as a direct reaction to the contextual condition of increased competition for labour. It is interesting however that HR turned to the experience of a different organizational function in order to address this problem. We now see HR practitioners drawing on expertise from outside of HRM and being forced to work closely with other departments. We have suggested the need for the HR function to work in association with the IT department in order to develop e-HRM solutions. We might also see a need for the HR function to work with strategists in order to be able to inform the development of and to implement business strategy, and with finance experts in order to assess the financial and economic value of HR activity. This is interesting, as, while we see the HR function itself breaking up into different specialist departments such as recruitment, talent management, training and development, etc., described by Tyson (1987) as the balkanization of HR, our discussion here suggests that we also see a disintegration of the barriers between different specialist functions and a reduction in 'siloed' working as departments are forced to work more closely together. A question posed by this text is whether, in the future, we will see groups of specialists in areas of HRM (for example, recruitment) from across organizational functions, therefore changing the way in which organizations are organized.

We suggest that this revolution in HRM practice has not yet gone far enough, therefore what is needed is an HR function that is flexible, agile, and resilient, and more fully integrated with the line. Organizational agility comes from close identification with the marketplace. We have yet to really see this being achieved in practice by the HR function. There is no such thing as business as usual since the economic downturn, and in order to address the new challenges that we have described, take advantage of the opportunities that present themselves, and to adapt to the longer term changes in the external context, firms and the HR departments within them need to be agile.

Heathfield (2013) defined an agile organization as one that could adapt readily to changing contexts and customer demands; can innovate rapidly and tailor products and services to customer needs. Indeed, as discussed in Chapter 4, many organizations have restructured in order to promote flexibility and agility (for example, networked and matrix structures, outsourcing, and virtual teams). Paradoxically, agile organizations need strong cultures which provide the 'glue', the accepted norms and behaviours based on common values to enable the high level of responsiveness to the marketplace and customers' demands. The HR function not only needs to support the organization in recruiting, motivating, and retaining agile people and in creating the systems and structures to adapt as an organization, but also needs to develop the above characteristics. Therefore an agile HR department needs to be able to create systems which facilitate improvisation, intelligent analysis of changing customer needs, producing changes within the organization and reacting to the external environment; adapting to the demands of the workforce and senior managers (their internal customers); and creating a workforce that provides the capabilities that such an agile and competitive organization needs. It is in these capabilities that the success of HRM lies in the future.

Bersin Associates (2013) suggest that agile HR departments have the following characteristics: they balance current and future needs when planning

HR staffing; invest in improving performance of the HR group; continuously evaluate HR performance; embed few or no layers of authority within the HR function; use technology to house or share information; optimize HR resources to maximize efficiency; and predict changes that are likely to occur affecting the HR group. Bersin Associates (2013) went on to suggest that the key to HR agility is in allowing HR practitioners the time to focus on strategic HR issues rather than being occupied by transactional and administrative tasks. We see here an alignment between the future requirements for an agile HR function and the increased devolution discussed above. A focus on strategic issues might be achieved via the removal of transactional and administrative activities to line managers, to technological and e-HRM solutions, or to HR outsourcing. In this way, devolution and revolution go hand in hand.

While some trends in HRM will continue to evolve, and other, apparent fashions (e.g. talent management) will become longer term necessities, the emphasis moving forward will be on flexibility and agility. The answer for the HR function is not to try to adapt to each change as it comes along as has happened so far, but about to create an HR system and organizational culture that allows the organization and HR practice to adapt and learn readily as contextual change occurs.

Throughout this text, we have discussed and built upon the themes that we introduced in the introductory chapter to this book. We have emphasized the need for organizations to develop dynamic capabilities and organizational agility so that they can adapt readily to contextual change. This applies to all forms of contextual change – both the longer term evolving changes such as technological advancement and increased diversity of the workforce, and the more sudden changes such as the economic downturn. The current operating environment is characterized by uncertainty, caused primarily by the economic context – this is problematic for any organization that is not agile and flexible. We have discussed the removal of HR activities, particularly those of a transactional and operational nature, to line managers and also to HR outsourcing providers and e-HRM. This devolution is linked ultimately to the changing role of HRM, and the pressure on HR practitioners to perform a more strategic and business partnering role within organizations. The removal of the burden of HR administration might allow the HR department to become closer to the business and therefore to play a more central role in identifying and developing the dynamic capabilities that the organization needs.

In the second part of this text, as well as discussing changes to the HR role, we also focused on two broad contextual changes that have a profound effect on the way that HRM is undertaken: the rapid development of technology, particularly the Internet, and the need to manage HRM in an increasingly international context, with diverse populations. We pick up the theme of diversity in our third part, where we consider the effects on policy of context. Increased diversity of the workforce means a growing need to differentiate between the preferences and values of different employees and thus moves us towards the individualization of the psychological contract. This need has commonly been addressed through HRM activities such as talent management, total rewards, and the use of concepts such as the employer brand and employer value proposition to attract and retain employees. These are HR policy areas that have evolved as a direct reaction to both labour market conditions and the changing values of the workforce.

It is difficult to predict what will come next for organizations and for HRM. After all, few people would have predicted that an economic downturn of the scale experienced since 2008 would have occurred. It is for this reason that we have chosen to emphasize the importance of agility and dynamic capabilities for the HR function and broader organization. We can predict that competition for labour will continue (albeit under differing constraints, depending on the economic context) and that it will be important to engage with employees and align their values with those of the organization in order to produce a competitive advantage for the firm. We have also suggested here that the way that HRM activity is structured within an organization is changing – with people management activities no longer the remit of only the HR department but being designed by multidisciplinary specialist teams and undertaken by line managers, with the support of e-HRM and HRO providers. There is no doubt: HRM actors need to analyse the external environment and be cognizant of contextual changes in order to be able to continue to be of value to the organization and to employees.

References

Abegglen, J. and Stalk, G. (1985) *Kaissha: The Japanese Corporation*, New York: Basic Books.

About.com (2012) *Single Parents*, www.singleparents.about.com [20 February 2013].

Ackermann, K.F. (1986) 'A contingency model of HRM strategy: Empirical research findings reconsidered', *Management Forum*, 13(6): 65–83.

Alas, R., Kaarselson, T., and Niglas, K. (2008) 'Human resource management in culture context: Empirical study of 11 countries', *EBS Review*, 1: 49–61.

Aldridge, H., Kenway, P., MacInnes, T., and Parekh, A. (2012) *Monitoring Poverty and Social Exclusion*, York: Joseph Rowntree Foundation and the New Policy Institute.

Ambler, T. and Barrow, S. (1996) 'The employer brand', *Journal of Brand Management*, 4(3): 185–206.

Ambrosini, V. and Bowman, C. (2009) 'What are the dynamic capabilities and are they a useful construct in strategic management?', *International Journal of Management Reviews*, 11(1): 29–49.

Armstrong, C., Flood, P., Guthrie, J., Liu, W., MacCurtain, S., and Mkamwa, T. (2010) 'The impact of diversity and equality management on firm performance: Beyond high performance work systems', *Human Resource Management*, 49: 977–98.

Armstrong, M. and Brown, D. (2005) 'Reward strategies and trends in the United Kingdom: The land of diverse and pragmatic dreams', *Compensation and Benefits Review*, 37: 41–53.

Armstrong-Stassen, M. (2008) 'Organisational practices and post-retirement employment experience of older workers', *Human Resource Management Journal*, 18: 36–53.

Arthur, C. (2011) 'Tablet use up during mornings and evenings', *The Guardian Online*, 19 November 2011.

Arthur, J. (1992) 'The link between strategy and industrial relations systems in American steel mini mills', *Industrial and Labor Relations Review*, 45(3): 488–506.

Arthur, J.B. and Boyles, T. (2007) 'Developing the human resource system structure: A levels-based strategic HRM framework', *Human Resource Management Review*, 17: 77–92.

Arthur, M. and Rousseau, D.B. (1996) *The Boundaryless Career: A New Employment Principle for a New Organizational Era*, New York: Oxford University Press.

Ashkenas, R., Ulrich, D., Jick, D., and Herr, S. (1995) *The Boundaryless Organization*, San Francisco: Jossey-Bass.

Astbury Marsden (2012) *Report on Job Prospects*, www.gotorecruitment.co.uk [25 March 2013].

Aston, C. and Morton, L. (2005) 'Managing talent for competitive advantage', *Strategic HR Review*, 4: 28–31.

Aston, L. (2013) 'Time to address engagement deficit', *People Management* [Online], 7 January, www.peoplemanagement.co.uk/pm/ [7 January 2013].

Aurand, T.W., Gorchels, L., and Bishop, T.R. (2005) 'Human resource management's role in internal branding: An opportunity for cross-functional brand message synergy', *Journal of Product and Brand Management*, 14(2/3): 163–9.

Axelrod, B., Handfield-Jones, H., and Michaels, E. (2002) 'A new game plan for C players', *Harvard Business Review*, January: 8–88.

Backhaus, B. and Tikoo, S. (2004) 'Conceptualising and researching employer branding', *Career Development International*, 9(4/5): 501–17.

Baden-Fuller, C. (1995) 'Strategic innovation, corporate entrepreneurship and matching outside-in to inside-out approaches to strategy research', *British Journal of Management*, 6: S3–S16.

Bak, C.A., Vogt, L.H., George, W.R., and Greentree, I.R. (1994) 'Management by team: An innovative tool for running a service organisation through internal marketing', *Journal of Services Marketing*, 8(1): 37–47.

Baker, E., Israel, B.A., and Schurman, S. (1996) 'The integrated model. Implications for worksite health', *Health Education Quarterly*, 23: 175–90.

Bakker, R.M. (2010) 'Taking stock of temporary organizational forms: A systematic review and research agenda', *International Journal of Management Reviews*, 12(4): 466–86.

Balain, S. and Sparrow, P. (2009) *Engaged to Perform: A New Perspective on Employee Engagement. White Paper 2009–04*, www.lums.lancs.ac.uk/research/centres/hr/whitepapers/ [1 December 2012].

Balmer, J. (1995) 'Corporate branding and connoisseurship', *Journal of General Management*, 21(1): 24–47.

Barney, J. (1991) 'Firm resource and sustained competitive advantage', *Journal of Management*, 17(1): 99–120.

Barney, J.B., Wright, P., and Ketchen, Jr., D.J. (2001) 'The resource based view of the firm: Ten years after 1991', *Journal of Management*, 27(6): 625–41.

Bartlett, C. and Ghoshal, S. (1989) *Managing Across Borders*, London: Hutchinson Business.

Bateson, J.E.G. (1991) *Managing Services Marketing*, Fort Worth, TX: The Dryden Press.

Batt, R. and Colvin, A. (2011) 'An employment systems approach to turnover: Human resource practices, quits, dismissals and performance', *The Academy of Management Journal*, 54: 695–717.

BBC Online (2010) 'UK ethnic minority numbers to rise to 20% by 2051', www.bbc.co.uk/news/10607480 [20 February 2013].

BBC Online (2013) 'Migration watch warning on Romania and Bulgaria immigration', www.bbc.co.uk/news/uk-21039087 [20 February 2013].

Bentham, M. (2011) 'UK ethic population has risen to 40 per cent in the last eight years', www.standard.co.uk [20 February 2013].

Berl, P. (2006) 'Crossing the generational divide', *Exchange*, March/April: 73–8.

Berry, L.L. (1980) 'Services marketing is different', *Business*, 30(3): 24–30.

Berry, L.L. and Parsuraman, A. (1991) *Marketing Services: Competing Through Quality*, New York: The Free Press.

Bersin Associates (2013) 'Enabling HR agility', www.bersin.com [22 February 2013].

Bird, A., Taylor, S., and Beechler, S. (1998) 'A typology of international human resource management in Japanese multinational corporations', *Human Resource Management*, 37: 159–72.

Bondarouk, T., Ruel, H., and van der Heijen, B. (2009) 'e-HRM effectiveness in a public sector organization: A multi-stakeholder perspective', *International Journal of Human Resource Management*, 20: 578–90.

Boon, C., Paauwe, J., Boselie, P., and Den Hartog, D. (2009) 'Institutional pressures and HRM: Developing institutional fit', *Personnel Review*, 38: 492–508.

Borney-Barrachina, M., De la Rosa-Navarro, D., Lopez-Cabrales, A., and Valle-Cabrera, R. (2012) 'Employment relationships and firm innovation: The double role of human capital', *British Journal of Management*, 23(2): 223–40.

Boselie, P., Dietz, G., and Boon, C. (2005) 'Commonalities and contradictions in HRM and performance research', *Human Resource Management Journal*, 15(3): 67–94.

Botero, J., Djankov, S., La Porta, R., Lopez-de-Silanes, S., and Shleifer, A. (2004) 'The regulation of labor', *Quarterly Journal of Economics*, 119: 1339–82.

Bowey, A.M. and Thorpe, R. (with Hellier, P.) (1986) *Payment Systems and Productivity*. Basingstoke: Macmillan.

Bowman, C. and Ambrosini, V. (2000) 'Value creation versus capture: Towards a coherent definition of value in strategy', *British Journal of Management*, 11: 1–15.

Boxall, P. (1995) 'Building the theory of comparative HRM', *Human Resource Management Journal*, 5(5): 5–17.

Boxall, P. (1998) 'Achieving competitive advantage through human resource strategy: Towards a theory of industry dynamics', *Human Resource Management Review*, 8(3): 265–88.

Boxall, P. and Purcell, J. (2011) *Strategy and Human Resource Management*, Basingstoke: Palgrave Macmillan.

Boxall, P., Ang, S.H., and Bartram, T. (2011) 'Analysing the "black box" of HRM: Uncovering HR goals, mediators and outcomes in a standardized service environment', *Journal of Management Studies*, 48(7): 1504–32.

Boyne, G.A. and Meier, K.J. (2009) 'Environmental change. Human resources and organizational turnaround', *Journal of Management Studies*, 46(5): 835–63.

Brewster, C. (1995) 'Towards a European model of human resource management', *Journal of International Business Studies*, First Quarter: 1–21.

Brewster, C. (1999) 'SHRM: The value of different paradigms', *Management International Review*, 39: 45–64.

Brewster, C. and Bournois, F. (1991) 'Human resource management: A European perspective', *Personnel Review*, 20: 4–13.

Brewster, C. and Mayrhofer, W. (2012) 'Comparative human resource management: An introduction', in eds. C. Brewster and W. Mayrhofer, *Handbook of Research on Comparative Human Resource Management*, Cheltenham: Edward Elgar, pp. 1–23.

Brewster, C., Mayrhofer, W., and Morley, M. (2004) *Human Resource Management in Europe: Evidence of Convergence?* Oxford: Elsevier.

Brewster, C., Sparrow, P., and Harris, H. (2007) 'Towards a new model of globalising HRM', *International Journal of Human Resource Management*, 16: 949–70.

Brewster, C., Wood, G., and Brookes, M. (2008) 'Similarity, isomorphism or duality: Recent survey evidence on the HRM policies of multinational corporations', *British Journal of Management*, 19: 320–42.

Brexendorf, T. and Kernstock, J. (2007) 'Corporate behaviour vs. brand behaviour: Towards an integrated view', *Brand Management*, 15(1): 32–40.

Briscoe, D., Schuler, R., and Tarique, I. (2012) *International Human Resource Management: Policies and Practices for Multinational Enterprises*, New York: Routledge.

Brookes, M., Croucher, R., Fenton-O'Creevy, M., and Gooderham, P. (2011) 'Measuring competing explanations of human resource management practices through the Cranet survey: Cultural versus institutional explanations', *Human Resource Management Review*, 21: 68–79.

Buchanan, D., Parry, E., Gascoigne, C., and Moore, C. (2013) 'Are healthcare middle management jobs extreme jobs?', *Journal of Health Organization and Management*, 27(5).

Budhwar, P.S. and Sparrow, P.R. (2002) 'An integrative framework for determining cross-national human resource management practices', *Human Resource Management Review*, 12: 377–403.

Burbach, R. and Dundon, T. (2005) 'The strategic potential of human resource information systems: Evidence from the Republic of Ireland', *International Employment Relations Review*, 11: 97–117.

Burns, T. and Stalker, G.M. (1961) *The Management of Innovation*, London: Tavistock.

Cable, D.M. and Graham, M. (2000) 'The determinants of organizational reputation: A job search perspective', *Journal of Organizational Behaviour*, 21: 475–82.

Cable, D.M. and Turban, D.B. (2003) 'The value of organizational image in the recruitment context: A brand equity perspective', *Journal of Applied Social Psychology*, 33: 2244–66.

Caligiuri, P., Lepak, D., and Bonache, J. (2010) *Managing the Global Workforce*, Chichester, UK: John Wiley and Sons.

Calo, T.J. (2008) 'Talent management in the era of the ageing workforce: The critical role of knowledge transfer', *Public Personnel Management*, 37(4): 403–16.

Cappelli, P. (2008a) *Talent on Demand: Managing Talent in an Uncertain Age*, Boston, MA: Harvard Business School Press.

Cappelli, P. (2008b) 'Talent management for the 21st century', *Harvard Business Review*, 86: 74–81.

Career Builder (2012) *Report on Percentage of Workers Living Pay Check to Pay Check*, Virginia, USA: SHRM.

Carlson, H. (2004) 'Changing of the guard', *The School Administrator* [Online], August, https://www.aasa.org/SchoolAdministratorArticle.aspx?id=14030&terms=changing+the+guard [25 March 2013].

Carroll, A.B. and Shabana, K.M. (2010) 'The business case for corporate social responsibility: A review of concepts, research and practice', *International Journal of Management Reviews*, 12(1): 85–105.

Carter, T. (1998) 'Legge and the problems of his time', in eds. R. McCraig and M. Harrington, *The Changing Nature of Occupational Health*, London: HSE Books, pp. 25–38.

Cartwright, S. and Holmes, N. (2006) 'The meaning of work: The challenge of regaining employee engagement and reducing cynicism', *Human Resource Management Review*, 16(2): 199–208.

Caudron, S. (1997) 'Can Generation Xers be trained?', *Training and Development*, 51: 20–4.

Certification Officer (2012) *Annual Report of Certification Officer*. London: HMSO.

CET Euronews (2012) www.euronews.com [31 December 2012].

Chambers, E., Foutlon, M., Handfield-Jones, H., Hankin, S., and Michaels III, E. (1998) 'The war for talent', *McKinsey Quarterly*, 4: 44–58.

Chandler, A. (1962) *Strategy and Structure: Chapters in the History of American Enterprise*, Cambridge, MA: MIT Press.

Chapman, J. and Kelliher, C. (2011) 'Influences on reward mix determination: Reward consultants' perspectives', *Employee Relations*, 33(2): 121–39.

Choi, J.N. (2009) 'Collective dynamics of citizenship behaviour: What group characteristics promote group-level helping', *Journal of Management Studies*, 46: 1396–420.

Chynoweth, C. (2012) 'Irrational fear', *People Management*, March: 43–48.

CIA Factbook (2013) https://www.cia.gov/library/publications/the-world-factbook/index.html [16 February 2013].

CIPD (2009) *The War on Talent? Talent Management under Threat in Uncertain Times*, London: CIPD.

CIPD (2011) *Talent Forward: Tackling the New Global Talent Realities*, London: CIPD.

CIPD (2012) *Annual Absence Management Report*, in partnership with Simplyhealth, October. Wimbledon: CIPD.

Claes, R. and Heymans, M. (2008) 'HR professionals' views on work motivation and retention of older workers: A focus study', *Career Development International*, 13: 95–111.

Collings, D. and Mellahi, K. (2009) 'Strategic talent management: A review and research agenda', *Human Resource Management Review*, 19: 304–13.

Collins, B. and Payne, A. (1991) 'Internal marketing: A new perspective for HRM', *European Management Journal*, 9(3): 261–70.

Collins, C.J. and Stevens, C.K. (2002) 'The relationship between early recruitment-related activities and the application of decisions of new labour market entrants: A brand-equity approach to recruitment', *Journal of Applied Psychology*, 87(6): 1121–33.

Conference Board (2012) *Feeling the Pain: Wage Growth in the United States during and after the Great Depression*, www.conference-board.org/publications/publicationdetail.cfm?publicationid=2182 [25 March 2013].

Conyon, M.J., Peck, S., and Sadler, G.V. (2001) 'Corporate tournaments and executive compensation: Evidence from the UK', *Strategic Management Journal*, 22: 805–15.

Cooper, C.L. and Cartwright, S. (1994) 'Healthy mind; healthy organisations: A proactive approach to occupational stress', *Human Relations*, 47: 455–71.

Cox, T. and Ferguson, E. (1994) 'Work environment and occupational health model', *Work and Stress*, 8: 98–109.

Cox, T., Leather, P., and Cox, S. (1990) 'Stress, health and organisations', *Occupational Health Review*, February/March: 13–18.

Cox, T.H. and Blake, S. (1991) 'Managing cultural diversity: Implications for organizational competitiveness', *Academy of Management Executive*, 5: 45–56.

Cranet (2009) www.cranet.org [16 February 2013].

Creelman, D. (2004) *What is Talent Management*, www.terraforum.com.br [9 June 2012].

Croucher, R., Tyson, S., and Wild, A. (2006) 'Peak employers' organisations: International attempts at transferring experience', *Economic and Industrial Democracy*, 27(3): 463–84.

Daniels, K. (2000) 'Measures of five aspects of affective well-being at work', *Human Relations*, 53: 275–94.

Danna, K. and Griffin, R.W. (1999) 'Health and well-being in the workplace: A review and synthesis of the literature', *Journal of Management*, 25: 357–84.

Davis, F. (1989) 'Perceived usefulness, perceived ease of use and user acceptance of information technology', *MIS Quarterly*, 13: 319–40.

Davis, N.J. (2005) 'Cycles of discrimination: Older women, cumulative disadvantages and retirement consequences', *Journal of Education Finance*, 31(1): 65–81.

DeJoy, D.M. and Southern, D.J. (1993) 'An integrated perspective on worksite health promotion', *Journal of Occupational Medicine*, 35: 1221–30.

Delery, J. (1998) 'Issues of fit in strategic human resource management: Implications for research', *Human Resource Management Review*, 8(3): 289–309.

Delery, J.E. and Doty, D. (1996) 'Modes of theorising in strategic human resource management, tests of universalistic, contingency and configurational performance predictions', *Academy of Management Journal*, 39(4): 802–35.

DelVecchio, D., Jarvis, C.B., Klink, R.R., and Dineen, B.R. (2007) 'Leveraging brand equity to attract human capital', *Marketing Letters*, 18: 149–64.

Denyer, D., Parry, E., and Flowers, P. (2011) ' "Social", "open" and "participative"? Exploring personal experiences and organisational effects of enterprise 2.0 use', *Long Range Planning*, 44: 375–96.

Dewettinck, K. and Remue, J. (2011) 'Contextualising HRM in comparative research: The role of the Cranet Network', *Human Resource Management Review*, 21: 37–49.

Dickmann, M. (2003) 'Implementing German HRM abroad: Desired feasible, successful?', *International Journal of Human Resource Management*, 14: 265–83.

Dickmann, M. (forthcoming) 'International human resource management', in eds. T. Redman and A. Wilkinson, *Contemporary Human Resource Management*, London: Prentice Hall.

Dickmann, M. and Baruch, Y. (2011) *Global Careers*, Abingdon: Routledge.

Dickmann, M. and Müller-Camen, M. (2006) 'A typology of international human resource management strategies and processes', *International Journal of Human Resource Management*, 17: 580–601.

DiMaggio, P.J. and Powell, W.W. (1983) 'The iron cage re-visited. Institutional isomorphism and collective rationality in organizational fields', *American Sociological Review*, 48: 147–69.

Docusign (2012) *Survey Reported in PM Daily HR Update*. CIPD. news@email. peoplemanagement.co.uk.

Doherty, N. (2002) 'Mental well-being in the workplace: Building the business case', in eds. D.M. Miller, M. Lipsedge, and P. Litchfield, *Work and Mental Health – An Employer's Guide*, London: Gaskill Publishing, pp. 28–33.

Doherty, N. and Tyson, S. (1993) *Executive Redundancy and Outplacement*, London: Kogan Page.

Doherty, N. and Tyson, S. (1998) *Mental Well-being in the Workplace – A Resource Pack*, Norwich: HMSO.

Du, S., Battacharya, C.B., and Sen, S. (2010) 'Maximizing business returns to corporate social responsibility (CSR): The role of communications', *International Journal of Management Reviews*, 12(1): 8–19.

Duncan, C. and Loretto, W. (2004) 'Never the right age? – gender and age-based discrimination in employment', *Gender, Work and Organization*, 11: 95–115.

Dunlop, J.T. (1970) *Industrial Relations Systems*, Carbondale: Southern Illinois Press.

Dyer, L. (1984) 'Studying human resource strategy', *Industrial Relations*, 23(2): 186–309.

Dyer, L. and Shafer, R. (1989) *From Human Resource Strategy to Organizational Effectiveness: Lessons from Research on Organizational Agility'*, CAHRS Working Paper No. 98.12. Ithaca, NY: Cornell University, School of Industrial and Labor Relations, Center for Advanced Human Resource Studies.

Dyer, L. and Shafer, R. (1999) 'Creating organisational agility: Implications for strategic human resource management', in eds. P. Wright, L. Dyer, J. Boudreau, and G. Milkovitch, *Research in Personnel and Human Resource Management. Supplement 4. Strategic Human Resource Management in the Twenty-first Century*, Stanford, CT: JAI Press, pp. 145–74.

Dyer, L. and Schafer, R. (2003) 'Dynamic organizations: Achieving market place and organizational agility', in eds. R.S. Peterson and E.A. Mannix, *Leading and Managing People in Dynamic Organisations*, Mahwah, NJ: Lawrence Erbaum Associates, pp. 7–40.

Easterby-Smith, M. and Prieto, I.M. (2008) 'Dynamic capabilities and knowledge management; An integrative role for learning', *British Journal of Management*, 19(3): 235–49.

Economist Intelligence Unit (2007) *Serious Business: Web 2.0 Goes Corporate*, London: EIU.

Edwards, M.R. (2010) 'An integrative review of employer branding and OB theory', *Personnel Review*, 39(1): 5–23.

Edwards, T. and Kuruvilla, S. (2005) 'International HRM: National business systems, organizational politics and the international division of labour in MNCs', *International Journal of Human Resource Management*, 16: 1–21.

Emery, F. and Trist, E. (1965) 'The causal textures of organisational environments', *Human Relations*, 18: 21–32.

EORY'S ENTR06/054 (2011) *Study on the Cost Competitiveness of European Industry in the Globalisation Era and Empirical Evidence on the Basis of Relative Unit Labour Costs (ULC) at Sectoral Level. Final Report.* DG Enterprise. Netherlands: EORY.

Eurostat (2010) www.epp.eurostat.ec.europa.eu [16 February 2013].

Falch, M. (2004) *A Study on Practical Experiences with Using e-learning Methodologies and Cooperative Transnational Development Methodology*. CTI Working Paper No. 97. Center for Tele-Information.

Farndale, E. and Paauwe, J. (2007) 'Uncovering competitive and institutional drivers of HRM practices in multinational corporations', *Human Resource Management Journal*, 17: 355–75.

Farndale, E., Paauwe, J., Morris, S.S., Stahl, G.K., Stiles, P., Trevor, J., and Wright, P.M. (2010) 'Context bound configurations of corporate HR functions in multinational corporations', *Human Resource Management*, 49: 45–66.

Fawcett Society (2012) *Are Women Bearing the Burden of the Recession?* www.fawcettsociety.org.uk [16 February 2013].

Ferner, A. (1997) 'Country of origin effects and HRM in multinational companies', *Human Resource Management Journal*, 7: 19–36.

Ferner, A., Tregaskis, O., Edwards, P., Marginson, P., Adam, D., and Meyer, M. (2011) 'HRM structures and subsidiary discretion in foreign multinationals in the UK', *International Journal of Human Resource Management*, 22: 483–509.

Ferris, G.R., Hochwarter, W.A., Buckley, M.N., Harrell-Cook, G., and Frink, D. (1999) 'Human resources management: Some new direction', *Journal of Management*, 25: 385–418.

Filella, J. (1991) 'Is there a Latin model in the management of human resources?', *Personnel Review*, 20: 15–24.

Filipczak, B. (1994) 'It's just a job: Generation X at work', *Training*, 31: 21–7.

Fisher, C.D. (2010) 'Happiness at work', *International Journal of Management Reviews*, 12: 384–412.

Fiske, R.P., Brown, S.W., and Bitner, M.J. (1993) 'Tracking the evolution of the services marketing literature', *Journal of Retailing*, 69(1): 61–103.

Flamholtz, E.G. and Lacey, J.A. (1981) *Personnel Management, Human Capital Theory and Human Resource Accounting*, Los Angeles: University of California, Institute of Industrial Relations.

Florowski, G. and Olivas-Lujan, M. (2006) 'The diffusion of human resource information technology innovations in US and non US firms', *Personnel Review*, 35: 684–710.

Foster, B. and Cadogan, J. (2000) 'Relationship selling and customer loyalty: An empirical investigation', *Marketing Intelligence and Planning*, 18(4): 185–99.

Fox, A. (1966) *Industrial Sociology and Industrial Relations*. Research Paper 3 of Royal Commission on Trade Unions and Employers Associations. London: HMSO.

Francis, H. and Keegan, A. (2006) 'The changing face of HRM: In search of balance', *Human Resource Management Journal*, 16(3): 231–49.

Friedman, T.L. (2005) *The World is Flat*, London: Penguin Books.

Gardner, S., Lepak, D., and Bartol, K. (2003) 'Virtual HR: The impact of information technology on the human resource professional', *Journal of Vocational Behavior*, 63: 159–79.

Gardner, T.M., Moynihan, L.M., Park, H.J., and Wright, P.M. (2001) *Beginning to Unlock the Black Box in the HR Firm Performance Relationship: The Impact of HR Practices on Employee Attitudes and Employee Outcomes*, New York: CAHRS, Cornell University, Working Paper 1–12.

Garrow, V. and Hirsch, W. (2008) 'Talent management issues of focus and fit', *Public Personnel Management*, 37(4): 389–402.

Gerhart, B. (2008) 'Cross-cultural management research: Assumptions, evidence and suggested directions', *International Journal of Cross-Cultural Management*, 8: 259–74.

Gerhart, B. and Fang, M. (2007) 'National culture and human resource management: Assumptions and evidence', *International Journal of Human Resource Management*, 16: 971–86.

Gerhart, B. and Rynes, S.L. (2003) *Compensation Theory, Evidence and Strategic Implications*, Thousand Oaks, CA: Sage.

Giancola, F. (2009) 'Is total reward a passing fad?', *Compensation and Benefits Review*, 4: 24–35.

Giddens, A. (1991) *The Consequences of Modernity*, Stanford, CA: Stanford University Press.

Gilleard, C. (2004) 'Cohorts and generations in the study of social change', *Social Theory and Health*, 2: 106–19.

Gingerbread (2012) *Statistics*, www.gingerbread.org.uk [20 February 2013].

Girard, A. and Fallery, B. (2009) *Human Resource Management on the Internet: New Perspectives*, Paper presented at the Third International Workshop of Human Resource Information Systems, Milan, Italy.

Gooderham, P.N. and Nordhaug, O. (2003) *International Management: Cross Boundary Challenges*, Oxford: Blackwell.

Goold, M. and Campbell, A. (1987) *Strategies and Styles: The Role of the Centre in Managing Diversified Corporations*, Oxford: Blackwell.

Gordon, S. (2006) 'Rise of the blog', *IEE Review*, 52: 32.

Greenberg, J. (1990) 'Organizational justice: Yesterday, today and tomorrow', *Journal of Management*, 16: 399–432.

Guest, D.E. (1987) 'Personnel and HRM; can you tell the difference?', *Personnel Management*, 21(1): 48–51.

Guest, D.E. and Peccei, R. (1994) 'The nature and causes of effective human resource management', *British Journal of Industrial Relations*, 32(2): 219–42.

Gummesson, E. (1990) 'Making relationship marketing operational', *International Journal of Service Industry Management*, 5: 5–20.

Gunnigle, P., Murphy, K., Cleveland, J., Heraty, M., and Morley, M. (2001) 'Human resource management practices of U.S. owned multinational corporations in Europe: Standardization versus localization?', *Advances in International Management*, 14: 259–84.

Gupta, V., Hanges, P.J., and Dorfman, P. (2002) 'Cultural clusters: Methodology and findings', *Journal of World Business*, 37: 11–23.

Hales, C. (2005) 'Rooted in supervision, branching into management: Continuity and change of the role of first-line manager', *Journal of Management Studies*, 42(3): 471–506.

Hall, C. (2013) 'Obama's White House – the diversity question', *Los Angeles Times*, 10 January 2013.

Hall, D.T. and Mirvis, P. (1996) 'The new protean career: Psychological success and the path with a heart', in ed. D.T. Hall, *The Career is Dead – Long Live the Career*, San Francisco: Jossey-Bass, pp. 1–12.

Hall, D.T. and Moss, J.E. (1998) 'The new protean career contract: Helping organizations and employees adapt', *Organizational Dynamics*, 26: 22–37.

Hall, P.A. and Gingerich, D.W. (2004) *Varieties of Capitalism and Institutional Complementarities in the Macroeconomy*. MPIfG Discussion paper 04/5. Berlin: Max Planck Institut fur Gesellschaftsforschung.

Hall, P.A. and Soskice, D. (2001) *Varieties of Capitalism: The Institutional Foundations of Comparative Advantage*, Oxford: Oxford University Press.

Hall, P.A. and Soskice, D. (2009) 'An introduction to *Varieties of Capitalism*', in ed. B. Hancke, *Debating Varieties of Capitalism*, Oxford: Oxford University Press, pp. 21–74.

Hamel, G. (2000) *Leading the Revolution*, Harvard, MA: Harvard Business School Press.

Hancke, B. (2009) 'Introducing the debate', in ed. B. Hancke, *Debating Varieties of Capitalism – A Reader*, Oxford: Oxford University Press, pp. 1–20.

Handel, M.J. (2003) *Implications of Information Technology for Employment, Skills and Wages: A Review of Recent Research*. SRI Project Number P10168. Arlington, WA: SRI International.

Handy, C. (1989) *The Age of Unreason*, Boston: Harvard Business School.

Harris, L., Foster, C., and Sempik, A. (2011) 'Employers' policies for third age employment – the case for action and the rationale for reaction', CIPD Conference, 24 June, Keele University.

Harrison, D.A., Price, K.H., Gavin, J.H., and Florey, A.T. (2002) 'Time, teams and task performance: Changing effects of surface and deep level diversity on group functioning', *Academy of Management Journal*, 45(2): 1029–45.

Harrison, D.A., Mohammed, S., McGrath, J.E., Florey, A.T., and Vanderstoep, S.W. (2003) 'Time matters in team performance: Effects of member familiarity, entrainment and task discontinuity on speed and quality', *Personnel Psychology*, 56: 633–69.

Harrison, R. (1987) *Organisation Culture and Quality of Service: A Strategy for Releasing Love in the Workplace*, London: Association for Management Education and Development.

Harzing, A.W. and Sorge, A.M. (2003) 'The relative impact of country of origin and universal contingencies on internationalization strategies and corporate control in multinational enterprises: World-wide and European perspectives', *Organisation Studies*, 24(2): 187–214.

Hathcock, B.C. (1996) 'The new-breed approach to 21st century human resources', *Human Resource Management*, 35(2): 243–50.

Hatum, A. (2010) *Next Generation Talent Management: Talent Management to Survive Turmoil*, Basingstoke: Palgrave Macmillan.

Heathfield, S.M. (2013) *Are you Ready for an Agile Future?* www.humanresources.about.com [22 February 2013].

Heifetz, R. and Bennis, W. (2003) *Harvard Business Review on Building Personal and Organizational Resilience*, Harvard, MA: HBR Paperback Series.

Hendrickson, A.R. (2003) 'Human resource information systems: Backbone technology of contemporary human resources', *Journal of Labor Research*, 24(3): 381–94.

Henkel, S., Tomczak, M., Heitmann, M., and Herrmann, A. (2007) 'Managing brand consistent employee behaviour: Relevance and managerial control of behavioural branding', *Journal of Product and Brand Management*, 16(5): 310–20.

Hennan, D.A. and Perlmutter, H.V. (1979) *Multinational Organizational Development*, Reading, MA: Addison-Wesley.

Herzberg, F., Mausner, B., and Snyderman, B. (1959) *The Motivation to Work*, New York: Wiley.

Heskett, J.L., Jones, T.O., Loveman, G.W., Sasser, W.E., and Schlesinger, L. (1994) 'Putting the service–profit chain to work', *Harvard Business Review*, 72(2): 164–74.

Hewlett, S.A. and Luce, C.B. (2006) 'Extreme jobs: The dangerous allure of the 70 hour workweek', *Harvard Business Review*, 84: 49.

Hieronimus, F., Schaefer, K., and Schroder, J. (2005) 'Using branding to attract talent', *The McKinsey Quarterly*, 3: 12–14.

High Pay Commission Report (2011) *Cheques with Balances: Why Tackling High Pay is in the National Interest*, London: High Pay Commission.

Hinchcliffe, D. (2009) *Enterprise Web 2.0*, http://blogs.zdnet.com/Hinchcliffe [29 November 2009].

Hofstede, G. (1980) *Culture's Consequences: International Differences in Work-related Values*, Beverly Hills, CA: Sage.

Hofstede, G. (1991) *Culture and Organizations: Software of the Mind*, London: McGraw-Hill.

Hofstede, G. (1993) 'Cultural constraints in management theories', *Academy of Management Executive*, 7: 81–93.

Hofstede, G. (1996) *Culture's Consequences: International Differences in Work-related Values*, Newbury Park, CA: Sage.

Hofstede, G. (1997) *Cultures and Organisations: Software of the Mind*, London: McGraw-Hill.

Hofstede, G. (2001) *Culture's Consequences: Comparing Values, Behaviours, Institutions and Organization Across Nations*, London: Sage Publications.

Hogg, M.A., Van Kippenberg, D., and Rast, D.E. (2012) 'Intergroup leadership in organizations: Leading across group and organizational boundaries', *Academy of Management Review*, 37: 232–55.

Hoover, J.N. (2007) 'Wells Fargo taps web 2.0 – financial services firm is using blogs, wikis and even Second Life's virtual world to connect employees and customers', *Wall Street & Technology*, 25: 25.

Hope Hailey, V., Searle, R., and Dietz, G. (2012) 'How trust helps', *People Management*, March: 30–6.

House, R.J. and Javidan, M. (2004) 'Overview of GLOBE', in eds. R.J. House, P.J. Hanges, M. Javidan, P.W. Dorfman, and V. Gupta, *Culture, Leadership and Organisations, The GLOBE Study of 62 Societies*, Thousand Oaks, CA: Sage, pp. 9–48.

Howell, C. (2003) 'Varieties of capitalism: And then there was one?', *Comparative Politics*, 36(1): 103–24.

Hudson, M., Phillips, J., Ray, K., and Barnes, H. (2007) *Social Cohesion in Diverse Communities*, York: Joseph Rowntree Foundation.

Hulberg, J. (2006) 'Integrating corporate branding and sociological paradigms: A literature study', *Brand Management*, 14(1/2): 60–73.

Humphrys, J. (2008) 'Virtual nightmare', *Daily Mail*, 5 January 2008.

IDS (2008a) 'McDonald's top reward menu', *IDS Executive Compensation Review*, 325: 11–13.

IDS (2008b) 'Getting into the talent mindset at Yahoo!', *IDS Executive Compensation Review*, 328: 10–12.

IDS (2008c) 'Making performance-related pay work at KPMG', *IDS Executive Compensation Review*, 327: 11–13.

IDS (2012a) 'Planning for reward in 2013', *IDS Pay Report*, 1105: October.

IDS (2012b) *The Director's Pay Report 2011/2012*. Incomes Data Services, London.

IEG (2013) 'Über sponsorship: Break the mold and shape the future', Annual Sponsorship Conference, April 2013, Chicago, IL.

Ignjatovic, M. and Svetlik, I. (2003) 'European HRM clusters', *EBS Review*, 17: 25–39.

ILO (2010) www.ilo.org [16 February 2013].

Jackson, S. and Schuler, R. (1987) 'Organisational strategy and organisational level as determinants of human resource management practices', *Human Resource Planning*, 10: 125–41.

Janson, R. (2012) 'Failing wage costs: Europe's light at the end of the tunnel?', *Social Europe Journal* [Online], www.social-europe.eu/2012/08/falling-wage-costs-europes-light-at-the-end-of-the-tunnel/ [February 2013].

Jensen, M.C. and Meckling, W.H. (1976) 'Theory of the firm: Managerial behaviour, agency costs and ownership structure', *Journal of Financial Economics*, 3: 305–60.

Johnson, G., Scholes, K., and Whittington, R. (2008) *Exploring Corporate Strategy*, London: Financial Times/Prentice Hall.

Johnson, L., Smith, R., Willis, H., Evine, A., and Haywood, K. (2011) *The 2011 Horizon Report*, Austin, TX: The New Media Consortium.

Karucz, E., Colbert, B., and Wheeler, D. (2008) 'The business case for corporate social responsibility', in eds. A. Crane, A. McWilliams, D. Matten, J. Moon, and D. Siegel, *The Oxford Handbook of Corporate Social Responsibility*, Oxford: Oxford University Press, pp. 83–112.

Kavanagh, M.J., Gueutal, H., and Tannenbaum, S. (1990) *Human Resource Information Systems: Development and Application*, Boston, MA: PWS Kent Publishing Company.

Kell, E. (2012) 'Manufacturing's great salary divide', *HR Magazine*, November: 41–5.

Kelliher, C. and Richardson, J. (2012) 'Recent developments in new ways of working', in eds. C. Kelliher and J. Richardson, *New Ways of Organizing Work: Developments, Perspectives and Experiences*, New York: Routledge, pp. 1–15.

Kerr, S. (1975) 'On the folly of rewarding A while hoping for B', *Academy of Management Journal*, 18(4): 769–83.

Khan, W.A. (1990) 'Psychological conditions of personal engagement at work', *Academy of Management Journal*, 33(4): 692–724.

Kijkuit, B. and Van den Ende, J. (2007) 'The organizational life of an idea: Integrating social network, creativity and decision-making perspectives', *Journal of Management Studies*, 44(6): 863–82.

Kim, J., York, K.M., and Lim, J.S. (2011) 'The role of brands in recruitment: A mixed-brand strategy approach', *Marketing Letters*, 22: 165–79.

Kim, K.H., Jeon, B.J., Jung, J.H.S., Lu, W., and Jones, J. (2012) 'Effective employment brand equity through sustainable competitive advantage, marketing strategy and corporate image', *Journal of Business Research*, 65: 1612–17.

King, S. (1991) 'Branding building in the 1990s', *The Journal of Consumer Marketing*, 8(4): 43–52.

Kirkman, B.L., Lowe, K.B., and Gibson, C.B. (2006) 'A quarter century of culture's consequences: A review of empirical research incorporating Hofstede's cultural values framework', *Journal of International Business Studies*, 37: 285–320.

Kirkpatrick, L., Davis, A., and Oliver, N. (1992) 'Decentralisation: Friend or foe of HRM', in eds. P. Blyton and P. Turnbull, *Reassessing Human Resource Management*, London: Sage, pp. 131–48.

Kirton, G. and Greene, A. (2009) 'The costs and opportunities of doing diversity work in mainstream organisations', *Human Resource Management Journal*, 2: 174.

Kivimaki, M., Nyberg, S.T., Batty, G.D., and Fransson, E.I. (2012) 'Job strain as a risk factor for coronary heart disease: A collaborative analysis of individual participant data', *The Lancet*, 380(9852): 1491–7.

Kotler, P. (1991) *Marketing Management: Analysis, Planning, Implementation and Control*, Englewood Cliff, NJ: Prentice Hall.

Kotter, J.P. (1973) 'The psychological contract', *California Management Review*, 15: 91–9.

Kumar, N., Stern, L., and Anderson, J. (1993) 'Conducting interorganizational research using key informants', *Academy of Management Journal*, 36: 1633–51.

Kupperschmidt, B. (2000) 'Multigenerational employees: Strategies for effective management', *The Healthcare Manager*, 19: 65–76.

Lai, L.S. and Turban, E. (2008) 'Groups formation and operations in the Web 2.0 environment and social networks', *Group Decision and Negotiation*, 17: 387–403.

Larsen, H. and Brewster, C. (2000) 'Human resource management', in eds. C. Brewster and H. Larsen, *Human Resource Management in Northern Europe*, Oxford: Blackwell Business.

Larsen, H. and Brewster, C. (2003) 'Line management responsibility for HRM: What is happening in Europe?', *Employee Relations*, 25: 228–44.

Lawler, E. and Boudreau, J.W. (2012) 'Creating an effective human capital strategy', *HR Magazine*, August: 57–9.

Lawler, E. and Mohrman, S. (2003) 'HR as a strategic partner: What does it take to make it happen?', *Human Resource Planning*, 20: 37–47.

Lawrence, P. (1993) 'Human resource management in Germany', in eds. S. Tyson, P. Lawrence, P. Poirson, L. Manzolini, and C.S. Vincente, *Human Resource Management in Europe*, London: Kogan Page, pp. 25–41.

Lawrence, P.R. and Lorsch, J.W. (1967) *Organisational and Environment: Managing Differentiation and Integration*, Boston, MA: Graduate School of Business, Harvard University.

Lazarova, M., Morley, M., and Tyson, S. (2012) 'International comparative studies in HRM and performance – the Cranet data', in eds. M. Lazarova, M. Morley, and S. Tyson, *International Human Resource Management: Policy and Practice*, Abingdon: Routledge, pp. 1–9.

Lazear, E.P. and Rosen, S. (1981) 'Rank order tournament as an optimal labor contract', *Journal of Political Economy*, 89: 841–64.

Le, H. (2007) *The Importance of Diversity to the American Society*, www.helium.com [16 February 2013].

Lee, M.P. (2008) 'A review of the theories of corporate social responsibility: Its evolutionary path and the road ahead', *International Journal of Management Reviews*, 10(1): 53–73.

Legge, K. (1995) *Human Resource Management – Rhetorics and Realities*, Basingstoke: Macmillan.

Legge, K. (2000) 'The ethical context of HRM: The ethical organisation in the boundaryless world', in eds. D. Winstanley and J. Woodall, *Ethical Issues in Contemporary Human Resource Management*, Basingstoke: Macmillan Press, pp. 23–40.

Lepak, D.P. and Shaw, J. (2008) 'Strategic HRM in North America: A look to the future', *International Journal of Human Resource Management*, 19(8): 1486–99.

Lepak, D.P. and Snell, S.A. (1998a) 'The human resource architecture: Towards a theory of human capital allocation and development', *Academy of Management Review*, 24: 31–8.

Lepak, D.P. and Snell, S.A. (1998b) 'Virtual HR: Strategic human resource management in the 21st century', *Human Resource Management Review*, 8: 215–34.

Lepak, D. and Snell, S.A. (1999) 'The strategic management of human capital: Determinants and implications of different relationships', *Academy of Management Review*, 24: 1–18.

Lepak, D. and Snell, S.A. (2002) 'Examining the human architecture: The relationships among human capital, employment and human resource configurations', *Journal of Management*, 28(4): 517–43.

Lertxundi, A. and Landeta, J. (2012) 'The dilemma facing multinational enterprises: Transfer or adaptation of their human resource management systems', *International Journal of Human Resource Management*, 23: 1788–807.

Levitt, T. (1983) 'The globalisation of markets', *Harvard Business Review*, May: 92–102.

Lewis, R.E. and Heckmann, R.J. (2006) 'Talent management: A critical review', *Human Resource Management Review*, 16: 139–54.

Libert, B. and Spector, J. (2008) *We are Smarter Than Me*, USA: Pearson Education.

Lings, I.N. (2000) 'Internal marketing and supply chain management', *Journal of Services Marketing*, 14(1): 27–43.

Lockett, A., Thompson, S., and Morgenstern, U. (2009) 'The development of the resource based view of the firm: A critical appraisal', *International Journal of Management Reviews*, 11(1): 9–28.

Lockwood, N.R. (2007) *Leveraging Employee Engagement for Competitive Advantage: HR's Strategic Role*, USA: Society for Human Resource Management.

Loretto, W. and White, P. (2006) 'Employers' attitudes and policies towards older workers', *Human Resource Management Journal*, 16: 313–30.

Loretto, W., Vickerstaff, S., and White, P. (2005) *Older Workers and Options for Flexible Work*. Working Paper Series No. 31. Equal Opportunities Commission.

LSE Growth Commission (2013) *Investing for Prosperity. Report of the LSE/IfG Growth Commission*. LSE Centre for Economic Performance, London.

Lyons, S., Duxbury, L., and Higgins, C. (2007) 'An empirical assessment of generational differences in basic human values', *Psychological Reports*, 101: 339–52.

McCafferty, F. (2003) 'The challenge of selecting tomorrow's police officers from Generations X and Y.', *American Academy of Psychiatry and the Law*, 88.

McDonnell, A., Lamare, R., Gunnigle, P., and Lavelle, J. (2010) 'Developing tomorrow's leaders – evidence of global talent management in multinational enterprises', *Journal of World Business*, 45: 150–60.

McDougall, M. (1998) 'Devolving gender management in the public sector: Opportunity or opt out?', *International Journal of Public Sector Management*, 11: 71–80.

MacGahan, A. (2000) 'How industries evolve', *Business Strategy Review*, 11(3): 1–16.

Macky, K. and Boxall, P. (2007) 'The relationship between high performance work practices and employee attitudes: An investigation additive and interaction effects', *International Journal of Human Resource Management*, 18(4): 537–67.

MacLachlan, R. (2011) 'Seek out an oasis of calm', *People Management*, December: 48–50.

McLeod, D. and Clarke, N. (2009) *Engaging for Success: Enhancing Performance through Employee Engagement*, www.bis.gov.uk [22 September 2012].

McVittie, C., McKinlay, A., and Widdicombe, S. (2003) 'Committed to (un)equal opportunities: "New ageism" and the older workers', *British Journal of Social Psychology*, 42: 595–612.

Malvin, S. and Girling, G. (2000) 'What is managing diversity and why does it matter?', *Human Resource Development International*, 3: 419–33.

Mannheim, K. (1952) 'The problem of generations', in ed. P. Kecskemeti, *Essays on the Sociology of Knowledge*, London: Routledge and Kogan Page, pp. 276–322.

Mannix, E. and Neale, M. (2005) 'What differences makes a difference? The promise and reality of diverse teams in organizations', *Psychological Sciences in the Public Interest*, 6: 31–55.

Manpower Group (2009) *The Global Talent Crunch: Why Employer Branding Matters Now?* www.manpowergroup.co.uk [10 February 2013].

Marks and Spencer Plan A (2013) http://plana.marksandspencer.com/ [7 March 2013].

Marler, J.H. (2009) 'Making human resources strategic by going to the Net: Reality or myth?', *International Journal of Human Resource Management*, 20: 515–27.

Martin, G. (2008) 'Employer branding and reputation management: A model and some evidence', in eds. C. Cooper and R. Burke, *Peak Performing Organizations*, Abingdon: Routledge, pp. 252–74.

Martin, G. and Beaumont, P. (2003) *Branding and People Management*, London: Chartered Institute of Personnel and Development.

Martin, G. and Hetrick, S. (2006) *Corporate Reputations, Branding and Managing People: A Strategic Approach to HR*, Oxford: Butterworth Heinemann.

Martin, G. and Reddington, M. (2010) 'Theorizing the links between e-HRM and strategic HRM: A model, case illustration and reflections', *International Journal of Human Resource Management*, 21: 1553–74.

Martin, G., Beaumont, P.B., Doig, R.M., and Pate, J.M. (2005) 'Branding: A new performance discourse for HR?', *European Management Journal*, 23: 76–88.

Martin, G., Reddington, M., and Kneafsey, M.B. (2009) *Web 2.0 and Human Resource Management: Groundswell of Hhype?* London: Chartered Institute of Personnel and Development.

Martin, G., Gollan, P., and Grigg, K. (2011) 'Is there a bigger and better future for employer branding? Facing up to innovation, corporate reputations and wicked problems in SHRM', *International Journal of Human Resource Management*, 22(17): 3618–37.

Martin-Alcazar, F., Romero-Fernandez, P.M., and Sanchez-Gardey, G. (2005) 'Strategic human resource management: Integrating the universalistic, contingent, configurational and contextual perspectives', *International Journal of Human Resource Management*, 16: 633–59.

Maxwell, R. (2010) *What Makes an Organisation's Corporate Identity Attractive to its Employees?*', Cranfield University, unpublished PhD Thesis.

Mayrhofer, W., Brewster, C., Morley, M.J., and Ledolter, J. (2011) 'Hearing a different drummer? Convergence of human resource management in Europe: A longitudinal analysis', *Human Resource Management Reviews*, 21(1): 50–67.

Meinert, D. (2011) 'Whistle-blowers: Threat or asset', *HR Magazine*, April: 27–32.

Mellahi, K. and Collings, D.G. (2010) 'The barriers to effective global talent management: The example of corporate elites in MNEs', *Journal of World Business*, 45: 143–9.

Michaels, E., Handfield-Jones, H., and Axelrod, B. (2001) *The Way for Talent*, Harvard, MA: Harvard Business School Press.

Migration Observatory (2012) *Immigration, Diversity and Social Cohesion*, www. migrationobservatory.ox.ac.uk [16 February 2013].

Miles, S. and Mangold, W. (2004) 'Conceptualisation of the employee branding process', *Journal of Customer Relationship Marketing*, 3(2/3): 65–87.

Ministry of Manpower (2003) *e-HR: Leveraging Technology. Case Study Series 2/2003*, www.employmenttown.gov.sg [16 February 2013].

Mintzberg, H. (1990) 'The design school: Reconsidering the basic premise of strategic management', *Strategic Management Journal*, 11: 171–95.

Mirza, B. (2011) 'Creative endeavours', *HR Magazine*, April: 34–8.

Monks, K. (2007) *The Business Impact of Equality and Diversity: The International Evidence*. The Equality Authority, National Centre for Partnership and Performance.

Morley, M., Gunnigle, P., O'Sullivan, M., and Collings, D. (2006) 'New directions in the roles and responsibilities of the HRM function', *Personnel Review*, 35(6): 609–17.

Moroko, L. and Uncles, M. (2008) 'Characteristics of successful employer brands', *Brand Management*, 16(3): 160–76.

Mosley, R. (2007) 'Customer experience, organisational culture and the employer brand', *Management*, 15: 123–34.

Mossholder, K.W., Richardson, A., and Setton, R.P. (2011) 'Human resource systems and helping in organisations: A relational perspective', *Academy of Management Review*, 36: 33–52.

Moyo, D. (2011) *How the West Was Lost*, London: Allen Lane-Penguin Group.

Muirhead, S.A., Bennett, C.J., Berenbeim, R.E., Kao, A., and Vidal, D.J. (2002) *Corporate Citizenship in the New Century: Accountability, Transparency and Global Stakeholder Engagement*, New York: The Conference Board.

Murphy, K.R. and Cleveland, J.N. (1995) *Understanding Performance Appraisal*, Thousand Oaks, CA: Sage.

Newman, K.L. and Nollen, S.D. (1996) 'Culture and congruence: The fit between management practices and national culture', *Journal of International Business Studies*, 27: 753–79.

Nijessen, M. and Paauwe, J. (2012) 'HRM in turbulent times: How to achieve organizational agility?', *International Journal of Human Resource Management*, 23(16): 3315–35.

Niven, M. (1967) *Personnel Management 1913–1963*, London: IPM.

Noland, J. and Phillips, R. (2010) 'Stakeholder engagement, discourse ethics and strategic management', *International Journal of Management Reviews*, 12(1): 39–99.

Norman, N. (2011) *Smartphones: A Smart Way Forward for Learning*, Brighton: Epic.

O'Cass, A. and Ngo, L.V. (2011) 'Examining the firm's value creation process: A managerial perspective of firm's value offering strategy and performance', *British Journal of Management*, 22: 646–71.

OECD (2007) *Offshoring and Employment Trends and Impacts*. Paris: OECD.

Olivas-Lujan, M., Ramirez, J., and Zapata-Cantu, L. (2007) 'e-HRM in Mexico: Adapting innovations for global competitiveness', *International Journal of Manpower*, 28: 418–34.

ONS (2008) *National Population Projections*, www.ons.gov.uk [1 March 2013].

ONS (2012a) www.ons.gov.uk [16 February 2013].

ONS (2012b, February) *Migration Statistics Quarterly Report*, www.ons.gov.uk/ons/rel/migration1/migration-statistics-quarterly-report.february-2012 [1 March 2013].

ONS (2012c) 'Gender pay gap falls to 9.6% in 2012', www.ons.gov.uk [16 February 2013].

Organ, D. (1988) *Organizational Citizenship Behaviour: 'The Good Soldier Syndrome'*, Lexington, MA: Lexington Books.

O'Toole, J. (1985) 'Employee practices at the best managed companies', *California Management Review*, XXXVIII(1): 35–66.

O'Toole, J. and Lawler, E.E. (2006) *The New American Workplace*, New York: Palgrave Macmillan.

Ozbilgin, M. and Tatli, A. (2011) 'Mapping out the field of equality and diversity: Rise of individualism and volunteerism', *Human Relations*, 64: 1229–53.

Paauwe, J. (2004) *HRM and Performance. Achieving Long-term Viability*, Oxford: Oxford University Press.

Paauwe, J. (2009) 'HRM and performance: Achievements, methodological issues and prospects', *Journal of Management Studies*, 46(1): 129–49.

Paauwe, J. and Boselie, P. (2003) 'Challenging strategic HRM and the relevance of the institutional setting', *Human Resource Management Journal*, 13: 56–70.

Paauwe, J. and Richardson, R. (1997) 'Introduction to special issue on HRM and performance', *International Journal of Human Resource Management*, 8: 257–62.

Paik, Y., Chow, I.H.S., and Vance, C.M. (2011) 'Interaction effects of globalization and institutional forces on international HRM practice: Illuminating the convergence-divergence debate', *Thunderbird Business Review*, 53: 647–59.

Panczuk, S. and Point, S. (2008) *Enjeux et outils du marketing RU. Promouvoir et vendre les resources humaines*, Paris: Eyrolles.

Pantouvakis, A. (2012) 'Internal marketing and the moderating role of employees: An exploratory study', *Total Quality Management and Business Excellence*, 23(2): 177–95.

Parry, E. (2011) 'An examination of e-HRM as a means to increase the value of the HR function', *International Journal of Human Resource Management*, 22: 1146–62.

Parry, E. and Harris, L. (2011) *The Employment Challenges of an Ageing Workforce*. ACAS Future of Workplace Relations Discussion Paper, www.acas.org.uk [25 March 2013].

Parry, E. and Tyson, S. (2007) *The UK Talent Report*, London: Capital Consulting.

Parry, E. and Tyson, S. (2009) 'Organisation reactions to UK age discrimination legislation', *Employee Relations*, 31: 471–88.

Parry, E. and Tyson, S. (2011) 'Desired goals and actual outcomes of e-HRM', *Human Resource Management Journal*, 21: 335–54.

Parry, E. and Urwin, P. (2010) *The Impact of Generational Diversity on People Management*, London: CIPD.

Parry, E. and Urwin, P. (2011) 'Generational differences in work values: A review of theory and evidence', *International Journal of Management Reviews*, 13: 79–96.

Parry, E. and Wilson, H. (2009) 'Factors influencing the adoption of online recruitment', *Personnel Review*, 38: 655–73.

Parry, E., Dickmann, M., and Morley, M. (2010) 'North American firms and their HR agenda in coordinated and liberal market economies', *International Journal of Human Resource Management*, 19: 2041–56.

Paul, R. and Townsend, J. (1993) 'Managing the older worker – don't just rinse away the gray', *The Academy of Management Executive*, 7: 67–74.

Peacock, L. (2013) 'More women on boards, but gender pay gap persists', www. telegraph.co.uk [16 February 2013].

Peel, Q. (2012) 'Merkel hints at cap on social spending', *Financial Times*, 17 December 2012.

Penrose, E.T. (1959) *The Theory of the Growth of the Firm*, New York: John Wiley.

Peretz, H. and Fried, Y. (2011) 'National cultures, performance appraisal practices and organizational absenteeism and turnover: A study across 21 countries', *Journal of Applied Psychology*, 97: 448–59.

Perlmutter, H.V. (1969) 'The torturous evolution of the multinational corporation', *Columbia Journal of World Business*, 4: 9–18.

Pew Research Center (2012) *The Lost Decade of the Middle Class*. Published 27 August. Washington DC: Pew Social and Demographic Trends.

Piercy, N.F. (1996) 'The effects of customer satisfaction measurement: The internal market vs. the external market', *Marketing Intelligence and Planning*, 14(4): 9–15.

Pitt, L.F. and Foreman, S.K. (1998) 'Internal marketing in organizations: A transaction-cost perspective', *Journal of Business Research*, 44: 25–36.

Pitt-Catsouphes, M., Sweet, S., and Lynch, K. (2009) *The Pressures of Talent Management*, www.bc.edu/research/agingandwork/projects/talentMgmt.html [29 May 2012].

Point, S. (2005) 'Accountability, transparency and performance: Comparing annual report disclosures on CEO pay across Europe', in eds. S. Tyson and F. Bournois, *Top Pay and Performance*, Oxford: Elsevier/Butterworth Heinemann, pp. 57–84.

Poole, M.S. and Van de Ven, A. (1989) 'Using paradox to build management and organisational theories', *Academy of Management Review*, 14(4): 562–78.

Powell, W.W. (1998) 'Institutional theory', in eds. C.L. Cooper and C. Argyris, *Concise Blackwell Encyclopedia of Management*, Oxford: Blackwell, pp. 301–3.

Prentice, G. (1990) 'Adopting management style for the organization of the future', *Personnel Management*, 22(6): 58–62.

Proudfoot, J.G., Corr, P.J., Guest, D.E., and Dunn, G. (2009) 'Cognitive behavioural training to change attributional style improves employee well-being, job satisfaction, productivity and turnover', *Personality and Individual Differences*, 46: 147–53.

Purcell, J. (1995) 'Corporate strategy and its links with human resource management strategy', in ed. J. Storey, *Human Resource Management: A Critical Text*, London: Routledge, pp. 63–86.

Rafiq, M. and Ahmed, P.K. (2000) 'Advances in the internal marketing concept: Definition, synthesis and extension', *Journal of Services Marketing*, 14: 449–62.

Remery, C., Henkens, K., Schippers, J., and Ekamper, P. (2003) 'Managing an aging workforce and a tight labor market: Views held by Dutch employees', *Population Research and Policy Review*, 22: 21–40.

Restubog, S.L.D., Hornsey, M.J., Bordia, P., and Esposo, S.R. (2008) 'Effects of psychological contract breach on organisational citizenship behaviour. Insights from the group value model', *Journal of Management Studies*, 45: 1377–400.

Reuters (2010) 'Chicago United survey shows impact of recent recession on diversity and inclusion', www.reuters.com [16 February 2013].

Reza, S., Javadin, S., Rayej, H., Yazdani, H., Esiri, M., and Aghamiri, S. (2012) 'How organizational citizenship behaviour mediates between internal marketing and service quality', *International Journal of Quality and Reliability Management*, 29(5): 512–30.

Rilla, N. and Squicciarini, M. (2011) 'R&D (Re)location and offshore outsourcing: A management perspective', *International Journal of Management Reviews*, 13(4): 393–413.

Ritzer, G. and Trice, H.M. (1969) *An Occupation in Conflict. A Study of the Personnel Manager*, Cornell: Cornell University Press.

Robinson, D., Perryman, S., and Hayday, S. (2004) *The Drivers of Employment Engagement*, Institute of Employment Studies, Report 408, Brighton.

Roden, M. and Williams, S. (2002) 'Individual and organizational stress', in eds. D. Miller, M. Lipsedge, and P. Litchfield, *Work and Mental Health. An Employers Guide*, London: Gaskell Publishing, pp. 47–52.

Roehling, M.V., Boswell, W., Caliguiri, P., Feldman, D., Graham, M., Guthrie, J., Morishima, N., and Tansky, J. (2005) 'The future of HR management. Research needs and directions', *Human Resource Management*, 44(2): 207–16.

Rokeach, M. (1973) *The Nature of Human Values*, New York: The Free Press.

Ronen, S. and Shenkar, O. (1988) 'Clustering variables: The application of nonmetric multivariate techniques in comparative management research', *International Studies of Management and Organizations*, 18(3): 72–87.

Rougeau, M. (2012) 'Smartphones and tablets account for more than 20% of US internet use', www.techrader.com/news [20 February 2013].

Rousseau, D.M. (1989) 'Psychological and implied contracts in organisations', *Employee Rights and Responsibilities Journal*, 2: 121–39.

Rousseau, D.M. (1995) *Psychological Contracts in Organizations: Understanding Written and Unwritten Agreements*, Thousand Oaks, CA: Sage.

Rousseau, D.M. and Ho, V.T. (2000) 'Psychological contract issues in compensation', in eds. S.L. Rynes and B. Gerhart, *Compensation in Organizations*, San Francisco: Jossey-Bass, pp. 273–310.

Roy, D. (1955) 'Efficiency and the fix: Informal intergroup relations in a piecework machine shop', *American Journal of Sociology*, 60: 255–66.

Rucci, A.J., Kirn, S.P., and Quinn, R.T. (1998) 'The employee-customer profit chain at Sears', *Harvard Business Review*, Jan–Feb: 83–97.

Ruch, W. (2000) 'How to keep Gen X employees from becoming x-employees', *Training and Development*, 54(4): 40–3.

Ruel, H., Bondarouk, T., and Loosie, J.K. (2004) 'e-HRM: Innovation or irritation? An explorative empirical study in five large companies on web-based HRM', *Management Review*, 15: 364–80.

Ruel, H., Bondarouk, T., and van der Vald, M. (2006) 'The contribution of e-HRM to HRM effectiveness', *Employee Relations*, 29: 280–91.

Saba, T. and Guerin, G. (2005) 'Extending employment in work attitudes and behaviour: The case of health care managers in Quebec', *Public Personnel Management*, 43: 195–214.

Saks, A.M. (2006) 'Antecedents and consequences of employee engagement', *Journal of Managerial Psychology*, 21(7): 600–19.

Sanchez-Hernandez, M.I. and Miranda, F.J. (2011) 'Linking internal market orientation and new service performance', *European Journal of Innovation Management*, 14(2): 207–26.

Schein, E. (1978) *Career Dynamics. Matching Individual and Organizational Needs*, Reading, MA: Addison-Wesley.

Scherer, A.G. and Palazzo, G. (2007) 'Toward a political conception of corporate responsibility: Business and society seen from a Habermasian perspective', *Academy of Management Reviews*, 32(4): 1096–120.

Schuler, R.S. (1992) 'Strategic human resource management: Linking the people with the strategic needs of the business', *Organizational Dynamics*, 21(1): 18–32.

Schuler, R.S. and Jackson, S.E. (1987) 'Linking competitive strategies with human resource management practices', *Academy of Management Executive*, 1(3): 207–19.

Schuler, R.S. and Jackson, S.E. (2005) 'A quarter-century review of human resource management in the US: The growth in importance of the international perspective', *Management Revue*, 16(1): 11–35.

Schuler, R.S. and Rogovsky, N. (1998) 'Understanding compensation practice variations across firms: The impact of national culture', *Journal of International Business Studies*, 29: 159–77.

Schuler, R.S. and Tarique, I. (2012) 'Global talent management: Theoretical perspectives and challenges', in eds. I. Bjorkman and G. Stahl, *Handbook of Research in International Human Resource Management*, London: Edward Elgar, pp. 205–19.

Schuler, R.S., Jackson, S.E., and Tarique, I. (2011) 'Global talent management and global talent initiatives: Strategic opportunities for IHRM', *Journal of World Business*, 46: 506–16.

Schultz, K.S. (2003) 'Bridge employment: Work after retirement', in eds. G.A. Adams and T.A. Beehr, *Retirement: Reasons, Processes and Results*, New York: Springer Publishing Company, pp. 214–41.

Schultz, M. and de Chernatony, L. (2002) 'The challenges of corporate branding', *Corporate Reputation Review*, 5(2/3): 105–12.

Schuster, J.R. and Zingheim, P.K. (1996) *The New Pay: Linking Employee and Organizational Performance*, San Francisco, CA: Jossey-Bass.

Schwartz, S.H. (1992) 'Universals in the content and structure of values: Theory and empirical tests in 20 countries', in ed. M. Zanna, *Advances in Experimental Social Psychology*, San Diego, CA: Academic Press, pp. 1–65.

Schwartz, S.H. (1994) 'Beyond individualism/collectivism: New dimensions of value', in eds. U. Kim, H.C. Triandis, C. Kagitcibasi, S.C. Choi, and G. Yoon, *Individualism and Collectivism: Theory Application and Methods*, Newbury Park, CA: Sage, pp. 85–122.

Schwartz, S.H. (2006) 'A theory of cultural value orientations: Explication and applications', *Comparative Sociology*, 5: 136–82.

Scullion, H. and Collings, D.G. (2010) 'Global talent management', *Journal of World Business*, 45: 105–8.

Scullion, H. and Collings, D.G. (2011) *Global Talent Management*, Oxford: Routledge.

Senge, P. (1990) *The Fifth Discipline*, London: Century Business.

Shepherd, J. (2011) 'Number of adults in England with poor numeracy rising', www. guardian.co.uk/education/2011 [20 February 2013].

Shrivastiva, S. and Shaw, J. (2004) 'Liberating HR through technology', *Human Resource Management*, 42: 201–22.

SHRM (2012a) *Employee Job Satisfaction and Engagement Report*. 3 October. Alexandria, VA: SHRM.

SHRM (2012b) *Survey Findings: Workplace Bullying*, www.shrm.org/research/ surveyfindings/articles/pages/workplacebullying.aspx [7 March 2013].

SHRM (2012c) *HR Knowledge Centre Report: Suicide in the Workplace*, www.shrm. org/hrinfo [7 March 2013].

SHRM (2012d) *Use of Monetary Incentives to Promote Wellness Grows*, www.shrm. org/hrdisciplines/benefits/Articles/Pages/Monetary-Incentives-Wellness-Grow.aspx.

SHRM (2013) *Round Two Sequestration Negotiations' Update. SHRM Public Policy 1/3/13*, www.SHRM.org [15 March 2013].

Sidle, S.D. (2008) 'Workplace stress management interventions: What works best?', *Academy of Management Perspectives*, 22: 111–12.

Sivakumar, K. and Nakata, C. (2001) 'The stampede towards Hofstede's framework: Avoiding the sample design pit in cross-cultural research', *Journal of International Business Studies*, 32: 555–74.

Slaughter, S.A., Ang, S., and Boh, W.F. (2007) 'Firm specific human capital and compensation: Organizational tenure and profiles: An archival analysis of salary data for IT professionals', *Human Resource Management*, 46: 373–94.

Smith, W.K. and Lewis, M.W. (2011) 'Toward a theory of paradox: A dynamic equilibrium model of organizing', *Academy of Management Review*, 36(2): 381–403.

Smola, K. and Sutton, D. (2002) 'Generational differences: Revisiting generational work values for the new millennium', *Journal of Organizational Behavior*, 23: 363–82.

Snape, E. and Redman, T. (2010) 'HRM practices, organized citizenship behaviour and performance: A multi-level analysis', *Journal of Management Studies*, 47: 1219–47.

Snell, L. and White, L. (2009) 'An exploratory study of the application of internal marketing in professional service organizations', *Services Marketing Quarterly*, 30(3): 195–211.

Snell, S., Yound, M.A., and Wright, P.M. (1996) 'Establishing a framework for research in strategic human resource management: Merging resource theory and organizational learning', in ed. G. Ferris, *Research in Personnel and Human Resource Management*, Greenwich, CT: JAI Press, pp. 61–90.

Sparrow, P. and Balain, S. (2009) 'Talent-proofing the organization', in eds. C. Cooper and R. Burke, *The Peak Performing Organization*, Abingdon: Routledge, pp. 108–28.

Sparrow, P. and Hiltrop, J.M. (1997) 'Redefining the field of human resource management: A battle between national mindsets and faces of business translations', *Human Resource Management*, 36(2): 201–19.

Sparrow, P., Schuler, R.S., and Jackson, S.E. (1994) 'Convergence or divergence: Human resource practices and policies for competitive advantage worldwide', *International Journal of Human Resource Management*, 5(2): 267–99.

Sparrow, P., Brewster, C., and Harris, H. (2004) *Globalizing Human Resource Management*, Abingdon: Routledge.

Sparrow, P., Scullion, H., and Farndale, E. (2011) 'Global talent management: New roles for the corporate HR function?', in eds. H. Scullion and D.G. Collings, *Global Talent Management*, New York: Routledge, pp. 39–55.

Stahl, G., Bjorkman, I., Farndale, E., Morris, S.D., Stiles, P., and Trevor, J. (2007) *Global Talent Management: How Leading Multinationals Build and Sustain their Talent Pipeline*, Fontinebleau: Faculty and Research Working Paper.

Strang, D. and Macy, M. (2001) 'In search of excellence: Fads, success stories and adaptive emulation', *American Journal of Sociology*, 107: 147–80.

Strauss, W. and Howe, N. (1991) *Generations: The History of America's Future, 1584–2069*, New York: William Morrow.

Strohmeier, S. (2007) 'Research in e-HRM: Review and implications', *Human Resource Management Review*, 17: 19–37.

Sturges, J. (1999) 'What it means to succeed: Personal conceptions of career success held by male and female managers at different ages', *British Journal of Management*, 10(3): 239–52.

Subeliani, D. and Tsogas, G. (2005) 'Managing diversity in the Netherlands: A case study of Radobank', *International Journal of Human Resource Management*, 16: 831–51.

Sullivan, S.E. (1999) 'The changing nature of careers: A review and research agenda', *Journal of Management*, 25: 457–84.

Sun, P.Y.T. and Anderson, M.H. (2010) 'An examination of the relationship between absorptive capacity and organizational learning, and a proposed integration', *British Journal of Management*, 12(2): 130–50.

Super, D.E. (1957) *The Psychology of Careers*, New York: Harper and Row.

Sweet, S., Besen, E., Pitt-Catsouphes, M., and McNamara, T. (Forthcoming) 'Do options for job flexibility diminish in times of economic uncertainty'.

Tansley, C., Newell, S., and Williams, H. (2001) 'Effecting e-HRM style practices through an integrated human resource information system', *Personnel Review*, 30: 351–70.

Tapscott, D. and Williams, A.D. (2007) *Wikinomics: How Mass Collaboration Changes Everything*, London: Atlantic Books.

Tarique, I. and Schuler, R.S. (2010) 'Global talent management: Literature review, integrative framework and suggestions for further research', *Journal of World Business*, 45: 122–33.

Taylor, S., Beechler, S., and Napier, N. (1996) 'Towards an integrative model of strategic human resource management', *Academy of Management Review*, 21: 959–85.

Teece, T.J., Pisano, G., and Shuen, A. (1997) 'Dynamic capabilities and strategic management', *Strategic Management Journal*, 18: 509–33.

The Lawyer Contributors (2007) *Linklaters Pilots Wiki for Shared Knowledge*, London: Centaur Communications Limited.

Thite, M. and Kavanagh, M. (2009) 'Evolution of human resource management and human resource information systems: The role of information technology', in eds. M. Kavanagh and M. Thite, *Human Resource Information Systems: Basics, Applications and Future Directions*, Thousand Oaks, CA: Sage, pp. 3–24.

Thurley, K. (1983) 'How transferable is the Japanese industrial relations system? Some implications of a study of industrial relations and personnel policies of Japanese firms in Western Europe', Paper presented at the 6th World Congress of Industrial Relations Association, 28–31 March, Kyoto, Japan.

Tichy, N., Devanna, M.A., and Forbrun, C. (1984) *Strategic Human Resource Management*, New York: Wiley.

Toh, S., Morgeson, F., and Campion, M. (2008) 'Human resource configurations: Investigating fit with the organizational context', *Journal of Applied Psychology*, 93: 429–62.

Topel, R. (1991) 'Specific human capital, mobility and wages: Wages rise with seniority', *Journal of Political Economy*, 99: 145–76.

Torrington, D., Hall, L., Taylor, S., and Atkinson, C. (2011) *Human Resource Management*, London: Financial Times/Prentice Hall.

Towers Watson (2012a) *The Next High Stakes Quest. Balancing Employer and Employee Priorities*. Global Talent Management and Rewards Study 2012–2013. London: Towers Watson/World at Work.

Towers Watson (2012b) *Global Workforce Study*. London: Towers Watson.

Trevor, C. and Nyberg, A. (2008) 'Keeping your head count when all about you are losing theirs. Downsizing, voluntary turnover rates and the moderating role of HR practices', *The Academy of Management Journal*, 51: 259–76.

Trevor, J. (2012) 'A rewarding crisis for HR', *People Management*, January: 40–44.

Trompenaars, F. and Hampden-Turner, C. (1998) *Riding the Waves of Culture: Understanding Cultural Diversity in Business*, New York: McGraw-Hill.

Tulgan, B. (1997) 'Generation X: Slackers? Or the workforce of the future?', *Employment Relations Today*, 24(2): 55–64.

Twenge, J.M. and Campbell, S.M. (2008) 'Generational differences in psychological traits and their impact on the workplace', *Journal of Management Psychology*, 23: 862–77.

Tyson, S. (1987) 'Managing the personnel function', *Journal of Management Studies*, 24(5): 523–32.

Tyson, S. (1995) *Human Resource Strategy: Towards a General Theory of Human Resource Management*, London: Pitman Publishing.

Tyson, S. (1997) 'Human resource strategy: A process for managing the contribution of HRM to organizational performance', *International Journal of Human Resource Management*, 8(3): 277–90.

Tyson, S. (2005) 'Fat cat pay', in eds. S. Tyson and F. Bournois, *Top Pay and Performance*, Oxford: Elsevier/Butterworth Heinemann, pp. 12–28.

Tyson, S. and Bournois, F. (2005) *Top Pay and Performance*, Oxford: Elsevier/Butterworth Heinemann.

Tyson, S. and Fell, A. (1986) *Evaluating the Personnel Function*, London: Hutchinson.

Ulrich, D. (1997) *Human Resource Champions: The Next Agenda for Adding Value and Delivering Results*, Cambridge, MA: Harvard Business Press.

Ulrich, D. and Brockbank, W. (2005) *The HR Value Proposition*, Cambridge, MA: Harvard Business Press.

United Nations (2008) *World Population Prospects: The 2008 Revision*, www.un.org [16 February 2013].

Urwin, P., Parry, E., Dodds, I., Karuk, V., and David, A. (2013) *Understanding the Business Impacts of Equality and Diversity: What Does the Evidence Tell us?* BIS/13/556. London: Business and Innovation Services.

US Bureau of Labor Statistics Report (2012) *Charting International Labor Comparisons*. September edition. Washington: US Bureau of Labor Statistics.

USA Today (2012) 'Gender pay gap persists', www.usatoday.com [16 February 2013].

Vance, R.J. (2006) *Employee Engagement and Commitment: A Guide to Understanding, Measuring and Increasing Engagement in your Organization*, Alexandria, VA: Society for Human Resource Management.

Varey, R.J. (1995) 'Internal marketing: A review and some interdisciplinary research challenges', *International Journal of Service Industry Management*, 6(1): 40–63.

Varey, R.J. and Lewis, B.R. (1999) 'A broadened conception of internal marketing', *European Journal of Marketing*, 33: 926–44.

Vickerstaff, S. (2010) 'Older workers: The "unavoidable obligation" of extending our working lives?', *Sociology Compass*, 4: 869–79.

Voermans, M. and van Veldhoven, M. (2006) 'Attitude towards e-HRM: An empirical study at Phillips', *Personnel Review*, 36: 887–902.

Vroom, V.H. (1964) *Work and Motivation*, New York: Wiley.

Walsh, D. (1972) 'Sociology and the social world', in eds. P. Filmer, M. Phillipson, D. Silverman, and D. Walsh, *New Directions in Sociological Theory*, London: Collier Macmillan, pp. 15–35.

Walsh, J.P. (2009) 'Are US CEO's overpaid? A partial response to Kaplan', *The Academy of Management Perspectives*, 23: 73–5.

Watson, T.J. (1977) *The Personnel Managers: A Study in the Sociology of Work and Industry*, London: Routledge and Kegan Paul.

Weber, H. (1947) *The Theory of Social and Economic Organizations*, New York: The Free Press.

Wernerfelt, B. (1984) 'The resource-based view of the firm', *Strategic Management Journal*, 5: 171–80.

Whitaker, A. (1992) 'The transformation of work. Post Fordism revisited', in eds. M. Reed and M. Hughes, *Rethinking Organizations: New Directions in Organizational Theory and Analysis*, London: Sage, pp. 184–206.

Whitley, R. (2000) *Divergent Capitalisms: The Social Structuring and Change of Business Systems*, Oxford: Oxford University Press.

Whittaker, S. and Marchington, M. (2003) 'Devolving HR responsibility to the line: Threat, opportunity or partnership?', *Employee Relations*, 25: 245–61.

Whysall, Z. (2012) *Talent Tactics: How Can you Plug the Talent Gap?*, Lane 4 Consultancy report.

Wilson, M.G., DeJoy, D.M., Vandenberg, J., Richardson, H.A., and McGrath, A.L. (2004) 'Work characteristics and employee health and well-being: Test of a model of healthy work organization', *Journal of Occupational and Organizational Psychology*, 77: 565–88.

Winstanley, D. and Woodall, J. (2000) 'Introduction', in eds. D. Winstanley and J. Woodall, *Ethical Issues in Contemporary Human Resource Management*, Basingstoke: Macmillan, pp. 3–22.

Witcher, B.J. and Chau, V.S. (2012) 'Varieties of capitalism and strategic management: Managing performance in multinationals after the global financial crisis', *British Journal of Management*, 23 Special Issue: S58–S73.

Wood, D.J. (2010) 'Measuring corporate social performance review', *International Journal of Management Reviews*, 12(1): 50–84.

Woods, D. (2008) 'Businesses lose vital opportunities because of poor talent management', *HR Magazine* [Online], www.hrmagazine.co.uk [25 March 2013].

Wright, P. and McMahan, G. (1992) 'Theoretical perspectives for strategic human resource management', *Journal of Management*, 18: 295–320.

Wright, P., Dunford, B.B., and Snell, S.A. (2001) 'Human resources and the resource based view of the firm', *Journal of Management*, 27: 701–21.

Yeh, R. and Lawrence, J. (1995) 'Individualism and confucian dynamism: A note on Hofstede's cultural root to economic growth', *Journal of International Business Studies*, 26(3): 655–69.

Yoon, S.J., Choi, D.C., and Park, J.W. (2007) 'Service orientation: Its impact on business performance in the medical service industry', *The Service Industries Journal*, 27(4): 371–88.

Youndt, M.A., Snell, S.A., Dean, J.W., and Lepak, D.P. (1996) 'Human resource management, manufacturing strategy and firm performance', *Academy of Management Journal*, 39: 836–66.

Zahra, S.A. and George, G. (2002) 'Absorptive capacity: A review, reconceptualization and extension', *Academy of Management Review*, 27: 185–203.

Zemke, R., Raines, C., and Filipczak, B. (2000) *Generations at Work: Managing the Clash of Veterans, Boomers, Xers and Nexters in your Workplace*, New York: Amacom.

Zhang, L. and Wang, H. (2006) 'Intelligent information processing in human resource management: An implementation case in China', *Expert Systems*, 23: 356–69.

Zingheim, P.K. and Schuster, J.R. (2000) *Pay People Right*, San Francisco: Jossey-Bass.

Index

References to tables are in *italics* and figures in **bold**